How Stories Teach Us

This book is part of the Peter Lang Education list.
Every volume is peer reviewed and meets
the highest quality standards for content and production.

PETER LANG
New York • Bern • Berlin
Brussels • Vienna • Oxford • Warsaw

How Stories Teach Us

Composition, Life Writing, and Blended Scholarship

Edited by Amy E. Robillard
& D. Shane Combs

PETER LANG
New York • Bern • Berlin
Brussels • Vienna • Oxford • Warsaw

Library of Congress Cataloging-in-Publication Data

Names: Robillard, Amy E., editor. | Combs, D. Shane, editor.
Title: How stories teach us: composition, life writing, and blended
scholarship / edited by Amy E. Robillard and D. Shane Combs.
Description: New York: Peter Lang, 2019.
Includes bibliographical references and index.
Identifiers: LCCN 2018057786 | ISBN 978-1-4331-6591-7 (hardback: alk. paper)
ISBN 978-1-4331-6592-4 (paperback: alk. paper) | ISBN 978-1-4331-6437-8 (ebook pdf)
ISBN 978-1-4331-6438-5 (epub) | ISBN 978-1-4331-6439-2 (mobi)
Subjects: LCSH: Narration (Rhetoric). | Blended learning.
Reflective learning. | Autobiography.
Classification: LCC PN212 .H67 2019 | DDC 808—dc23
LC record available at https://lccn.loc.gov/2018057786
DOI 10.3726/b15451

Bibliographic information published by **Die Deutsche Nationalbibliothek**.
Die Deutsche Nationalbibliothek lists this publication in the "Deutsche
Nationalbibliografie"; detailed bibliographic data are available
on the Internet at http://dnb.d-nb.de/.

The paper in this book meets the guidelines for permanence and durability
of the Committee on Production Guidelines for Book Longevity
of the Council of Library Resources.

© 2019 Peter Lang Publishing, Inc., New York
29 Broadway, 18th floor, New York, NY 10006
www.peterlang.com

Printed in the United States of America

Contents

Foreword

SOCIAL WORKERS

I'd been teaching undergraduates to write, semester after semester, for close to twenty years when I accepted an invitation to help develop a writing curriculum for practicing social workers enrolled in a new doctoral program at my university. I desperately needed a change. I was tired of thinking the same old thoughts, of having the same old conversations, of grading and re-grading the same kind of papers. I got the jolt I needed and more from the three years I spent reading and responding to writing by the working adults in the social work program. Some of my students were counselors in public schools or prisons or half-way houses; others helped vets or addicts or victims of domestic abuse or sex offenders; others had private practices that specialized in trauma or grief or adolescence or divorce. Regardless of the client population and the practitioner's specialization, story was central to all members of the doctoral program. To gain access to the suffering of others, these professional caregivers depended on narrative's ability to open a window into the mysteries of personal experience.

The lesson I learned during those three years is the lesson that is at the heart of *How Stories Teach Us*, this remarkable collection of essays edited by Amy Robillard and Shane Combs: because we are the stories we tell about ourselves to ourselves, we can initiate change by learning to tell new stories about ourselves in new ways. In the therapeutic environment of the social work program, this change was triggered by having the students contend, over and over again, with the question, "what is a person?" Stories of mental illness and mental health, of practices that lead from decline to recovery, of research that points the way to improved care: all such stories assume a shared understanding of what it means to be a person. By moving that question to the forefront, we were able to get the students to question their own assumptions about the end point of the care they were providing in their varied settings.

The question that implicitly drives the stories in this volume is a different one: here, the essays composed by teachers reflecting on their lives together bid the reader to ask, "what is a teacher?" This is an important question, because it exposes the fact that scholarship on teaching and learning assumes that teaching methods are its proper subject. This assumption has led much of the work in the field to be an argument for one method over another, as if *who* is doing the teaching is an irrelevant detail to be filled in later. And, indeed, the emergence of the first-year Writing Program is, itself, founded on this same assumption: there is the program, with its method and values, and then there is the infinitely substitutable teaching force, comprised of an ever-churning pool of teaching assistants, part-timers, full-time instructors, program administrators, and the odd faculty member or two. But the assumption that who does the teaching is irrelevant is counter-factual. Each teacher in each classroom arrives with an archive of stories that shapes what form the teaching can take, what kind of writing will be solicited, what kind of writing will be rewarded, which students will be recognized, and what kinds of conversations will be permitted and which ones discouraged.

How Stories Teach Us breaks from this assumption, giving us direct access to actual teachers, with personal histories, reflecting on what it means to teach specific student populations at specific institutions right now. In each of the essays collected here, the teachers emerge as individuals whose concerns are shaped by past experiences, current events, and hopes for certain versions of the future. And this is what makes this book so important: it is a radical argument against the overwhelming pressure in public education at this time to flatten, to norm, to simplify, and to render generic. (Think high stakes testing; think Common Core.) In place of calls for sweeping educational reform, the contributors to this volume model varying ways to engage in acts of self-reflection. And then they contend with the disruptive results that inevitably arise when one looks and looks again into one's own past.

In the Doctoral Program in Social Work, we had a shorthand phrase for this kind of work: we called it "n = 1." What we meant by this was that the only way to responsibly deliver mental health care was to see every potential patient or client as an individual case rather than as a collection of diagnosable symptoms for which there were automatically proscribed treatment regimes. Working against a health care system designed for speed and profit, the approach we were teaching required slowing down, learning to see both the patient and the care provider as unique constellations of stories. To be responsible caregivers, we argued, practitioners had both to engage in the ceaseless hermeneutics of self-reflection and to help their patients imagine life stories not as destinies, but as possibilities.

Readers of *How Stories Teach Us* will quickly determine that there is not one method here for using life writing to reimagine the classroom nor is there is a single way to produce writing that blends scholarly aspirations with self-disclosure. Professors Robillard and Combs provide us with a set of essays that show that who does the teaching determines to a very large degree what becomes possible for the other learners in the writing classroom. Each contributor here comprises a set of $n = 1$; as the teacher-scholars learn to tell their stories in new ways, new meanings emerge for them and what can happen in their classrooms begins to change. That's the gift of this volume: it shows teachers how constructing and reconstructing the narrative of one's life leads to imaginative acts of interpretation that have the power to change how one teaches, what one teaches, and how one reads, understands, and assesses student responses to those changes. Or to put it another way, what the co-editors call here "blended scholarship" might also be called transformational scholarship, because it: cuts across both literary forms and generic conventions; captures the teacher in the act of experiencing the transformative effects of rethinking a past position; and invites readers to invent their own ways of generating writing that moves between the personal and the scholarly, the individual and the general, the specific and the universal.

Richard E. Miller

Rutgers University

Acknowledgements

Amy

I would like to thank Sarah Hochstetler for reading drafts of my chapter and for always encouraging me to say what I need to say, Bill White for helping me figure out how to say those things, and Steve Field for listening, always. I also want to extend sincere thanks to this volume's contributors for heeding the call to tell their stories.

Shane

I would like to thank Demet Yiğitbilek, who was first to read each of my drafts. Moreover, she listened and encouraged when I was living those 45 days of untested story. I would also like to acknowledge anyone who chooses to take up the messy and meaningful work of blended scholarship. The process is the reward.

Introduction: Learning How to Tell the Story

AMY E. ROBILLARD AND D. SHANE COMBS

Composition studies courts a paradoxical relationship to personal writing. On the one hand, our first-year anthologies are filled with essays, a large percentage of them personal, and we teach students how to write by asking them to read and respond in writing to these essays. On the other hand, we have engaged for decades in a debate about the relationship between the personal and the academic in our own writing, most often coming down on the side of the academic, for the personal itself should remain, we argue, outside of academe. Scholars in the field position themselves on either side of this debate, a debate in which the terms are reduced to, simply, the personal or the academic, a debate that is represented by, for instance, David Bartholomae and Peter Elbow in the mid-1990s, a debate that has us stymied when it comes to understanding ourselves as writers whose work grows out of impulses that are more than simply academic. The work collected here leaves this debate behind. We believe that rehearsing the debate only persuades us to choose a side; indeed, the debate suggests that there are only two sides from which to choose. More persuasive and more fruitful, we have found, is doing the work of imagining the agentive potential of story: how do stories *act* in our lives to direct our attention, to teach us what to value, what to believe, what to suspect, and what to do and not to do? What we should take seriously and what we should dismiss? How, in short, do stories teach us?

This is not to say that personal writing is to be equated with storytelling; indeed, the work we have gathered in this book demonstrates instead that good storytelling is both personal and academic, that there is a continuum on which what we are calling blended scholarship exists, and that scholarship and storytelling feed into one another in ways we have not yet recognized. We want to not just recognize that work but celebrate it here.

Introducing Blended Scholarship

We are certainly not the first in composition studies to suggest that the personal and the academic be combined. Deborah Holdstein and David Bleich's collection, *Personal Effects: The Social Character of Scholarly Writing* showcases what they call "the human in the humanities," making a strong case for "how fundamental it is in humanistic scholarship to take account, in a variety of ways and as part of the subject matter, of the personal and collective experiences of scholars, researchers, critics, and teachers" (1). Holdstein and Bleich argue that the work in *Personal Effects* forms the "basis for new pedagogical initiatives—ones that permit the risks, the personal reflections, the experiments, the errors, the awkward moments characteristic of real teaching and real research" (4). Similarly, in their collection, *Alt Dis: Alternative Discourses and the Academy*, Christopher Schroeder, Helen Fox, and Patricia Bizzell note in 2002 that "many academics and students have been developing new discourse forms that accomplish intellectual work while combining traditional academic discourse traits with traits from other discourse communities" (viii). The editors of *Alt Dis* spend some time discussing what to call these forms of discourse—hybrid, mixed, constructed. In his contribution to the collection, Christopher Schroeder observes that "the legitimacy of stories as a form of intellectual work often depends upon who does the telling" (183); no doubt this remains true today. In 2013, Robert J. Nash and Sydnee Viray published *Our Stories Matter: Liberating the Voices of Marginalized Students Through Scholarly Personal Narrative Writing*, a book that comes as close to blended scholarship as any of the work we've yet seen. Nash and Viray understand Scholarly Personal Narrative writing as a methodology for underrepresented students in the academy and characterize it this way: "Rather than directly challenging the mainstream, normative story, SPN writing describes the multidimensional personal qualities scholars need to make meaning of their lives within a heterogeneous society" (4). All of this work has made possible our own; we extend the work of Holdstein and Bleich, of Schroeder, Fox, and Bizzell, and of Nash and Viray to offer blended scholarship as a genre that recognizes that the academic is personal and the personal is academic and the bleeding that happens between these categories cannot be contained. What we add to their work is an explicit focus on life writing. For, until now, no work in composition studies has explicitly asked scholars to write blended scholarship—to write from their lives in a way that showcases the effects of their scholarship and teaching on their lives and the effects of their lives on their scholarship and their teaching.

The essays we've collected here are examples of blended scholarship, work that interrogates the relationship between the academic and the personal, insisting on the importance of story for any understanding of who we are, how we move through this world, how we relate with and to others, how we make it to the end of the day, when, as we all know, what matters most is how we manage to live with ourselves. Blended scholarship combines the self-reflexive, self-analytical, culturally aware analysis of the stories we tell ourselves with the moves of good scholarship, tackling an issue from multiple perspectives, theorizing potential reasons for and responses to difficult issues, and working toward insights that may prove helpful to others in different contexts. Blended scholarship is writing that explicitly blends the personal and the academic in order to understand, in ways that either alone cannot, the ways in which our life experiences influence our teaching and scholarship and our teaching and scholarship influence the stories we make of our lives.

As we read proposals for this collection, we looked for work that highlighted the ways that stories teach us something about what it means to be human in this world but also that demonstrated the ways that the critical work of scholarship—either explicit mention of theoretical and scholarly work or the critical moves of scholarship—made possible insights into one's story that storytelling alone could not. Concerning these insights, we made it a point throughout this process, from selection of essays to editing to completion, to resist placing a formulaic percentage upon how much "academic" and how much "personal" is necessary to constitute blended scholarship. If, for example, Jonathan Alexander is using a rhetorical framework to critique a podcast, he might make more traditional scholarly moves than say, Laura Gray-Rosendale, who is writing of her experiences with cancer for the first time. There exist already spaces where the demand would be to do "the academic" or "the personal" in some hard-and-fast way. What we sought from this collection is what we seek for scholars, teachers, and students alike, a *blending* of components personal and scholarly that, depending on where we are in our lives and in the moves we are making, might blend more in one direction in one essay and more in another the next. With this approach to writing in mind, we looked for writers who could blend story and scholarship in ways we did not see when we opened up the most recent edition of *The Best American Essays*; we wanted to understand how scholars and teachers of writing understand what it means to write and teach life writing and essays in what some have come to call the Golden Age of the Essay.

Collected here are scholars of composition and rhetoric coming to terms in writing with what it means to deal with loss, with grief, with illness, with trauma, depression, abuse, gender identity, the ravages of time. What it means to learn how to tell, and perhaps one answer to the question of how stories teach us has to do with time: the time it takes to prepare to tell, the time it takes to tell, the time it takes to tell again, the time it takes to tell in a different way this time, the time it takes to revise those earlier versions of the story. The time it takes to gather the courage to write the story. Many of the essays collected here narrate the authors' processes of preparing to tell stories that had not yet—even *have* not yet—been told. Storytelling about the self is not the simple thing it is often made out to be. It is, in fact, one of the most difficult tasks we undertake, as doing so forces us to come to terms with versions of ourselves that perhaps we'd prefer remain hidden, with secrets we'd prefer remain buried, with truths we'd prefer remain muddled. And always, this coming to terms takes time—sometimes weeks, sometimes months, often years. And once we come to a set of terms, we are often not finished. We often return to those terms only to revise. Because a story told once is just that—a story told in a particular way at a particular time for a particular purpose. It is rhetorical. It serves. It will do for now. It may not do later. We may need to tell it another way. The writers collected here theorize time both explicitly and implicitly, and it is this, perhaps more than any other characteristic of the blended scholarship collected here, that demonstrates most clearly what combining storytelling with scholarship can do. This kind of writing can help us understand in more complex ways the relationship among time, narrative, writing, and our evolving understanding of events in our lives.

Why Life Writing?

In *Nowhere Near the Line: Pain and Possibility in Teaching and Writing*, Elizabeth Boquet poses a question that begins to get at the heart of why we've collected these essays in one place: "What more is a university made of than its people? Not much, as it turns out" (35). And what more do people do at a university than seek to create meaning? Not much, as it turns out.

One way we seek meaning is by storying our lives. Story shapes all of our experiences, whether we consciously story our experiences or not, whether we want to acknowledge it or not, and what we do in this collection is go beyond acknowledging that truth to celebrating it. Life writing is by its very nature political; when we tell the stories of our lives, we are drawing from the narrative resources at our disposal, and the narrative resources at our disposal are culturally shaped. Jerome Bruner, in *Making Stories*, makes the important point that one of the crucial functions of narrative is to help us come to terms with the unexpected. Bruner further observes,

> No human culture can operate without some means of dealing with either the foreseeable or the unforeseeable imbalances inherent in communal living. Whatever else it must do, culture must devise means for containing incompatible interests and aspirations. A culture's narrative resources—its folktales, its old-hat stories, its evolving literature, even its modes of gossip—conventionalize the inequities it generates and thereby contain its imbalances and incompatibilities. (93)

When we write our lives against these narrative resources—when we defy them, for so much life writing is defiant, is talking back—we resist the conventionalized narratives that have told us for so long who we are, who we are supposed to have been. Vivian Gornick puts this a different way when she writes that "modern memoir posits that the shaped presentation of one's life is of value to the disinterested reader only if it dramatizes and reflects sufficiently on the experience of 'becoming'; undertakes to trace the internal movement away from the murk of being told who you are by the accident of circumstance toward the clarity that identifies accurately the impulses of the self that [Willa] Cather calls inviolable" (93). Our narrative resources so often label us by positioning us in that murk that Gornick speaks of—who we are by accident of circumstance—and it is through life writing that we talk back to those storylines, negotiating a self as we consider the ways story acts on us and the ways we act on story.

We write our lives for any number of reasons, but perhaps the number one reason we write our lives is to create a permanent record, to say, with some degree of (temporary) certainty, "This is how it was for me." One of the functions of life writing is *persuasive*: this is how it happened. Let me give you my side of the story. Life writing is corrective. Life writing is defiant. Life writing aims to create a version of events that we can live with. In good life writing, we witness a writer shed the cultural scripts she has inherited from family and adopt new scripts she can adapt to her present circumstances. Sidonie Smith and Julia Watson write that, "in autobiographical narratives, imaginative acts of remembering always intersect with such rhetorical acts as assertion, justification, judgment, conviction, and interrogation. That is, life narrators address readers whom they want to persuade of their version of experience" (7). And that's what any story is: a version of experience requiring interpretation, revision, and reinterpretation.

While anybody can and does write parts of their lives on social media, there's something about spending an extended amount of time writing our lives in the context of the academy that tends to pull us in, to grab our attention, to work on us in ways we haven't yet, as a field, articulated the reasons for. We want to know how others have done it, how others have gotten through, have carried on when faced with something like serious illness or having been stymied by a colleague's death. We want to know how others negotiate complex identities in the academy or how they cope with a family member's death. How do others survive trauma and still manage to teach others to write? We're not asking for a friend. We're asking for ourselves because we want to learn something for ourselves about how to live.

In "A Cure for Bitterness," Dorothy Allison writes,

> What we learn when crafting the story of our lives is some way to love ourselves even in the midst of our horror. To forgive ourselves, our broken damaged hurt places, an appreciation for the muscle we have created in order to survive.

An appreciation for the muscle we have created in order to survive. For many of us, that muscle is writing. Or reading. Literacy. Allison continues,

> And what we learn as theorists and practitioners, academics, writers, is to look at scary impossible situations with complex, reasonable, nuanced attention. We create a way to understand what is unexplainable, and two or three things I tried to figure out what I genuinely know. (252–53)

But it is the things we do not know, Allison writes, that "become the subjects of our lectures, our stories" (253). We write our lives to figure out a little bit more about the things we do not know. Life writing does not require that we disavow the parts of our lives or ourselves that we do not understand; indeed, life writing insists that we dwell with those parts.

Stories are about making selves; blended scholarship asks that we approach that making with a particular stance toward inquiry, complexity, analysis, and uncertainty. Blended scholarship is political; it asks that we understand that values and beliefs are tied up in the personal, that the personal is tied up in the public, that the personal and the public are revealed in our scholarship, and that artificially separating our values from our stories renders us identity-less.

Stories are rhetorical. Stories act. Stories slow us down.

The writers brought together in this book have collectively slowed down to consider the relationships between life writing and scholarship in ways that can only encourage *us* to slow down and consider how our own life stories have influenced our scholarship and how our scholarship has influenced our life stories.

Coming to Terms, Revising, and Surviving: Who Will Witness Our Stories?

If it feels to some that this introduction does more to explicate life writing than the critical elements of blended scholarship, this would be because composition, in its history, has borne witness to the scholarly far more than the personal. In "The Place of Creative Writing in Composition Studies," Douglas Hesse details this history. Hesse writes about how composition "has turned away from the imaginative and toward argument, civic discourse, academic genres, and rhetorical moves" (37). He chronicles a history where creative nonfiction was once part of composition. In fact, Hesse writes that by the late 1980s "it looked like creative nonfiction would gain a firm home within CCCC and composition studies. But exciting developments in rhetoric and theory...channeled more of the field's attention" (37). As creative nonfiction became more popular in the public, writes Hesse, "creative writing 'discovered' creative nonfiction and, finding no staked claims, was more than happy to annex its genres" (37). Hesse adds: "CCCC still has a creative nonfiction special interest group; the 2009 meeting attracted thirteen people" (37).

It is our stance, in providing a treatment for blended scholarship, that we must bear witness to the parts that have been overlooked and underdeveloped. This doesn't mean that life writing is more or less important than the critical scholarship. It just means, in composition, we've far outpaced ourselves in practicing the critical. To make both the critical and the personal accessible, then, we must continue with the critical but do decades of catch-up with the personal. This is why we stress life writing here. This is why we stress life writing in our classroom spaces when teaching blended scholarship.

In our own classrooms, both editors of this collection have been mindful to teach students what it means to bear witness to one another at the site of storytelling. Both of us, at one time or another, have leaned on works that bring in the empathetic witnessing needed in a community where writers-turn-reader and readers-turn-writer. Both of us, together with our students, have done close readings of works like Leslie Jamison's *The Empathy Exams*, in which the author theorizes a radical witnessing where we "enter another person's pain as [we'd] enter another country, through immigration and customs, border crossing by way of query: *What grows where you are? What are the laws? What animals graze there?*" (6). From this very text, we have witnessed, with our students, a paradoxical relationship between bearing witness to another and coming back to our own narratives with more compassion, more open-mindedness, more value. In a recent course taught by Shane, in an assignment that required vulnerability and personal narrative in shared storytelling, one of the students responded after by stating, "I am…guilty of judging people before I get to know them, and I think the worst thing I do is assume that people haven't been through much in their [lives] and have it easy. I really don't like that I do that and this section of the semester… really opened my eyes to what other people go through" (Heidkamp). It is a fascinating point that, in writing the call for what is now *How Stories Teach Us: Composition, Life Writing, and Blended Scholarship*, we experienced more curiosity, sometimes more concern, wondering what scholars and teachers might submit, if they *would* submit, than we spent worried about what our students might submit. This is not a critique of what we, as scholars, are capable of doing. It is, rather, a critique of what we as scholars have and haven't valued, including the worthiness of our own stories. In fact, it is a fair statement that more students have likely been taught to bear witness to each other by professors teaching such theory and practice than there have been spaces for those of us who share these beliefs to practice what we teach with each other.

Lisa Ruddick, in a presentation on "Literature and the Feeling of Aliveness," strikes a similar tone when she says that, "There is…a need for more conversation in English, not in classrooms where we talk and think about this all the time, but in the expert discourse, colleague-to-colleague, in the field, about what it is that makes a work of literature seem like a living thing, and what it is that makes us feel that we're living beings, that we're dwelling in three dimensions." Ruddick continues, stating that a certain kind of "professionalization, at least in the field of English… sucks the aliveness out of the object that we're studying." This is a troubling point for those who take it up, but perhaps especially so, for those of us who would suggest we do life writing and bearing witness as scholars and teachers, with each other. If Ruddick's concerns have merit, we might ask the following: How much "life" do we give the stories of our colleagues who surround us? Said differently, when faculty come together, let's say, at a required weekly meeting, how alive, or not, do we feel, to ourselves and to each other? How seldom do we feel like living beings in three dimensional spaces and how often do we feel the life sucked from us? Despite what some of our initial responses may be, the collection that follows proves a positive: for many of us, it is more a lack of *opportunity* to bear witness to our lives within our scholarship and the lives of those around us in professional settings than an *unwillingness* to do so that is the problem. In other words, nothing but our own constructions dictate an inability for the personal to function alongside what we call the scholarly and the professional.

The responses we received for this collection, more than five times the number we could actually publish, demonstrate the potential for the personal and scholarly to exist together. The submissions we received are from scholars and teachers who are seeking the blended witnessing that we have described above. Indeed, many times, during the editing process, the writers would mention to us their excitement to eventually read everyone else in this collection and their curiosity concerning the types of blended scholarship we were receiving from colleagues in the field. The responses we received, unlike many spaces in social media and unlike too many academic spaces, allow for longform storytelling, allow for a tension between storytelling and scholarship, and allow for a potential bearing witness, colleague-to-colleague, that we assert is long overdue. The responses we received, now essays, now formed to tell nuanced stories independently and together as a collection, are organized into three categories: "How We Come to Terms With Our Lives," "How We Revise Our Lives," and "How We Survive Our Lives." With these categories, then, we think of the framework offered by Arthur Frank, that in writing our lives and living our writing, "people need terms of *selection*—what to pay attention to—and following immediately is the need for *evaluation*, or what to think about what has been selected. Stories work as people's *selection/ evaluation* guidance system" (46).

In the first category, "How We Come to Terms With Our Lives," we see authors learning to name and thereby give shape to the situations that have been preoccupying them, drawing on their understanding of life writing and rhetoric to shape a story that will do for now. In the first essay, "Before the Heavens Open Up," Elizabeth Boquet traces the process of thinking with and through the letters her mother wrote to her over their more than twenty years of living apart. To do so, she draws on the work she is assigning at the same time to her first-year writing students, assignments that ask them to write about the experience of looking closely and quietly at their own faces. Together, they grapple with how to make sense of such strangely familiar experiences, and they work to organize the ineffable. Rona Kaufman, in "An Arrangement," juxtaposes a history of the canons of rhetoric with her search for her paternal grandmother, a Polish Jew who migrated to Pittsburgh between the World Wars and who died before the author was born. Her grandmother's recorded historical life begins around age 30, when she is married, the mother of two, and a settled immigrant. While Aristotle would have us march linearly through the canons, privileging invention and appeals to reason all the way through, the author explores what can be known and learned when historical records are limited, when stories aren't recorded or heard or remembered, and when storytellers can work only with fragments and fog. Kaufman plays with the five canons of rhetoric and pursues a new-to-her genealogical lead: her grandmother's first marriage was arranged. That arrangement is the reason for her grandmother's migration—an arrangement, then, that almost certainly saved her life and the family line. The author reflects on how what appears to be constraint can be a life preserver and how the messy simultaneity of invention, arrangement, memory, style, and delivery can bear fruit.

In "Collecting and Coding Synecdochic Selves: Identifying Learning Across Life-Writing Texts," Bump Halbritter and Julie Lindquist explore the potential of reflective narrative writing to make learning available to students through (1) their understanding of the affordances of narrative production for self-awareness as observed by researchers and theorists, (2) a curriculum of iterative knowledge-making moments that develop the potential for students' stories over time, (3) the corpus of storied, reflective texts as resources for inquiry into and discovery of evidence of student learning and development within a curriculum of iterative knowledge-making moments that develop the potential for students' stories over time, and (4) the corpus of storied, reflective texts as resources for ongoing inquiry into and discovery of evidence of student learning and development. With this in mind, Halbritter and Lindquist advocate for an approach to first-year writing organized around opportunities for facilitated, iterative storytelling. They suggest that to be most productive, students' stories must be situated as data on experience within a learning environment—a curriculum—that allows students to do both deconstructive and reconstructive work.

And, in "Writing Backwards: Adventures With Time and Structure in Life Writing," Sam Meekings focuses on what he learned as a writer and writing instructor through writing about his younger brother's life (and death). The essay explores how memory is negotiated through the act of writing, and how writing about memory might be seen as a performative action that goes some way to creating an agreed-upon version or interpretation of the past. The essay documents how the process of writing encouraged him to reconsider traditional notions of narrative structure and linearity, and explains the rationale behind eschewing a chronological and biographical structure running from birth to death, in order to show how our conception of lives in writing (and indeed the way we imagine our own lives) often resists such a restrictive conception. It examines a variety of influential life writing texts, and considers the challenges inherent in trying to construct an "accurate" portrait of life through writing. It ends by discussing the issues and stumbling blocks that need to be addressed in terms of remembering, reassembling and reclaiming the past.

In the second category, "How We Revise Our Lives," we see writers reevaluating the stories they've come to tell about their lives, choosing to retell them through different frameworks and with different concepts and perspectives. The writers in this section arrive at spaces, internally and externally driven, where they find themselves needing to update their outdated narratives. Lisya Seloni's "Moving Literacies: A Need to Tell Transnational Stories," is about moving across languages, literacy practices, and cultural narratives. Through an autobiographical narrative of what movement means in transnational lives and how it affects one's storytelling, this essay addresses the following questions:

1. What does it mean to navigate a cross-cultural life with multiple literate histories?
2. How do we write our way back to ourselves as academics and teachers blending public and private writing?

Jessica Weber's "(Dis)Arming With Stories: Power and Narrative Reconciliation in Retelling" offers a series of vignettes in which a young professional reconciles two paradoxical trajectories in her life—the excitement of a suddenly successful career in a big city, and the quiet terror of escaping an abusive relationship after an assault. Throughout her experience, she finds herself grounded in the work of creating and directing a workplace writing center. While encouraging the professionals around her to be honest and to tell the story of their findings, she begins to apply the same lens of openness, support, and storytelling within and beyond the workplace. In the process, she also begins to reframe her own stories of abuse, isolation, [in]visibility, growth, building community, and starting over.

Karen-Elizabeth Moroski's essay describes their experience as a gender-orphan, and the ways in which life writing has served as a mystery of faith through which they've come to re-learn and re-know themselves apart from polarities of gender, sexuality, and body. Using affective neuroscience, trauma studies, and critical theory to give shape to the amorphous work of creating a "self," the essay challenges notions of temporality and method—ultimately carving space for joyful excavation/exploration of a radical, vibrant self. This essay posits queer memoir and queer life writing as the work of developing an *architext*—a master narrative, still flexible, that allows for healing, growth and reconstellation in the process of queer identity development. A tender love-letter to the self who becomes, unbecomes, and becomes anew, this essay's weaving together of hard sciences alongside theory and lived experience provides generative ground for understanding not only the complex relationship between queerness and life writing, but also the ways in which trauma, bibliotherapy, and imagination can conspire to break the wheel of a painful world and arrange its kaleidoscopic pieces into something new that catches the light. And in "The Me I Don't See *Unless*: Life Writing, Play Studies, and an Untested Story," D. Shane Combs attempts to write himself out from under an untested story in his life while demonstrating how life writing and play studies can be an avenue for individuals to move beyond untested stories in their own lives. When we cease to challenge the narratives that form around our lived experiences, according to Combs, we "trod…down a lived-and-narrativized path only to find ourselves somehow shocked to be on it." In calling on play studies, Combs seeks a narrative-building approach with *stretch*, one that, according to Thomas Henricks, allows us "to render creatively the conditions of [our] lives" in order to "create and then to inhabit a world of one's own making." With play as the activity, Combs imagines life writing as a narrative-building and narrative-sustaining playground, one that allows us to frame the *acts of play*, in order to complicate and/or alleviate the untested stories in our lives while beginning to build identities based in the intentionality and friction of a life lived and written, written and lived.

The final section, "How We Survive Our Lives," moves us to those moments in life, and in life writing, where surviving is not a guarantee. In "Hearing Voices," we learn that, after spending twenty years as a community-engaged writing specialist, a colleague's death from ALS prompted Brooke Hessler to re-examine her own narrative and to pursue a more story-worthy life. Hessler's essay explores the importance of paying attention to spoken voices (in and beyond academic life), why they matter, and how preserving them can help us learn some fundamentals about life writing: that every story matters, that the stories we tell about other people are only ever about ourselves, that speaking our own truths takes practice, and that listening itself is an ethic and a craft. Next, Jonathan Alexander models his attempt to "write alongside" the experience of listening to the award-winning and provocative podcast, *S-Town*, which Alexander analyzes as a "memoir-by-proxy" or attempt to render the complicated life story of a rural gay man legible to a diverse audience. Part of what complicates *S-Town* as memoir or life writing, however, is its central "character's" inability to give consent to the life story told about him. In the podcast producer's rendering of this life narrative, then, particularly one involving complex issues of sexuality and intimacy, the producer generates multiple "versions" or interpretations of how listeners might understand this fascinating and difficult life story. By "writing alongside" *S-Town*, Alexander attempts to tease out how he, as a gay man, is understanding this life story in ways that might diverge from the interpretations offered by the producer. For instance, Alexander re-situates *S-Town* as (unconsciously) emulating the genre of the sexological case study, which has been used over the past century to document deviant or perverse sexual behavior. Such rhetorical listening allows us to understand how this important podcast ideologically contributes to the continued pathologizing of gay subjects even as it attempts to render such subjects as sympathetic.

In her essay, "Narrating Depression," Amy E. Robillard juxtaposes the difficulty of telling stories about the semester during which she suffered from severe depression with an undergraduate student's developing awareness that she is in a relationship in which she is being gaslighted. The difficulty with narrating depression stems from the fact that *nothing* happens: all feeling is lost, all desire is lost, all movement is stopped. At the same time however, Robillard had to continue teaching, and one thing she taught that semester was rhetoric. Gaslighting can be understood as the erasure of reality, while rhetoric is a contest for what is real. Robillard considers the extent to which depression can be understood as a form of gaslighting as she struggles to come to terms with the difficulties of narrating an experience that defies narration, highlighting as she does the vital need to speak depression. The last essay in the collection belongs to Laura Gray-Rosendale, who writes about her experiences composing *College Girl: A Memoir* aside several other crucial, traumatic events that have occurred in her life but that she has never published anything about. At 34 she was diagnosed with aggressive breast cancer. She underwent extensive chemotherapy, massive surgeries. And, in the midst of the travel for *College Girl*, she was diagnosed with a second form of cancer, multiple myeloma. Drawing on both scholarly and creative approaches, her essay tells pieces of these cancer stories and attempts to explain the various reasons—both conscious and unconscious—why she has not yet published pieces about these experiences. She theorizes about the complex nature of the memoir genre, about identity itself, about why we necessarily need to share certain identities at certain moments, in certain ways, and in certain contexts and other identities at other moments, in other ways, and in other contexts—and the potential effects of doing so. What is the exact nature of writing about traumatic experiences? Is it different when we are dealing with a trauma like sexual violence that—in Gray-Rosendale's case— may be well in the past, time- and space-bounded, rather than those such as illnesses that are ongoing, terminal, and in the present? When do we reveal various parts of ourselves to various audiences and with what potential costs and benefits? Gray-Rosendale also considers how these experiences continue to shape her as a person. And, finally, she describes how they impact the ways in which she teaches rhetoric and life writing as well as publishes scholarship about their interconnections.

In these twelve essays, readers may see overlap between the categories. Just as writers select and evaluate, just as editors do so, readers will as well. In fact, the essays that attract us most one day might not be the ones that draw us in the next. Or, even still, the *particulars* of a single essay that we focus on, as readers, may change from day to day. In *The Storytelling Animal: How Stories Make Us Human,* Jonathan Gottschall compares the witnessing of story to Navy pilots using flight simulators before taking flight for the first time. "Landing a jet on an aircraft is complicated," writes Gottschall, "but navigating the intricacies of human social life is more so, and the consequences of failure can be almost as dramatic" (56–57). If, then, as Gottschall asserts, "story is where people go to practice the key skills of human social life," (57) perhaps we should ask how few stories are written, by us in academe, about the lives we live. If those who work among us, or students considering a life in academe, don't tell stories that reflect what the life of a teacher and scholar is like, there will always be those outside this experience who will portray, if not caricature, the life of the academic. It is the blending of scholarship—the critical and rhetorical moves compositionists are able to make in and with story—that will separate the caricatured and the one-time told, one-themed telling, from what we are capable of doing with a multi-angled approach.

In this way, the *us* that we begin with—writers and editors of this collection—is not the *us* who comes next. *How Stories Teach Us: Composition, Life Writing, and Blended Scholarship* is a collection that aims to *demonstrate,* with the hope of persuading others, instructors and students alike, to take up their own writing, to blend it with the scholarly, to demonstrate their lives, to move from simulation to a constant, concentrated living, writing, and re-writing of their lives.

References

Allison, Dorothy. "A Cure for Bitterness." *Critical Trauma Studies: Understanding Violence, Conflict, and Memory in Everyday Life.* Ed. Monica J. Casper and Eric Wertheimer. New York: New York UP, 2016: 244–55.

Boquet, Elizabeth H. *Nowhere Near the Line: Pain and Possibility in Teaching and Writing.* Logan: Utah State UP, 2016.

Bruner, Jerome. *Making Stories: Law, Literature, Life.* Cambridge: Harvard UP, 2002.

Frank, Arthur W. *Letting Stories Breathe: A Socio-Narratology.* Chicago: U of Chicago P, 2010.

Gornick, Vivian. *The Situation and the Story: The Art of Personal Narrative.* New York: Farrar, Straus and Giroux, 2002.

Gottschall, Jonathan. *The Storytelling Animal: How Stories Make Us Human.* New York: Mariner Books, 2013.

Heidkamp, Halie. "Final Uptake." 10 May 2018. Illinois State University, Normal, Illinois.

Henricks, Thomas. "The Nature of Play: An Overview." *The American Journal of Play* 1.2 (2008): 157–80.

Hesse, Douglas. "The Place of Creative Writing in Composition Studies." *College Composition and Communication* 62.1 (2010): 31–52.

Holdstein, Deborah H., and David Bleich, eds. *Personal Effects: The Social Character of Scholarly Writing.* Logan: Utah State UP, 2001.

Jamison, Leslie. *The Empathy Exams: Essays.* Minneapolis: Graywolf Press, 2014.

Nash, Robert J. and Sydnee Viray. *Our Stories Matter.* New York: Peter Lang, 2013.

Ruddick, Lisa. "Lisa Ruddick lectures on 'Literature and the Feeling of Aliveness.'" *YouTube*, uploaded by College of the Holy Cross, 11 Sep 2015, www.youtube.com/watch?v=qEyThLHSS3w&t=3443s.

Schroeder, Christopher, Helen Fox, and Patricia Bizzell, eds. *Alt-Dis: Alternative Discourses and the Academy.* Portsmouth: Boynton/Cook, 2002.

Smith, Sidonie, and Julia Watson. *Reading Autobiography: A Guide for Interpreting Life Narratives.* Minneapolis: U of Minnesota P, 2010.

I

How We Come to Terms
With Our Lives

1. *Before the Heavens Open Up*

Elizabeth Boquet[1]

I make a run for it. To pick up a baby present, to the bakery, and finally to Fisherman's Seafood on Magazine, where I grab the last two pounds of boiled crawfish and a grape Fanta for five bucks. That's dinner. All the while I keep my eye to the sky, where the mid-summer late afternoon storm clouds are gathering. New Orleans' public radio station, WWOZ 89.9, is playing Corigliano's "Voyage for Flute and Strings" and there is something about being behind the wheel with the sky looming and the crepe myrtles draping and the piercing clarity of Edmund-Davies' articulation that is simultaneously wearying and edifying. "You better get your little butt home," I can hear my mom saying, "before the heavens open up." "I'm on my way," I think to myself. "I am on my way."

Home for the moment is an AirBnB in New Orleans, a cottage behind a camelback on Camp Street. It has a lovely courtyard shaded by a majestic oak tree so I am not surprised to find myself shooing feral cats from my doorstep, scooping up roach carcasses, and chasing lizards around my bathroom with a tin pie plate and a plastic Krewe of Endymion cup. I haven't lived down South for a long time but that shit is like riding a bike. It comes right back. I'm in New Orleans for a week, writing. Or doing some approximation of it. New Orleans is home, or some approximation of it. When I tell the bus driver I am from here but I live now in Connecticut, he says, "Damn, you a long way from home." As we talk more, I tell him I'm actually from Thibodaux, a small town about 50 miles south of the city. He says, "Thibodaux? To Connecticut? Well you a real long way. I mean, New Orleans, that's a long way. But Thibodaux's a whole nother thing."

When I planned my summer writing time, I expected to have a lot of material to work from—the scores of letters my mom wrote me over the nearly three decades we spent living apart. When I realized how scattered they were—tucked in drawers, stuck in file folders, crumpled in moving boxes—I made it my early summer project to gather them all, to slip them one by one into translucent sleeves, and to clasp them in 3-ring binders. I made a special trip to Staples to buy these items brand new, though we had some gently used ones at home. My mom would have said that was good enough. She made do with other people's leftovers her whole life. Even her letters are written on outdated stationery from the defunct family insurance agency or on leftover sheets of a yellow legal pad. Not only does she not let this stop her, she narrates her noticing, like when she writes, "Oh oh, I didn't notice this page was torn." No, for this project, for these letters, she will have new things.

By the end of July, the binder sat on my office desk, empty. The carton of translucent sheets next to it, unopened. I thought this would be the least of the tasks I could accomplish in a summer. All the letters are dated, some even with the day of the week and a time stamp ("Thursday—February 25, 1999, 11:30 a.m."). All I needed to do was stack them and page through the upper right-hand corners to put them in order. Would not have even needed to read her writing about this newspaper clipping she is sending or this photo she thought was funny or how much she misses her sister, her brother, her son, or her daughter, me. Still, I couldn't.

*

When classes began in the fall, my first-year writing students purchased their own 3-ring binders, with their own translucent sleeves. We compiled our portfolios together. The first item I placed in my binder was a class reunion booklet from May 18, 1991, when the Thibodaux College/Mount Carmel Convent Classes of 1950 and 1951 gathered in our small South Louisiana hometown. I didn't slide it into a sleeve. Instead I tucked it in the front pocket. Provisional, but it was progress. Two paragraphs on page 28 are devoted to my mother's life in the fifty years between her graduation and this gathering. They note her "Associate's Degree in Secretarial Science" from Francis T. Nicholls Junior College and name her two children ("Bert Jr. and Elizabeth"). Her mini-autobiography reads like this: "Once her children started school, Pat began working for her husband and continued to do so until 1989 when she 'retired.' She now enjoys fishing with Bert and spoiling her granddaughter, Jessica."

Some readers might wonder why she would put "retired" in quotes, but I know my parents closed the insurance agency my father had run for more than 40 years because the business tanked during the recession in the late 1980s. I also know she was continuing to work, for no pay (which is how she had been working in the agency for more than 20 years) in a quirky "wellness center" my father set up in 1990. My mother doesn't mention this work. At the time of the reunion, in 1991, I'm sure she was hoping her involvement in this venture would be minimal but, as it turns out, she ended up keeping the books, making out orders, and when necessary working the floor and standing behind the counter selling vitamins and herbs for nearly 20 years. She retired (no quotes) in 2008, when they closed that business for good. Also, she did not enjoy fishing and certainly by 1991 her arthritis would have prevented her from climbing into a boat to do it, even if she were so inclined. She did enjoy spoiling her granddaughter Jessica. That part is true.

Clipped to the inside of the reunion booklet's front cover are two yellowing pages from what must have been my mom's original yearbook, a prose poem entitled "Senior Class Prophesy Their Futures." It is told in the voices of an assortment of animals in a spring garden where "Birds were singing sweetly/Bees were busy, too/And butterflies were flitting high/High into the blue." Each of the fourteen young women in the Mount Carmel Class of 1951 has a couplet devoted to her, their cap-and-gown portraits appearing in some proximity to their stanzas. My mom's is told in the voice of a raven, who says, "Some day a novelist Pat will be/Her tales will be carried across the sea."

When I found this record among her things, when I read this rhyme about her stories, I broke wide open for the girl who became the woman I never saw read a book, other than the ones she recited tirelessly to her children and grandchildren. Who spent her days poised at an IBM Selectric, typing claims forms in triplicate. Who wrote recipes in a shorthand no one now can read. Her novel, as far as I can tell, she wrote only to me.

*

In "Argument as Emergence, Rhetoric as Love," Jim W. Corder writes,

> What happens if the merest glimpse into another narrative sends us lurching, stunned by its differentness, either alarmed that such differentness could exist or astonished to see that our own narrative might have been or might yet be radically otherwise than it is? Do we hold our narratives? Keep telling the story we have been telling? At all costs? (19)

The shock of discovering our parents are people without us is a familiar trope. We walk in on our parents having intimate moments just as we are coming to wonder, or understand, what that means. We see photos of our mothers when they were objects of desire, maybe even before they were wives, back when they were as close as ever to feeling like their own women. I always knew my mother had been Liz-Taylor beautiful and a masterful flirt, but a novelist? That, I never knew. I never knew her to aspire. Is this the truth? When she offered this tidbit for her yearbook, was it like her saying she was "retired"?

That she liked fishing? Or that she enjoyed spoiling her granddaughter? Was it somehow all of that? Or none of the above. "Sometimes we turn away from other narratives," Corder writes. "Sometimes—probably all too seldom—we encounter another narrative and learn to change our own" (19).

*

After my mom died, friends encouraged me to write my way through the grief. They gave me notebooks for my birthday, for Christmas, for the trip to bury her. I had never been a journaler, but this unmooring, this untethering was so profound. Maybe it required new modes. Maybe, I thought, I should try it.

My therapist also told me to write—but not like the writing I normally do, she said. Not writing that someone else might see. Writing that was, instead, just for me, where I could write whatever I was feeling. As though writing wasn't already that. As though I had a category for writing that didn't include an audience. I don't. It was not helpful. None of this was helpful. Mostly what it made me feel was that I was mourning badly, that I was grieving wrong. I stopped writing. I stopped trying to write.

For months, I swallowed my sadness. My body told my stories for me. When I couldn't breathe, the pulmonologist took one look in my throat and said I had heartburn so bad it was spilling over and scorching my esophagus. "Haven't you felt it?" he asked. I said no, I had not. When a filling needed to be replaced, the dentist gave me a shot of novocaine to numb my lower jaw. I went home after the procedure and waited for the feeling to return in my mouth. It never did. Hours, days, weeks later, I felt nothing on the left side but the occasional prickle in my lip, my tongue, my cheek. A neurologist and a potent course of steroids shocked my face back to life. When my period started in November and didn't stop ever, my gynecologist put me under in February for a D&C. I woke to tears running down my cheeks, pooling in my ears, to a nurse with a purple glove wiping them away. "She's crying," I heard her say. "I had a bad dream," I said, thick-tongued. "She says she had a bad dream," the nurse repeated. A man behind my head touched my shoulder and said, "You couldn't have had a bad dream. I gave you only the happy juice." I never saw his face.

I have since found my way to writing about my mom, about her life, about her death, the only way I've ever known how—for and with others. I now have thousands of words—poems, flash nonfiction, lyrical essays, a more-than-partial outline of a memoir. Last summer, I pulled out one draft and asked a friend for feedback. "This piece," I said to him, "this one is special." I had already submitted it to, and had it rejected by, a few favorite journals. My friend said, "It needs more of your mother's voice." I mentioned that I might have a few letters I could look through.

*

My favorite letter of hers, and the first one I managed to slip into a sleeve, is the only one I have that is not addressed to me. The envelope reads "To Miss A. H. Hoffmann. Thibodaux, LA." It is written in a child's cursive, in pencil, on unlined pulp paper, folded in half, then in quarters, then in half again:

Dear Mama,

I am going to play with Olver [Olive] at 2 thirty. And your answer is going to be no. But I don't care I am still going. And to morrow I am going to school so that is setele now. You don't want me to go too school but I am going there to. And I am not taktinek castoroil to morrow morning. And I never going to either. I hope Sally [my mom's older sister] does'nt mine me using her ditonary. If she gets mad well that's going to far. Love from Pat.

I was dumbfounded (to use one of my mom's favorite words) when I read this letter. I know my mom's mother (whom all the grandchildren called "Ma") only through family stories—she died when my mom was 25, eight years before I was born. Through those tellings, I learned Ma was proper and wealthy. The matriarch. That she expected deference. Respect. I couldn't imagine my mom mouthing off to Ma like that, the way I was assured she never had, the way I used to smart off, the way that earned me a good mouth-soaping and, when I didn't complain enough about the lather, a desperate tongue-peppering.

*

My mom kept a photo of Ma on her dresser in the bedroom. In it, she wore an all-black shirtwaist dress with a white corsage on her left lapel. If I had to guess, I would have said she was seventy, but I know she couldn't have possibly been. She died in her mid-50s, not much older than I am now, about the same age my mom was when I left home, when she began writing her letters to me. Ma looks straight into the camera, her salt-and-pepper hair gathered loosely in a bun at the nape of her neck, her lips drawing a thin straight line. I see that same expression in photos of my mom. No teeth. No smile. An expression only of regard. Once my mom held on to a picture my husband took of me on a ferry crossing Lake Champlain. "You're wearing my expression," she said, which I was. She could just have easily have said it was Ma's, which it was. "I didn't know you made that face," she said. "Neither did I," I said.

I don't know what happened to the photo of Ma that stood on the dresser all those years. I only remembered this story when I began doing this writing alongside my first-year composition students, who were reading Ruth Oze-ki's *The Face: A Time Code* and writing their own versions of that essay. I was teaching this piece for the first time. First-year students often need encour-agement to write in the first person. I thought Ozeki's format would provide helpful constraints: "The experiment is simple: to sit in front of a mirror and watch my face for three hours." Students needed only to regard their faces for 30 minutes. "Really look at yourself," I told them. "Don't look away. Record everything you are thinking."

I underestimated how terrifying the writing would be for them. "This is unbearable," several students said. As I sat with their resistance to this assignment one evening, I started archiving a few more of my mom's letters, and the memory of these photos resurfaced—Ma in her shirtdress, me on the ferry, my mom holding us each in her hands. I heard my students again, only now with my heart, not with my head: This is unbearable. Of course it is. Why didn't I know this.

The first-year students at Fairfield are only beginning to encounter the foundational questions that animate the Jesuit Catholic mission of our uni-versity: "Who am I? Whose am I? Who am I called to be?" The daily practice of discernment in Ignatian Spirituality requires quiet self-regard and deep contemplation as preparation for action. These are questions with no final answer, only the mindful consideration of at least one next step.

*

When I say I miss my mom, my friend Liz replies, "She is still in you." At times, I want to stamp my feet in response, like a five-year-old: "I don't want her there. I want her *here*." Like that little girl who wanted to play with her friend Olive and go to school so bad she wrapped her chubby little fingers around a pencil and put her mom in her place, if only on paper. I want to tell her to get her little butt home before the heavens open up. Before the earth swallows me whole. I don't expect Ma let my mom go play with Olive or go to school the next day. I don't expect my mom to get her little butt home. But that doesn't mean it don't need to be said. I want my mom in the world with me.

I want my mom in the world with me so much I have spent years com-mitting her stories to the page. They are in me, as Liz says. When I trail out a memory, my cousins say, "I miss Aunt Pat and her stories." My stories of her stories are not the same. But I haven't trusted her to tell her own sto-ries, which was one of her true joys. I have ignored her, just like everybody else.

*

Despite much encouragement and several scaffolded writing exercises, in their first drafts, most students used the mirror as an occasion to write about themselves in the broadest terms possible. Reading these early efforts, I couldn't tell whether they had even looked in a mirror before starting to write. I certainly couldn't see how sustained attention to the contours of their faces had led them to the stories they were composing.

I considered abandoning the assignment. Maybe this was asking too much. The transition to college is such a tricky time. I could see why sitting and staring at your face in a mirror for 30 minutes seemed pointless or weird, why it might make them feel too vulnerable. I decided to give it one more go. For homework, I asked them to model Ozeki's first chapter, entitled "Time Code 00:00:00." In it, she time-stamps each paragraph, describes her most mundane actions ("I've put the mirror on the altar where the Buddha used to be.") and signals her procrastination through a series of frantic questions and stream-of-consciousness observations ("Okay. Ready. No, wait, there's dust on the mirror. Must clean it. Do I have vinegar? Yes, under the sink.") Finally, they get it. Or I get it. We all get it.

*

4/27/98—Monday
Dear Bethy—
I just got through doing my books for the store & everything balanced the first time. I thought I'd celebrate by writing you a short letter.

I am an accidental archivist at best, an inept one at worst. I come by my disorganization honestly. When my parents moved to Connecticut to live near my husband and me, my mom dumped generations of memorabilia into gray Country Life Vitamin shipping bins: photos, letters, photos, trophies, photos, diplomas, photos. Nothing and no one is identified. Back home, there was no need. The guessing games were rapport-building. Who is this, when was this, where was this—questions were our conversation starters. So this 1998 letter is filed right behind my mom's letter to Ma, even though there are many letters from her that come before it. I file it first because of its celebration of writing. I haven't found another instance where she acknowledges such explicit pleasure in having a chance to write. More to the point, perhaps, she is celebrating finishing the books, a task she hated. At any rate, she is celebrating, and that is rare enough.

*

Once my first-year writing students completed their initial portfolios ("The Face"), they began their writing inventories. In much the same way they struggled with looking at their faces, they struggled to *see* their writing.

Their initial attempts, brainstormed in class, were abbreviated. It took effort and attention to draw out all the writing they did in a day: Instagram captions, texts to parents, whiteboard notes on residence hall doors. "All of that," I tell them, "is writing. You are all writing all the time." But is this *writing*? Or is it "writing"? I press forward with the premise that all "writing" is *writing*, practically a commandment in my field. But is it the truth? Am I doing my students a disservice when I encourage them to shed their skepticism that the notes they took in accounting class and the notes they took on their faces are simply different in degree, not in kind? In "'You Can't Make This Stuff Up': Complexity, Facts, and Creative Nonfiction," Chris Mays writes, "The primary source of writing's power is not its simplicity, but its ability to *disguise* its own incredible complexity" (320).

To begin our work on Portfolio 2, we shared students' reflections on Portfolio 1. We considered how Joan Didion's "On Keeping a Notebook," the first reading they did for our class, prepared them to turn the time-stamped Writer's Notebook entries observing their faces into their braided personal essays on the self, how waking up to a new zit above an eyebrow or seeking out the barely-there scar from a mole removed on a chin became a meditation on the koan Ozeki poses in her prologue: "What is your original face?" We talked about how much heavy-lifting these entries, these lists, did in the end.

I don't keep a notebook, despite my devotion to Didion, but I do save scraps of paper that tell stories no one but I can remember. A random assortment of them lives beneath my clear desk protector. As I type, they peek out from beneath my laptop, my iPad, the latest issue of *CCC*. In the top left corner is a list my mom sent me to the grocery store with, probably ten years ago now. In a desperate moment of grading procrastination, faced with the mound of Portfolios 1, I spied that list and wondered whether I could do anything with it, whether I could translate that "writing" to *writing*. I remembered, if not the specific day, at least the general time (spring of my 2007 sabbatical) when my mom sent me to Rouse's for lettuce, tomatoes, Chex cereal, and corn. Oh and—last minute addition—crawfish. I searched for places that might publish something inspired by a list like this, and I found one (Boquet). The memory spilled out.

My mom didn't keep a notebook either. At work she took dictation and typed. I don't recall ever hearing her refer to these activities as writing. I'm fairly certain she would not have regarded them that way. I never found among her personal effects, either when she was alive (I was an unrepentant snoop) or after she died, any evidence that she wrote in a journal. Like me, she does not appear to have had a category of writing that was for her and her alone.

My mom was a woman of letters. Growing up, I understood this mostly through her devotion to the prompt and proper thank-you note. I also knew she had been a devoted correspondent when my father was in the Army, but I had only his replies (tied with a string in a box in the attic) as evidence. For almost 40 years, she seems to have had no occasion to put her thoughts down on paper, aside from expressions of sympathy or congratulations—narrow genres. It's possible, I suppose, that there was someone else somewhere, but I have nothing to go on. Sometimes I wish I did. That trail is ice cold.

When I lived at home, my mom and I were hard on each other. She hovered, I bristled, we fought. Doors were slammed, tears were shed. My long-distance move turned out to be the best one for our relationship. Once I was out of the house, we talked on the phone every single day, with very few exceptions, at a time when people still paid by the minute. Between minutes to spare, which she had plenty of, and money, which was scarce, she somehow always found the money. Still, she wrote—I hadn't realized how often, not until I started gathering her letters to me in one place, a project that is ongoing. I won't even venture a count at this point. I am too far from being certain I have gathered them all.

As for me, I was a much less faithful correspondent. I rarely wrote her back. I didn't really see the point. It took a full seven days for mail to travel between us. By my calculations, we would have talked nearly a dozen times by then, sometimes more. My mom knew it too. "Well, Boo," she writes on Tuesday, 4/8/97, "I have work to do so I'd better close. Take care & I will be talking to you soon—today as a matter of fact. I love you, Mom." But the duplication does not seem to have dissuaded her from posting.

For a while I hoped I wrote more often than I remembered, but I've come to think that is not the case, as she appears to have saved whatever I sent to her, mostly special occasion cards with rote and repetitive messages: "I'm sorry I can't be there for [fill-in-the-blank]" or "I can't believe we're spending another [fill-in-the-blank] apart." From me, I found only two items so far that I would call letters: one written in block print on Big Chief paper, dated (by my mom) 2/25/73, when I was six years old; the other, from my senior class retreat and addressed to both my parents. On its original envelope, my mom wrote, "We treasured this. Thank you. Love, Mom." Neither of these letters represents what I would call self-sponsored writing, prompted as they were in response to some assignment, with some oversight by a teacher. Despite my lack of reciprocity, my mom continued to write. The corpus of her letters is rich and varied. I am only beginning to code them.

This summer it will be seven years since my mom passed away—Thursday, 07/28/11. I wish I didn't remember that morning as well as I do. She went

from home to ambulance to ER to morgue in just under three hours. Before
the day was out, I had written a set of thank-you notes to the emergency
room staff, to the physician, to the nurse who stayed with me through my
mom's final stages of respiration. Then I put my pen down for a long while.

This summer I will be writing an application for a sabbatical. At our Jesuit
Catholic university, colleagues remind each other of that word's Latin roots:
sabbath. A holy time. A time of worship. A time of rest. A time when the
land lies fallow. In farming, we don't hew to this notion anymore. Agricul-
tural science methods allow for continuous crop rotation, and modern universities press for ever more productivity—including, perhaps especially, from
those faculty at institutions still supporting these extended leaves. A proposal
for a semester to worship and rest probably would not carry the day on my
campus, in spite of our mission, but that's okay. My mom's words have lain
fallow long enough. It's time to till the soil.

Note

1. Elizabeth Boquet, Professor of English, Fairfield University. eboquet@fairfield.edu

References

Boquet, Elizabeth H. "How to Make a Grocery List." 01 March 2018. *Dead House-
keeping.* http://www.deadhousekeeping.com/entries/how-to-make-a-grocery-list.
Accessed 01 November 2018.
Corder, Jim W. "Argument as Emergence, Rhetoric as Love." *Rhetoric Review* 4.1 (1985):
16–32.
Didion, Joan. "On Keeping a Notebook." *Slouching Toward Bethlehem.* New York: Farrar
Straus and Giroux, 1968, 131–41.
Mays, Chris. "'You Can't Make This Stuff Up': Complexity, Facts, and Creative Nonfic-
tion." *College English* 80.4 (2018): 319–41.
Ozeki, Ruth. *The Face: A Time Code.* Brooklyn, NY: Restless Books, 2015.

2. An Arrangement

Rona Kaufman[1]

In my parents' living room, in a gold-plated, two-part, hinged frame, my photo adjoins one of my paternal grandmother. We both focus past the camera lens, each of us looking alert, as though we are listening with interest and pleasure to someone with persuasive charm just out of frame. I am a sitting-up baby in a red dress, white tights, and white lace-up shoes, holding a squeaky toy, which blends into my dress and distracts my hands. My grandmother also appears to be in a photographer's studio, in a dark V-neck dress with buttons and puffed shoulders. She wears light-rimmed glasses, her hair braided and pinned to her head like a crown. Her lips are painted and her cheeks flushed, though it's not clear how much color comes from her and how much from the processing of the print. She is heavier in this photo than in most of the ones I've seen of her, her hair ungrayed and her smile easy. I imagine she is in her 40s. She has not yet lost her second husband. She has not yet had to rent out the third floor of her Pittsburgh home. She has not yet gotten sick. I know neither grandmother—neither the vibrant one nor the wizened one. Our photos, divided by thin borders of plated gold, are the closest we ever get to touching. My grandmother died 18 months before I was born, so there is no picture of her holding me. I have always felt connected to her—am, in fact, named after her—yet the closest I can physically get to her are these photos arranged on built-ins in my parents' home, our images hinged, our gazes parallel, but never sharing the same frame.

My parents' living room is full of framed family photos. I am responsible for several of them, taking the photos, buying the frames, and moving the images to the room in which my now-almost-octogenarian parents spend most of their time. I was the child in the family who poured through family photo albums, making homemade glues for pages that had lost their stick and complaining about my under-representation as the youngest child who followed twins. Now in my 40s myself, a new mother and a new wife, I have taken a different, deeper interest in these photos and in my family's histories. I have been aware for most of my life that I am a child in this clan, but it is now, in my middle age, that I am trying to find my place in a line of mothers.

I set off to find my grandmother. I take what I know—that she was born in Poland around 1900, that she migrated to the United States around 1920, that she lived in Pittsburgh until her death in 1968, that she was married twice and had four children, that she was Jewish and primarily spoke Yiddish—and I plug the details into search engines. I find nothing before a 1930 census. No Rose Adler in Warsaw, no Rose Adler immigrating through Ellis Island, or Philadelphia, or Baltimore, or Boston, no Rose Adler in Pittsburgh before a husband and two sons. I call my father in Pittsburgh, who restates the facts he knows and apologizes for all he doesn't, for not paying better attention. I call my uncle, now 88, who recalls less than my father but less apologetically, who tells me that my other uncle, deceased in 1985, would have been a better source. I write to cousins who don't respond or who don't know. I question my facts. Maybe she wasn't born in Warsaw but somewhere else in Poland, and maybe not then-Poland but now-Poland. Maybe Rose Adler was her Anglicized name. The gap between my grandmother and me widens rather than narrows. My uncle, 11 years older than my father and a son of the first husband, remembers one detail long forgotten: Rose's first marriage was arranged. I hold onto this new piece and lay it beside the others and try to make a story.

On Rhetoric

In classical rhetoric, the work of making a persuasive text is organized into five stages: invention, arrangement, style, memory, and delivery. Called the canons of rhetoric, these five steps provide a scaffold for speakers to formulate arguments; to order the parts of a speech persuasively; to find the best language to present the argument; to employ mnemonics to help the speaker practice the speech; and to modulate the voice and the body to present the speech. Moving systematically—and sometimes concurrently: as Cicero explains, "the structure of memory, like a wax tablet, employs places [*loci*] and in these gathers together images" (Ede, et al, 232)—through the canons allows the speaker to develop a full and complete speech. These speeches should also cover Aristotle's three different appeals: to reason (*logos*), to emotion (*pathos*), and to the speaker's authority (*ethos*). While all three appeals should be present in a speech, Aristotle has a hierarchy. Logical appeals are at

the heart of the argument. Pathos and ethos are in the introduction and conclusion—ways to bring listeners in and out, but not to hold them. Arrangement, hinging content and (imagined) audience response, swims in emotion.

On Invention

What I know about my paternal grandmother:

> She was born in Poland around the turn of the twentieth century.
> She migrated to the United States around 1920.
> She lived in Pittsburgh until her death in 1968.
> She was married twice. Though unrelated, each man was named Kaufman.
> She was Jewish and spoke Yiddish.
> She had four children: two sons with her first husband, and a daughter
> and a son, my father, with her second.
> She became a naturalized citizen in 1943.
> She died a year and a half before I was born.
> I was named after her. In Hebrew: Rachel.

What I don't know about my paternal grandmother:

> If her name in Poland was Rose Adler, as my father says.
> If she came from a family of rabbis and if she had diamonds and salami
> sewn into the lining of her coat as she crossed, as my father believes.
> Why she migrated to the United States.
> If she had family who migrated with her, or before her, or after her.
> Why she chose Pittsburgh.
> How she met her husbands.
> If her first marriage was arranged, as my uncle suspects.

On Arrangement

I sign up for an Ancestry.com account and dive in. What I learn about Rose
from the 1930 census is that, as of April 1, 1930, she was married to Paul
Kaufman; listed as either 20 or 30 years old (there is a cross out and correction in this column, but the correction is not clear); lived on Devilliers
Street; paid $16 a month in rent (the least of any of their neighbors on the
page); had two sons, Hyman J. (four) and Bernard N. (nine months); was
20 at her first marriage; immigrated at 20; was understood as white; was
from Poland, as were both her parents; spoke Yiddish in the home before

coming to the United States; was able to speak English; had no occupation; and was an "alien." Many of her neighbors were Polish and spoke Yiddish. (A good number of neighbors were also from the American South—Georgia, Atlantic, and Virginia—which seems much more surprising to me than the Eastern-European-populated street.) Her husband Paul was 12 years her senior, had migrated in 1910, was the owner of a confectionary store, had his first papers for naturalization, had worked the day before the census worker came to record their socio-economic facts, and was not a veteran.

My uncle casts doubt on this record. He tells me that he thinks his mother was younger when she came over, that she was 16 or 18 years old in 1917 or 1918 or 1916. He thinks that she went through Ellis Island ("My impression was that she came by herself") and traveled straight to Pittsburgh, where she met Paul Kaufman, a third cousin, also from Warsaw, who had been arranged to be her husband. My uncle, who lost his father before he turned two years old, believes that Paul Kaufman was 41 or 42 when he died and that he was not the owner of a candy store but someone who sold apples on the street corner. Paul died of pneumonia. My uncle thinks there was already a cousin in Pittsburgh—Hymie Gordon, a Communist and successful baker. He doesn't think she ever went to school (something supported in the 1940 census) and spoke Yiddish, Polish, Russian, and English. She couldn't read or write in English—in fact, "I never saw her read or write at all." My uncle stretches for more details. Rose's mother's name was Bella, and my uncle was named for her; her father was Huskel. My grandmother married her second husband, Nathan, when my uncle says he was six years old. (My grandparents' marriage license, which my father has in his nightstand, puts him at nine. I see that her parents are listed as Beatrice Joey and Henry Kaufman, and I wonder which story is being told here, and by whom.) He doesn't know how they met and never thought to ask. "I'm not a good info person, Rona," my uncle says, "Uncle Chick had it all down pat." His parents were "very private about stuff, especially Nathan. It was his way. He was the most taciturn guy you ever saw. He would sit in the living room and listen to the radio for hours."

My uncle really wants to tell me more about the nearer past and the present—his close but fractious relationship with Uncle Chick and his family, his lifelong disdain of my aunt, the magnetism of California, his frustrations with my father's memory gaps but his belief that my father is a "good soul," and his love for his cherished grandchildren. I keep returning him to his mother, to her life and family in Warsaw. But my uncle doesn't remember Rose's communicating with any of her family other than Hymie Gordon—not in Poland, "no city in the U.S. either," he adds. "She didn't keep in touch that I knew. Never a phone call. I don't remember any mail. She might have been in some touch through Hymie Gordon. He would come to the house every day with fresh bread." My uncle can't remember much about Hymie Gordon either, other than that he was a baker; "that he was very active in the Communist Party," which kept my father out of the Intelligence Corps when he enlisted in the army in the late 1950s; and that "he treated Rose like a little sister." When I check a distant cousin's family tree, I see that Paul Kaufman's mother's name was Rachel Adler and wonder if that echo of name is as much confirmation as I'm going to get that Rose and Paul were cousins.

On Rhetoric

So strongly is Aristotle associated with the five canons that it is disorienting to go looking for them in his *Rhetoric*, tidy in a row, and not find them there. Books I and II address invention. Book III addresses arrangement, style, some delivery, but not memory. All five canons have to be teased out of the Rhetoric, with rhetoricians who know the framework and trust the parts are there to find. The clear, balanced organization of the canons comes after one has read all the way through not just the *Rhetoric* but all of Aristotle's works.

On Arrangement

I email the Rabbi, tell him briefly about my grandmother, and ask him what he knows about arranged marriage and Eastern European Jews. He writes back immediately and says "it would not surprise me if she was married to a distant relative and that it was arranged. On my father's family tree there are a number of marriages between relatives, although it is not clear if they were arranged since it was in Germany." He points me toward a few books and articles. "By the way," the long- and happily married rabbi closes, "if you Google *arranged Jewish marriage Poland*, you get Polish dating and single sites!"

One of the articles the rabbi sends me to is about *Briefenshtellers*, a book of sample letters about family, community, and business activities and events, including courtship and arranged marriage. These letters would often be copied word for word—either by the sender or by a paid letter writer if the sender were illiterate—and would be a way of expressing love, extending invitations, giving thanks, and conducting business. The earliest known Briefenshteller was published in 1610, and the most recent in the late 1920s; the majority were published between 1880 and World War 1. In the early-twentieth-century, New-York-published *Briefenshteller* that sociologist Nathan Hurvitz studies, courtship and marriage letters—written by matchmakers, potential betrotheds, parents, and friends—account for 15% of the letters in the book, showing the normalcy if not centrality of arranged marriages in Eastern-European Jewish culture. They also show that they involved trans-Atlantic relationships, as some of the sample letters come from a friend in New York who is helping to guide her Eastern-European friend on a potential match. They are also far livelier— *The subject of this inquiry, your daughter that is, is certainly not an exceptional beauty nor is she well educated. Apparently you want to hide these shortcomings with a lot of money—which is, I must tell you, a good cover—for with it one can even cover a hump on her back too. So it occurred to me to propose a match* (Hurvitz 426)—than one might expect a template letter to be.

Marriages were arranged in order to build or maintain the prestige of a family, to ensure economic stability or mobility, to encourage procreation, and to control the family line. Had my grandmother's first marriage been arranged at a young age, long before Paul Kaufman migrated to the United States? My father says she came from a religious family—my father grew up with a now-missing portrait of her father wrapped in a tallit, a Jewish prayer shawl, in the dining room—and so perhaps the arrangement came from a desire to maintain a religious family. Or was the marriage arranged after he was settled in the New World and the arrangement was strategic, a way to get a daughter from one place to another? A way to keep her safe?

On Invention

On my paternal grandfather's side, I am lucky. A third cousin, Cindy, has already done considerable genealogical work, and while she doesn't go beyond my great grandparents, she has amassed a lot of records, including those about my great grandmother, who is listed as Nahoma, Norma, Annie, and Dorothy in various documents. A photograph shows her to be a singularly unattractive woman in a white dress and white head covering in a dark room. I learn that my great grandmother bore eight children, only five of whom lived, and died in 1919 of senility and heart failure; my grandfather Nathan is listed as the informant of her death. One of best things I discover from Cindy's archival collection is my paternal grandfather's initial naturalization papers in 1919, 24 years before my grandmother's. One of his witnesses was named Max Americansky. Literally *Max from America*. A complete invention.

My cousin has little, though, on my grandmother Rose, who was my grandfather's second wife (I come to learn) and who, as someone not genetically related to Cindy, is on an outer limb of her family tree. The website shows that my cousin has been collecting this material for just shy of a decade, and so perhaps it is unfair to say that she's untroubled by the lack of certain detail attached to my grandmother, that she is untroubled that my grandmother's birthyear is listed as 1898, 1900, and 1901. Perhaps she, too, has spent hours, keystrokes, and phone calls trying to place my grandmother specifically in the world. My cousin tells me several times in our phone call that most of her information comes from living people and that I should bring skepticism into the written record. One of my great uncles, for example, left the United States several times because he did not like America very much—"did not like being a small fish in a big pond"—which is something the record doesn't show. "I talk to living people as much as I can," she says, "because they have more information." And also, she says, "because it's more fun than talking to dead people." I do enjoy talking to my cousin, but she isn't getting me closer to my grandmother.

And so I keep searching. Ship manifests. Naturalization records. Newspaper archives. Birth. Death. Censuses. Cemeteries. Pittsburgh. Pennsylvania. The United States. Poland. Warsaw. Russia. Adler. Kaufman. One F, two Fs, one N, two Ns. Rose, Rachel, Ruchel. I learn a little—details that flesh out the skeleton I already knew—but the historical record starts in 1930 with her already married and the mother of two small boys. When I try to find her in Poland, I'm not sure what blocks me more: not knowing Polish, the scarcity of digital records, or the scarcity of Jewish records, period. At one point in my family research, I am so hungry to find the facts of my grandmother that I consider hiring a genealogist, whose initial fee is $2,500. I even write a preliminary inquiry but then, not yet ready to turn over my family search to a stranger, duck the phone calls I get from a Salt Lake City area code in response. My husband, Ken, who has roots in Salt Lake and whose family was long-ago Mormon, gets excited to try his hand. But when his digital queries don't lead to answers, he gives up and pursues his own family lines. In the evening, after we put our daughter to bed, I sit on the sectional and Ken sits ten feet away at his desk. As I search in vain for my grandmother, I hear him call, "I can go back ten generations! No, wait! Eleven!" The privilege of being a descendant of the record keepers. That night when he gets into bed next to me, I want to smother him, briefly but purposefully, with my pillow.

On Rhetoric

In the thirteenth century *Poetria Nova*, Geoffrey of Vinsauf writes that arrangement has two paths: "on the one hand, it may labor up the footpath of art; on the other, it may follow nature's main street." The natural path follows an event's actual happenings and "does not deviate from the natural order of the events." The artistic path, however, plays with the order, "places ensuing things first," transposes order—and all without shame or tension: "on the contrary, without strife they take up their alternate positions, and freely, and in a spirit of good humor they cede to one another willingly." Artistic order *improves* natural order, rendering it more sophisticated and fertile. Natural order is "barren," but in artistic order, "one branch miraculously grows up into many, the single into several, one into eight. Now in the area of this technique the air may seem to be dark, the path rugged, the doors closed, and the problem knotty" (Bizzell and Herzberg 507).

The *Poetria Nova* provides tender reassurance for a granddaughter who loves the craft of a sentence and who can't go very far down the natural path, even to a relation as near as a grandmother.

On Style

When I learn that I am pregnant with a girl, Ken and I quickly settle on her name. In Judaism, parents name a baby after a family member who has died, and my family's version of this is to play with the first letter of the English name and give the same Hebrew name. My father asks me to consider naming my child after my Uncle Jerome, his oldest brother who died when I was a teenager—he is troubled that his brother has been dead for almost thirty years with no children named after him—but he does not have to ask. I did not know my uncle well at all—he had moved to California not long after I was born, and I had never been west of the Mississippi until after he died—but I know how important he was to my father. He is also the closest relative on my Jewish side to have died in my lifetime. Ken quickly agrees so long as our daughter can have the middle name of Lynn, a tradition for first-born daughters in his family. We brainstorm *J* names. *Jane. Julia. Jacqueline. Josie.* Ken suggests *Juniper* for his love of the natural world and for its evocation of Utah, where he grew up. I immediately say no but the next day say yes. Juniper can be June can be Juny can be Junebug. I hear so many possibilities—names and personas for her to play with. *Juniper.* It's in choosing a name for my daughter that she becomes most real to me—a cluster of cells turned into a baby turned into a person turned into my daughter. Even more so than my changing body, genetic tests, pictures from sonograms, and flutters and kicks in my belly, her name becomes an idea to think with.

Elie Wiesel writes, "In Jewish history, a name has its own history and its own memory. It connects beings with their origins. To retrace its path is then to embark on an adventure in which the destiny of a single word becomes one with that of a community; it is to undertake a passionate and enriching quest for all those who may live in your name." But figuring out Juniper's Hebrew name becomes more difficult than settling on her English one. When I work with the rabbi to prepare for her baby naming ceremony shortly after her birth, I cannot give him a straightforward path to her Hebrew name. I tell him she was named after Jerome Kaufman, who was referred to only as Chick in my lifetime. But Chick was not only called Chick in *his* lifetime: it's a nickname that stuck when he fought as a Marine in World War 2. My father was not entirely sure of Chick's Hebrew name. He says that my grandmother called him Chaim Yonkel. My other uncle thinks that Chaim Yonkel was Jerome's Yiddish name, not Hebrew name. My aunt thinks that his name was actually Yonkel Chaim and that, according to his birth certificate, his American name was Jerome Hyman Kaufman. She says that my uncle hated his middle name so much that he dropped it. She also says that my uncle was named after his great, great grandfather who had the same exact name. Years later, when I look up the 1930 census, I see that he is listed, at four, as Hyman J. Even figuring out Juniper's families' Hebrew names is complicated. Mine is Hebrew for Rachel, from my grandmother. Ken, who isn't Jewish, doesn't have a Hebrew name, but it's important to both of us that he be named in the ceremony. My father, Herb, is Huskel, from his grandfather, and my mother, Mary, is Miriam, a solipsistic invention when she converts at 24. The rabbi sorts through this murky history and suggests Chaya Ya'akova. He welcomes her into the world and guides us as we offer her the gifts of tradition, unconditional love, Jewish education, and independence—and, of course, her name. Her name is not merely a matter of style, something ornamental, but a pathway in the world, connecting her with her past—*a* past—and carrying her into the future.

On Arrangement

Also called *dispositio* or *disposition*, arrangement is a way of understanding the importance of organization, of moving readers or listeners to a new position of knowledge. G.S. Howard writes in 1788 that we order a subject "as it is fittest to gain the clearest knowledge of it." For Aristotle, this means marching through a preconceived ordering of movements: introduction, statement of issue, the argument, and the conclusion. For Cicero, arrangement has five parts and covers all of the appeals. For Erasmus, arrangement speaks to a range of orders, from syntax to propositions to parts of individual arguments to the whole argument. For Erasmus, arrangement is embodied, "what the sinews are in an animal's body," and joins the speaker's body to the audience's disposition, "since we both learn more easily and remember more accurately something that is said in a scattered and confused manner (in fact, the place where everything is said is quite important for persuasion, since it is improper to entrust some things to minds without prior preparation)." Language joins us, "supplies the words and figures suited to the subject: this is in language what flesh and skin are in the body, and gives a seemly covering to the bones and sinews" (Bizzell and Herzberg 631–632).

But arrangement can also help us learn what it means to know when our statement of fact doesn't hold, when the facts evaporate from the center. Arrangement can help us with the turn of the mind—another way of understanding disposition—that encourages connections in gaps that otherwise do not speak.

On Memory

During my first sabbatical in 2009, I decided to spend several months in Pittsburgh. I was doing a project on Jewish cookbooks in America, considering recipes and cookbooks as a form of life writing and researching how Jewish women in particular used this ready-made form to navigate faith and place. Living in Pittsburgh made it easier for me to get to libraries with strong cookbook holdings—in Boston, in Ann Arbor, in Lansing. I also wanted to interview my mother, who had converted to Judaism at 24 before marrying my father and who, without a Jewish parent to teach her, had cooked her way in part into Judaism. I wanted to read her cookbooks through this academic lens. But this was also a flimsy excuse to spend real time with my parents and with some of my closest friends, who had themselves recently returned to Pittsburgh, but for good. Just tenured, I was living happily in the Pacific Northwest but not deeply rooted—no partner, no children, no mortgage. I decided to take my flexibility, which could at times feel like loneliness, and go to my childhood home and be with the people who knew me the best and longest.

Driving to Pittsburgh from Tacoma in a Mini Cooper and with a 17-pound cat without pushing too hard and without wandering too far from the Interstate takes about six 500-mile days. I did the first two myself, leaving Tacoma right after the election that saw Referendum 71 pass, making domestic partnership equivalent to marriage in Washington State and extending LGBTQ rights. I drove 15 hours to my friend Jennifer's house in Logan, Utah, and then drove with her first to Cheyenne, Wyoming, where we walked to a statue of Esther Hobart Morris in the dark of night, and then to Grand Island, Nebraska to stay with her beloved aunt and uncle. I dropped Jennifer off at the Omaha airport and drove three hours alone to pick up my father at the Kansas City airport, who was wearing a Steelers jersey and standing outside Arrivals on a sunny day as though I were picking him up from the grocery store. He spent the next three days, with overnight stops in St. Louis and Indianapolis, telling me stories about our family.

It wasn't accidental that I organized my extended stay around the election. I stayed in Tacoma to vote. I stayed to be heard in a way that would register. The red-state/blue-state divide was not new, but it felt deepening to me, playing out legislatively, most prominently through marriage rights, and rhetorically, with a language of "real Americans." Barreling across country in a Mini Cooper with a checkerboard top and a big-boned cat, I carried my resentment of this phrase—designed, as I heard it, to dismiss people like me not living in the center—through the Intermountain West, through the plains, through the historical Midwest, into the Rust Belt. I thought a lot about my father, from working-class roots, Jewish, a state employee, long-time treasurer of his union, heart patient, Steelers fan, and marveled at how anyone could reject his realness. I wondered about our out-of-placement—as in, I wondered if we *were* out of place more than felt ourselves to be—and at times saw us, birds-eye, a blue dot driving through all that red. I drove the whole time while my father, who had taught me how to drive a stick-shift on a 1976 Ford Pinto but wasn't eager to test his skills two decades later, told me stories. He told me about his extended family in Pittsburgh, about growing up with his own heart-patient father, about working at a bakery as a boy with parents who wanted him to be a baker, about learning that his brothers were his half-brothers when his father died, about being a mediocre student who gave his teenaged paycheck to his mother, about his decision to join the army at 18. My father refers to those conversations all of the time. *Remember how I told you,* he'll say. *You know this story from our drive.* But the truth is that I have forgotten many of the details, especially when it comes to the extended family, the history before my father, one of the people of this world to whom I'll tether my life. How I wish I had recorded all 1,000 miles of conversation. How I wish my father himself remembered more of what he said. But I hope I never forget the feel of those miles on my skin, my father by my side, two real Americans carefully maneuvering their way through places they'd never been, enjoying the company and finding their way home.

On Style

My whole life, I have been told that I look like my grandmother. I don't
see it, perhaps because I never knew her in motion, perhaps because the few
photos I've seen of her place her in middle age or older. But I have dark hair
and eyes like her, fair skin like her, and for a long time I was short like her.
I was slow to grow, and my parents wondered if I would make it to five feet
tall (a late teenaged growth spurt got me to 5'3.5"). On her naturalization
certificate, Rose is listed as 5'1"—an exaggeration, says my father, who insists
she was 4'11". When I look at the photos of her in my parents' living room,
I think I see my own eyes, which means I now also see my daughter's. I can
remember as a child running errands with my parents in Squirrel Hill, one of
the historically Jewish parts of Pittsburgh and where my grandmother lived,
and being asked by strangers whom I did not know if I am Rose Kaufman's
granddaughter. They have located the past in me. And while I will not learn
the concept until I am in graduate school, I experience the sublime.

My father tells me that I not only look like Rose but share her ways. My
father's favorite nickname for me is Ronala—little Rona. But often enough he
calls me Mumala—little mother. Once during an argument with my father's
sister, my aunt got so angry with me that she placed me in a pattern I'm not
part of. "Mummy!" she yelled, "You always do this!" before she remembered
that she was talking to her niece. It is an aunt on my mother's side, Aunt Pat,
who most often connects me to my paternal grandmother. This aunt met my
grandmother only a few times, but she was clearly struck by her warmth, her
capacity for love and inclusion, her welcoming of my mother, the daughter
of two poor Irish Catholic immigrants, and her gift of letting go of people's
pasts to meet them in the present. When my aunt wants to praise me, she tells
me I remind her of my grandmother. It is a logic that guides my days.

On Delivery

One day at school, when I'm walking through the library, saying hello to the
librarians and student workers at the circulation desk, I see one particular
woman with new eyes. Ilona, one of my favorite librarians, grew up in Poland,
migrating to the United States in 1988 when she was 26. I tell her that I'm
trying to find the records of my Polish grandmother and ask if she can help
me. Ilona takes a piece of paper and writes carefully *Róża Adler*. "This is your
grandmother's name in Polish," she says. She is happy to help. She asks for
the facts I know, and she delivers her responses carefully, words balanced with
silence.

"She was Jewish?" Ilona asks.

"Yes. She migrated around 1920—definitely between the wars."

"That's good. If she hadn't...if she hadn't...you would not be standing here....
The Jews in Poland...in Eastern Europe...you would not be standing here."

These ellipses, these hesitations, sound loudly in all my grandmother-related conversations with Ilona. I do not know how to fill them. Does she worry that I worry that her family were perpetrators? that they were bystanders? that they could have fueled my grandmother's interwar migration? Or does she want me to know that her family were not "those" Poles who were active or complicit in Jewish persecution? Or is she figuring out what *I* know about Jewish-Polish history? Does she worry about what I might find?

"Adler is a common name," Ilona tells me.

"Is it? Is it a Polish name?"

"Well, it is a Jewish name."

I am reminded that *Jewish* and *Polish* are incompatible descriptors.

Ilona's own family does a lot of boundary crossing in the twentieth century. In the 1910s, her grandmother had migrated to the United States where she married and had two sons. She returned to Poland between the wars with her children. When she and her family began to hear rumors about Hitler, her husband said, "You should go back to America." She did. Ilona says she has always been interested in Jewishness in Poland and reads Isaac Bashevis Singer in particular for stories about Jewish life and culture in Poland. "Jewish culture is steeped into Poland," she tells me, "but there are no Jews." She tells me of Warsaw's flattening, how many youth were lost in the Uprising, how entire high school classes were wiped out.

Looking for Rose Adler means considering the Holocaust, even though she fled Poland roughly (likely) 20 years before the Nazis invaded Poland. This is not a surprise for Eastern European Jews who migrated at the beginning of the twentieth century. Even my cousin Cindy, whose archive focuses on the fecundity and success of the family, including one of the first female doctors in Pittsburgh in the 1920s, tells me that the Kaufmans left Tomashpol, Russia (now in Ukraine) because of pogroms. "It was unsafe to be there," she learned from her grandparents, my father's aunt and uncle. "They were pushed around and shoved around and killed and threatened." But this is general language that is delivered softly.

And so I'm surprised by the exacting bluntness I hear in searching for my grandmother. I write to a number of people I find on a Jewish genealogical site who have connections to Adlers in Warsaw. One writes me back immediately, telling me her grandmother's and great-grandparents' names. "There is no connection to Rose Adler Kaufman," she writes. "My grandparents died in Warsaw Ghetto. Hope you'll find information about your grandmother." Another person lists her grandparents and uncles and writes that one "ran away to USSR and was killed as a soldier in the Red Army. My father left after his brother and later became a soldier too and survived. The rest of the family died in the Ghetto. If you have more questions write again. We are not related but friends." I follow a lead about a Haskiel Adler, whose name is similar to my grandmother's father, the man whose portrait hung in my father's childhood dining room, who is not from Warsaw but from Tyszowce, a town in southeastern Poland that was incorporated in the mid-fifteenth century. I learn from Wikipedia that on April 16, 1942, the Nazis gathered the Jews of Tyszowce in the public square and shot them, dumping their bodies in a ditch.

And then there is the exacting silence. In February 2018, the Polish Senate passed a bill making it a crime to say that Poland or its people were complicitous with Nazis. A U.S. president who doesn't mention Jews on International Holocaust Remembrance Day and who fails to condemn Neo-Nazis. Two members of Parliament in Britain who propose changing Holocaust Memorial Day to "Genocide Memorial Day—Never Again for Anyone," because, after all, all genocides matter. Aristotle says that delivery itself is not "an elevated subject of inquiry" (III.3), that it is "unworthy" compared to the other canons. Yet he also acknowledges that "we cannot do without it," as "the way in which a thing is said does affect its intelligibility" (III.3). Not saying a thing delivers a different kind of intelligence, one that terrifies as it obscures.

On Rhetoric

Feminist scholars have reminded us that studying classical rhetoric requires troubling who the traditional rhetor is—"for until recently, the figure of the rhetor has been assumed to be masculine, unified, stable, autonomous, and capable of acting rationally on the world through language. Those who did not fit this pattern—women, people of color, poorly educated workers, those judged to be overly emotional or unstable—those people stood outside of the rhetorical situation, for they were considered neither capable of nor in need of remembering and inventing arguments" (Ede, et al, 232–233). Questioning who is included in rhetorical situations requires locating subjectivity "within the larger context of personal, social, economic, cultural, and ideological forces, impossible not to notice not only the context itself, but also who is absent from this context as well as what exclusionary forces (regarding knowledge and argument, for example) are at work there" (Ede, et al, 233). Lisa Ede, Cheryl Glenn, and Andrea Lunsford also insist that in addition to considering who is included in the study of rhetoric, we ask *what counts as knowledge*: "Women have also sought to include the intuitive and paralogical, the thinking of the body, as valuable sources of knowing, as sites of invention" (233). They call for feminist scholars to take Aristotle's dictum that "a speech has two parts. You must state your case, and you must prove it" (Ritchie and Ronald 14) and look instead for ways in which women's texts have "resist[ed] the linearity of beginning, middle, and end, preferring to alternate warp and woof, to move in circular or spiral rhythms, to weave and dance rather than march in a straight line" (Ritchie and Ronald 14).

An Arrangement

After years of searching, I cannot say that my grandmother Rose as an individual person has come into any clearer focus for me. She remains largely obscured in the historical record. Her life seemingly begins in the middle of things—largely rooted in place as a wife and mother. The exact place will change—my grandmother will live in a number of rented houses before ending her days in her own home on Darlington Road—but she will stay within a four-mile radius in Pittsburgh. Her husband will change: within eight years of losing her first Kaufman, she will marry another. And her number of children will change: she will have four children in 15 years (and, according to my father, a number of miscarriages in between). Despite the fact that she outlived him by 13 years, I have far more evidence of how my grandfather lived in the world than I do my grandmother. This may be, in part, because I have yet to discover a distant cousin who is equipped with genealogical skills and who is in the Adler line of my family. It is also in part because some of the ways that people are recorded in history are tied to traditional gender roles— draft cards, occupations outside the home, home ownership. But other factors in my grandparents' historical visibility are about the circumstances of their migrations: my grandfather's with his nuclear family before the wars; my grandmother's alone, between the wars, from a place razed and erased of Jews.

What marked my grandmother most was her role as wife and mother. Her married, maternal status is not just about the official record of the United States—not just the censuses. It determined her final affiliations: her obituary notes that she was a member of a Russian synagogue, despite the fact that my Polish grandmother was far more religious than my Russian grandfather, and she is buried on the Russian side of the Jewish-Russian-Polish cemetery in Pittsburgh, next to her second husband. The institution of marriage is also what moved her across the world: to be a wife and ideally mother moved her to safety and enabled her to mother four children who would go on to have seven children who would go on to have seven children. Eighteen people out of a single arrangement—and who knows how many more to come? That arrangement almost certainly saved her life and the line. My grandmother's story is a reminder that what appears to be a leaden anchor may in fact be a life preserver. And it's a lesson about how the weight of the linear at times takes priority over all else. If she stayed there, I could not be here. No artistic path can matter more than this natural one.

And yet who knows which stories aren't told here—stories about happiness, and purpose, and security, and assimilation, and connection? What choices did my grandmother believe she had—to marry the first time, the second time, to have children, to turn her head away from the Old Country and keep her gaze on the New? According to my father and my uncle, my grandmother was a woman who lived in the present. My father says that when he doubted himself, when he hesitated, his mother would say, "You're American born. Just do it!" as though all possibility begins with and in America. And so I will be left to invent an early life for my grandmother, one that seeks context and confronts exclusion, that embraces the gifts of the gaps, and that delights in the concurrence of the canons, the ways that invention, arrangement, memory, style, and delivery awaken and shape each other. The failures of the linear, the scarcity of historical proof, even the frustrations of fabrication, whether they be innocent or strategic and in service of someone else's story, have tilled some fertile ground. They have opened up more lines of dialogue and thinking than I could have imagined, and that I could have known I longed for, as I set out to find my young grandmother.

At my daughter's baby-naming ceremony, the Rabbi told this Midrash—a story, explanation, or commentary on Hebrew scripture:

> [W]hen the Jewish people had gathered at Mount Sinai to receive the Torah, God said to them: "I will give you My Torah, if you will prove to me that you deserve it."
>
> They answered, "Our ancestors are our proof."
>
> God said: "Your ancestors are not sufficient. Bring me better proof, and I will give you My Torah."
>
> The people replied: "Our prophets are our proof."

God said: "Your prophets are not sufficient. Bring me better proof, and I will give you My Torah."

They responded: "Our children are our proof."

God said: "They are certainly sufficient proof. For their sake I give My Torah to you."

Locating myself in a line of mothers means thinking through my daughter and what she will receive—directly and through the gaps.

I continue to add to the photo collection in my parents' living room, not only in terms giving them new framed photos every year but in terms of beings. I have brought a husband and child to the arrangement. Even the big-boned cat has made the gallery. My wonderful dog through marriage by all rights should be next. A photo of my husband and me on our wedding day, informal though it was, is placed near formal portraits of my parents and my Irish grandparents on their wedding days. And a photo of me and my daughter, just after her first birthday, as we both look to the camera and smile squinty smiles into the late-summer sun, is on the same shelf as the hinged photos of me and my grandmother. The next time I am in Pittsburgh, I will move them side by side and see what the new arrangement reveals.

Note

1. Rona Kaufman, Associate Professor of English, Pacific Lutheran University. kaufman@plu.edu

References

Aristotle. *The Rhetoric and Poetics of Aristotle*. Trans. W. Rhys Roberts and Ingram Bywater. New York: The Modern Library, 1954.

Bizzell, Patricia, and Bruce Herzberg, eds. *The Rhetorical Tradition: Readings from Classical Times to the Present*. 2nd ed. Boston: Bedford/St. Martin's, 2001.

Ede, Lisa, Cheryl Glenn, and Andrea Lunsford. "Border Crossings: Intersections of Rhetoric and Feminism." *Rhetorica: A Journal of the History of Rhetoric* 13.4 (Autumn 1995). 401–41.

Hurvitz, Nathan. "Courtship and Arranged Marriages Among Eastern European Jews Prior to World War I as Depicted in a *Briefenshteller*." *Journal of Marriage and Family* 37.2 (May 1975): 422–30.

Ritchie, Joy, and Kate Ronald, eds. *Available Means: An Anthology of Women's Rhetoric(s)*. *Pittsburgh:* U of Pittsburgh P, 2001.

3. Collecting and Coding Synecdochic Selves: Identifying Learning Across Life-Writing Texts

BUMP HALBRITTER AND JULIE LINDQUIST[1]

We begin our story of storying by inviting you to imagine the following scenario—one that, if you are a dedicated Pandora user (or even a not-so-dedicated, but moderately familiar one), may have some reference to your experience:

You are a committed control freak, and a connoisseur of esoteric music. You make mix "tapes." You give them to your friends as demonstrations of your good taste and judgment. You also do so as a demonstration of your generosity: you are generous with your time, your money, and your acumen. Good for you!

Now, however, you are confronted with a problem. You are also a control freak when it comes to hosting well-staged dinner parties, and you find yourself responsible for hosting such an event now, at the last minute. And your guests will, if dictates of fashionable lateness hold, be arriving in 20 minutes.

What to do? Could you, as a control freak, find a reason to entrust the evening's playlist to ... Pandora? Heresy, you think. But there are rugs to be swept, guacamole to be made, candles to be selected and rose petals to be scattered in a manner that looks random but is by no means random! You find yourself doing a quick and pragmatic cost-benefit analysis: which of the evening's features are you most determined to control? Which are you willing to relinquish control over, so that the entire event might impress upon your guests that they would do well to return for another such occasion?

And, having come around to such a devil's bargain, could you, having relinquished control of the mix to Pandora's algorithm, ever admit to yourself that your favorite track of the evening was the third song in the queue, a song you'd

never, until now, heard? Even after discovering that the song is one that is per-
formed by ... Bon Jovi?

If you're a Pandora user, you know that you are faced with choices and inter-
ventions, and that these are different from those you encounter if you use, for
example, a service like Spotify. If you've spent some time with Pandora, you have
come to see that by shifting the things you value most—that is, your usual criteria
for assessment—you may open yourself to preferable outcomes—in some circum-
stances, if not all. Pandora liberates you from your own habits and inclinations
to pay attention to, and possibly value, other things. It is, therefore, pedagogical:
it presents you to yourself as a learner, and teaches you to pay attention to things
made invisible by the force of your own habits and routines. In freeing you from
the burden of making every possible choice, Pandora manages the labor of deci-
sion-making in a way that makes it possible to attend in new ways, and learn the
value of things you would otherwise be disinclined to prefer.

We thus begin our inquiry into the potential of story with a story—a
fiction, specifically. More specifically, a story of a will to tell a story (via a
soundtrack), and of the things that might facilitate or interfere with this process. We find the analogy to Pandora to be productive because it suggests
that those who wish to create stories—in this case, a story of a discerning,
knowledgeable consumer of music—can experience their stories as a more
generative vehicle of discovery within intentionally designed, decision-mak-
ing spaces than they might otherwise be inclined to experience them. With
Pandora, listeners enlist the help of an algorithm—a curriculum, of sorts—to
return their experiences to them in such a way as to present new possibilities
for making new stories of their experiences as music listeners. In return for
giving up control over every music-listening story they may be inclined to tell
by virtue of their habitual (and habituated) listening choices, Pandora helps
listeners learn music-listening selves they've not yet discovered.

Pandora listens to the data listeners give it—that is, it listens for qualities in
the music that listeners have told it they like, and the music they've told it they
do not like—in order to construct a story of a particular kind of listener. Pandora
constructs partial listeners: partial in that they are constructed by way of their
preferences, and partial in that their partialities are fractured from their other
partialities. Pandora helps listeners recognize partial selves. As such, Pandora has
the ability to circumvent established music-listening identities of its users, and
return to them new stories of themselves. Holy Cow, I like ... Bon Jovi!?!

Please don't misinterpret our fascination with Pandora as some sort of
inherent faith in and/or endorsement of artificial intelligence technologies.
We are writing teachers. We teach writers. And, as writing teachers who teach
writers, we are not, in fact, interested in creating a story-selecting algorithm.

We are, however, interested in creating a story-selecting curriculum—one that, similar to Pandora's algorithm, returns to storytellers opportunities to not only tell stories, but to subsequently study them as artifacts of the story-tellers' former selves. We will return later to this story, and its analogic possibilities, to explore some ideas about how a writing curriculum that makes the most of storytelling and its predicaments might function as a space in which students may engage multiple and partial selves—past, present, future; doubting and believing; knowing and learning—in surfacing their needs and goals as learners.

In *After-Education: Anna Freud, Melanie Klein, and Psychoanalytic Histories of Learning*, feminist philosopher of education Deborah Britzman suggests that learning is implicated in histories and experiences that live in spaces beyond the pedagogical, calling for "a more intimate sense of education and the ongoing work of having to make education from experiences never meant to be educative" (150). This, too, is our goal: to create a pedagogical approach that invites stories that are as-yet-un-storied (or, on the other hand, overly-storied), and makes available for learning experiences (those that happen both prior to the classroom and within it) other stories that have not likely been accessed for the purposes of education—at least not yet.

So let us begin from the premise that storytelling is a generative practice for learners in transition. We have learned, from our work as researchers and as teachers, that stories have the potential to enable productive, inclusive learning experiences because, unlike genres that have no expression in vernacular discourse (e.g., the "research paper"), they

1. are the rhetorical practice available to those who have not had prior access to academic genres (and are therefore inclusive of all experience);
2. can make students' past experiences—of whatever kind, and of whatever value to academic pursuits—available as assets for present and future inquiry; and
3. are the primary mode of reflection, which we believe to be essential for creating opportunities for low-stakes, transferable learning.

And yet—and this is key—we suggest that to be most productive, students' stories must be situated as data on experience within a learning environment—a curriculum—that allows students to do both deconstructive and reconstructive work. In the hopes of provoking an inquiry into how such a learning environment can function, we make two moves in the discussion to follow:

- We first look *away* from the classroom and its usual routines, and toward the practice of interviews as facilitated storytelling events.
- We then offer an approach to storytelling *in* the classroom that is an expression of understandings of the self-inventive potential of story from disciplines associated with narrative inquiry and their interview-based methodologies, and we situate this within a program of curricular moves that allows this self-inventive potential to develop.

In such a curriculum, students become not only producers of, but *researchers* attentive to, the discoveries made available by a growing archive of their own stories, which they come to understand as an important source of *data* on the operations of their learning.

We have found, as first-year writing program directors (Julie served as WPA at MSU for four years; Bump is currently in his fourth year in the job), that making our pedagogical approach—inasmuch as it treats storytelling as the primary activity and means for learning—intelligible to our colleagues requires its own form of pedagogical ingenuity. Others have observed (as the very premise of this collection would suggest), that within the field of Writing Studies, stories continue to be undertheorized (and therefore, underused) in their potential to facilitate learning. We are reminded of the truth of this observation whenever we hear (especially when we describe our mostly narrative-based FYW curriculum) the baffled question: "Yes, but when do they get to the *real* writing?" While it is tempting, in those moments, to simply invoke Dewey's insights into experience and learning, we understand that the commonplaces about "personal narrative" run far too deep to dismiss such skepticism with a reference to the most well-developed educational philosophy of the 20th century. As Deborah Britzman teaches us, "If we make education from anything, we can make education from experiences that were never meant to be education, and this unnerves our educational enterprise" (*After-Education* 1).

The pervasive disciplinary anxiety about narrative writing not being "real" or "analytical" or "critical" has had the unfortunate effect of deferring the work of putting our teaching practice in relation to a theory of learning and in relation to the needs of our students. When our claim that life writing is ideally suited for FYW students is met with skepticism, we find ourselves explaining that telling stories relevant to the self *is*, in fact, a way of engaging the world, developing critical capacity, and engaging in a practice with rhetorical impact—especially when the practice is situated within programs of instruction designed to ensure that these outcomes are likely to be realized. And yet, stories continue to be off the radar both in conversations about "critical" practices and in many discussions of inclusivity and access. Julie found herself at a panel session at a recent *CCCC*, at which presenters expressed concerns for inclusivity and access, and who then went on to debate the superiority of "threshold concepts" as an organizing principle of FYW versus critical reading as the primary content of that course. Nowhere in evidence was the idea that students' experiences might be useful to the mission of FYW, much less questions about what forms of rhetorical practice might help to make these experiences available for learning.

We are writing teachers. We teach writers.

At the same time, we are quite aware that we are not the first to advocate for the place of narrative in FYW, or to take issue with the idea that the exclusive business of rhetorical study is the teaching of arguments (either making or evaluating them). Those associated with imaginative writing, for example, have made this case for some time now. In "The Place of Creative Writing in Composition Studies," for example, Douglas Hesse takes up this very challenge, inviting the field to reconsider the role of non-deliberative, non-disciplinary writing in how we conceive and practice our work. Hesse is skeptical about the continuing relevance of approaches to rhetoric that assume that the primary mode of persuasion is argumentation, especially given that the traditional agora has been largely replaced by fragmented audiences, virtual networks, and dispersed media markets: "The aesthetic," writes Hesse, "has a rhetorical force ... of image and identification, metaphor and symbol, of narrative arc as actor and acted upon, of Burkean ratios enacted in possibility rather than constrained by given formations." This rhetorical work, Hesse explains, "may not have the full frontal assault of argument," but to "imagine it has no effect beyond killing time is to misunderstand what is actually possible in an age surfeited by texts" (48).

Hesse knows, however, that he's got his work cut out for him. The idea that it is the business of rhetoric—and therefore writing instruction—to teach argument as *the* form of public engagement is a durable commonplace, established by its role in disciplinary formation, and made durable by continued institutional and disciplinary challenges. Gerald Graff's "Hidden Intellectualism" is a good example of the depth and intractability of the commonplace. In that piece, Graff argues that everybody can learn to argue, provided that the business of teaching argument is approached in the right way. Meanwhile, the question of whether teaching argument, exclusively or even primarily, is the most productive means for students to learn ethical discourse practices—much less, about their own places in the university and in the world—seems to be largely off-radar.

In "Hoods in the Polis," a response to Graff, Julie applauded the inclusive move Graff wants to make, but made the case that argument (informed by her own research on practices of argument in a working-class bar, *A Place to Stand*) is a culturally variable practice with uncertain rewards for those who lack social and institutional power in the first place—and that what was needed is a view of rhetoric—informed by qualitative studies of rhetorical practice—that will help to describe rhetoric as it is actually used. But if it is true, as Graff suspects, that first-generation students are often ill-suited to the production of academic arguments—and our goal is inclusivity—then perhaps the invitation is not, in fact, to build a better pedagogy of academic argument (at least, as a first step), but rather, to develop curricula around the rhetorical forms and practices (such as storytelling) with which students *do* have deep experience. And yet we are not, unlike Hesse and others, making a case for FYW as an experience in "creative writing," as it is our mission to treat stories as *practices,* for which the goal is not, in fact, to create good examples of narrative genres, but to put them in relation to other possible stories in other moments. In this scenario, a "better story" is not necessarily a more well-crafted, but rather, a more productive, one (see Halbritter and Lindquist, "It's Never," "Witness"; Lindquist and Halbritter, "Documenting").

If we believe that storytelling accesses, renders, and participates in experience, and that experience situates all learning, then we would not imagine that inviting students to reflect on their own experiences is beside the point of education. However, if we want to ensure the engagement of certain forms of learning from experience—to "make education from experiences that were never meant to be educative," as Britzman (*After-Education* 1) says—then we have to create *pedagogical* experiences that facilitate such engagements. The theories and practices of life history researchers can be instructive in this regard, as those who do such work begin from the idea that stories can be the invitations to, and materials of learning: Goodson and Gill, for example, suggest that narratives of the self have the capacity to "present various past selves and diverse evaluations of these selves within the same story" (8). They write: "Narrative is not a product nor is it a set of tales about individuals and their communities. It is a process, a journey that leads to learning, agency and better understanding of oneself, others, and one's purpose in the world" (102). In other words, no single story is necessarily reliable in the truths it reveals about experience—nor is it necessarily reliable in the synecdochic truths it suggests about the storyteller. But sequences of stories may reveal truths about an author's experiences of storytelling, even if the stories themselves contain little (objective) truth about the specific experiences that they each represent. In fact, should such a pattern of falsehoods emerge, that would, itself, suggest a truth about the storyteller's storytelling experience(s). It may also help us posit a truth or two about the storyteller as well. Goodson and Gill have provided us with an understanding of the learning potential in narrative; we have made it our mission to provide a set of pedagogical moves we believe may best realize that potential.

In other words: it may be hit or miss whether any given story is a potent vehicle for providing insight into the lived experiences of its author; however, an archive of stories—especially chronological sequences of stories—are certain to offer insight into the storyteller's experiences of being a storyteller.

With this in mind, we advocate for an approach to FYW organized around opportunities for facilitated, iterative storytelling. We believe that this approach can be useful not only for those seeking to apply rhetoric to qualitative inquiry on narrative practice and those who seek to move narrative to the foreground as something available for rhetorical theorizing, but also (as an added benefit) as a more general challenge to the primacy of argument as the real business of rhetoric, to the disciplinary tendency to overdetermine argument's relationship with persuasion. We suspect that the disciplinary attachment to argument as the proper site of rhetoric not only has the effect of rendering us myopic in seeing what the (various and diverse) discourse functions of argument are, but that it also cuts us off from the insights of other disciplinary approaches to, and methodologies for understanding, argument as discourse (and discourse more generally). Expanding the purview of rhetoric to include not only narrative, but narrative practice, is a way to create a more nimble, fluid disciplinary space that accommodates the exploration of rhetoric in its multiple capacities. In what follows, we explore work outside the discipline that theorizes the inventive work of stories, and the scenes in which we might facilitate such work.

Storytellers and Their Accomplices:
Narrative Encounters and the Inventive Work
of Storytelling Events

> Autobiographical narratives have power not because they foreground one coherent set of characteristics, but because they help narrators express and manage multiple, partly contradictory selves and experiences. (Wortham 7)

The idea that narratives are functionally complex events and practices is a given in many other disciplinary traditions. Theorists and researchers of narrative in fields outside rhetoric have, as it turns out, given a good deal of thought to how autobiographical narratives work as rhetorical acts. We have found work in narrative inquiry, particularly phenomenological interviewing and life history research—research traditions governed by questions such as, how do narratives work, what occasions them, and how can we understand how they operate?—to be especially useful in thinking about the kinds of social and rhetorical work stories of life experience do (see, for example, Bruner; Clandenin and Connolly; Goodson and Gill; Grumet; Gunn; Schleifer and Vannatta; Thomson). Life historians Goodson and Gill observe that although life narratives predictably participate in constructive and interpretive work, there is considerable variation across individuals and groups in the kinds of invention work their storytelling practices do—in their "narrative capacity." Narrative can be more or less elaborated, more or less descriptive or analytical: "For some, the scripted narrative is open to re-construction, and for others, it is fixed in a strong version of his/her life and may prevent the narrator from engaging in a different account and hence may hinder any learning or action" (60). The authors go on to describe a continuum of narrative inventive potential, with "more 'scripted' narratives at one end and more elaborate and reflective/analytical narratives at the other." The act of narrativizing (not simply narrating, but fashioning into a narrative) one's experiences can, therefore, function as a "somewhat passive process," on the one hand, and as more dynamic "retrospective recounting of what has happened to the narrators and a transformative encounter with others," on the other (61).

If, as Goodson and Gill claim, narrative is "a process, a journey that leads to learning, agency and better understanding of oneself, others, and one's purpose in the world" (102), then, when it comes to the production of narratives, the opportunities for learning are as much a function of the *narrativizing* as the narrative itself. While we see this as an important shift in emphasis, we do not wish to suggest that, once the narrativizing process is complete, its pedagogical value has been exhausted. What is produced through narrativizing is also of value, even if the approach we are suggesting locates its value in the future learning it will expose and inform, more so than in the past learning for which it is taken as an indicator.

We first learned, as researchers, how much the *scenes* in which storytelling happens matter. Research we have done using phenomenological interviews to learn more about the literacy sponsorship of first-year writers (Halbritter and Lindquist, "Time"; "Sleight"), has taught us just how generative interview encounters—themselves rhetorical situations in which stories are solicited and facilitated—can be in thinking about the inventive and reflective potential of stories, and the conditions under which they may make good on this potential for their tellers. When we began our research in 2007, however, we found that there was little engagement in our mainstream journals with interview-based research models that work from a sufficiently theorized methodology of listening for stories and make meaning from them once they emerge (a situation that persists in 2019). To conceive a methodology for our research using a sequence of scaffolded interviews with students, we had to look to scholarship on narrative inquiry in disciplines of education and anthropological linguistics for sufficiently well-developed methodological models (Schuman; Seidman; Mishler). Rich treatment of narrative, as has been done in other fields, such as discourse studies and educational philosophy, continues to be peripheral to the conversations that typically take place in mainstream Composition and Rhetoric venues.

We have learned much from this body of interdisciplinary research and scholarship about how stories can be facilitated by purposeful interventions in scenes of learning. In contrast to treating interviews as information-gathering endeavors, we have used them as occasions to facilitate stories that are not likely to be produced in other situations. In fact, we understand the potential of interviews to produce dynamic inventions of self through story as their most generative affordance. We assume, with Deborah Britzman, that "the process of studying practices cannot conclude once practices are narrated" (*Practice* 67), and that "when practices become a text, they must be read not as guarantees of essential truths, or recipes for action, but as representations of particular discourses" (68). Others (e.g., Gunn; Grumet) echo the claim that storytelling selves are engaged in constructive and reconstructive activity that may be more or less conscious of its own motives, and which practice uses history and experience strategically to accomplish some end, whether realized or unconscious. Central to our understanding about narratives of self and what it means to work with them are the claims voiced by linguistic anthropologist and educational theorist Stanton Wortham:

1. Autobiographical narrative does self-inventive work.
2. Any account of this work has to address the dynamics of interpersonal interaction, of positioning and repositioning.
3. Any analysis of this process needs powerful methodological tools for understanding narrative discourse. (1)

As an example of research that honors these principles, Wortham references Kathleen Stewart's ethnographic work on Appalachian ethnopoetics as an approach to narrative research that "evokes the fragmented and particularistic character of ... experience by describing the complex, divergent stories [her Appalachian subjects] tell about themselves" (7). As a postmodern researcher interested in ethnopoetics, Stewart sees culture as rendered through aesthetic acts, through invocation and evocation. For Stewart, *culture* is in no way declarative or deliberative: it is slowly, collectively, and obliquely rendered in accumulations of mnemonic episodes and performative fragments. Experience is rendered through narrative practice, even if the *narratives* in question aren't always transparent in their integrity as such. Similarly, we see the cultural "stuff" that emerges through interviews—scenes of narrative practices—as emergent, in relation to the actors in these scenes. As an instructive example, Wortham describes a scene of interview with a woman named Jane. As evidence of the constructive work the process of narrativizing experience does for Jane, Wortham points to cues in Jane's delivery that indicate the emotional effects of the storytelling process on her: "she pauses often, her voice breaks, and she even cries at one point." Wortham concludes: "While describing her transformation from passive to active at the orphanage, Jane herself enacts an analogous shift in her projected relationship with the interviewer" (4). In other words, the inventive work Jane's storyteller is performing is contingent on the scene of its production.

The claims of researchers such as Gunn, Grumet, Stewart and Wortham to the effect that narrative coherence is a function of the storytelling scene as much as form or genre is consistent with postmodern challenges (e.g., Bourdieu) to the idea of biographical coherence on experiential and representational grounds. Yet, as Norman Denzin writes, "The point … is not whether biographical coherence is an illusion or a reality. Rather, what must be established is how individuals give coherence to their lives when they write or talk self-autobiographies" (62). To ask this question is, as Holstein and Gubrium indicate, to focus less on narrative form, *per se*, and more on storytelling as a practice. When the storytelling happens in an interview situation, then practices of all interlocutors become relevant to the interpretation of narrative practice as a social activity. Narrative data of this sort is highly interactive, mediated, and co-constructed. As practices, narratives are compositions (Holstein and Gubrium 66). When they happen in interviews, they are, to some extent, collaborative compositions—and this is true regardless of the extent to which interviews intend to *reveal voices* or *get out of the way* of emerging stories. We have called these voices that surface in interview-based texts "third-voice: … the voice of the product of speaker and editor/author" (Halbritter and Lindquist, "Sleight," Reprise). In short, try as we may, there is just no *getting out of the way* of someone else's voice. The moment we step in, no matter how lightly we (think we) tread, there we are.

Viewing narratives as "an ongoing process of composition rather than the more-or-less coherent reporting of stories," point out Holstein and Gubrium, "opens to view the developing construction of personal stories, revealing the process by which narratives are connected, assembled, rearranged, and revised, but under the auspices of decidedly practical circumstances" (166).

To describe these compositional processes and to fully account for the inventive nature of narrative practice, Holstein and Gubrium foreground the activity of narrative editing. It may be obvious how researchers function as editors with an interest in making the stories they hear from participants serve their own (that is, the researchers') stories. However, Holstein and Gubrium remind us that storytellers themselves are largely responsible for such editorial work: "As much as the storyteller can be the author of his or her narrative, he or she is also an editor who constantly monitors, manages, modifies, and revises the emergent story" (170).

If narratives in storytelling encounters are co-constructed, then to enable the production of stories, the scene of interviewing is more about good listening than it is a matter of delivering a script of questions formulated in advance. It is a dynamic, rhetorical human encounter, defined at every moment by principles of *kairos* and *phronesis*. As Irving Seidman explains, "Listening is the most important skill in interviewing," adding that "the hardest work for many interviewers is to keep quiet and listen actively" (78). Seidman describes the process this way, explaining that interviewers must listen to their participants on more than one level:

> First, they must listen to what the participant is saying. They must concentrate on the substance to make sure that they understand it and to assess whether what they are hearing is as detailed and complete as they would like it to be. They must concentrate so that they internalize what participants say. Later, interviewers' questions will often flow from this earlier listening....On a second level, interviewers must listen for what George Steiner (1978) calls "inner voice" as opposed to an outer, more public voice (78). ... On a third level, interviewers—like good teachers in a classroom—must listen while remaining aware of the process as well as the substance. (79)

Seidman characterizes the kind of "active listening" necessary for a good interview as a difficult act that "requires concentration and focus beyond what we do in everyday life" (79). It entails a kind of rhetorical slalom, a busy negotiation of competing needs and impulses—for example, management vs. receptivity. Seidman suggests that interviews require that the interviewer manage her impulse to talk at the same time she remains ready to speak "when a navigational nudge is needed" (79). He compares this kind of conversational two-step to what is required for effective teaching: "They [interviewers] must be conscious of time during the interview; they must be aware of how much has been covered and how much there is yet to go. They must be sensitive to the participants' energy level and nonverbal cues" (79). The analogy to teaching is key: in interviewing, we are teaching participants to teach us how to learn from them, and we are learning to diagnose the learning situations they present us so that we may respond with appropriate courses of action. This entails practicing the art of abduction—hypothesis formation—both during and following the interview session.

For Seidman, interviewing is a rhetorical methodology (though he doesn't name it as such): interviews are treated as inventive acts, in which invention happens interactively, collaboratively, over time. Similarly, Holstein and Gubrium, writing for an audience of sociologists, begin from the premise that social science researchers have moved well beyond the notion that stories can be approached as transparent windows to subjective experience: "Methodologically self-conscious narrative analysts," they declare, citing Joan Scott, "no longer view storytellers and their accomplices as having unmediated access to experience, nor do they hold that experience can be conveyed in some pristine or authentic form" (103).

Holstein and Gubrium offer us what they call an "analytic vocabulary" for accounting for coherence as it is produced in personal narratives. An important term in this vocabulary is *narrative practice*, which they use to describe "the activities of storytelling, the resources used to tell stories, and the auspices under which stories are told," taken together (164). This idea of *practice*, explain the authors, points to an interest both in performativity (as described by Bauman), and the resources and "auspices" activated in storytelling events. Among these auspices are normative institutions in which narrative practices are produced and regulated: "Schools, clinics, counseling centers, correctional facilities, hospitals, support groups, and self-help organizations....provide narrative frameworks for conveying personal experience through time, for what is taken to be relevant in our lives, and why the lives under consideration developed in the way they did" (164).

Holstein and Gubrium cite Rose to describe these as the "technologies" of narrative, mechanisms that "constitute experience in accordance with local relevancies" (164). Holstein and Gubrium admit that finding a productive analytical relationship between the what and the how of storytelling can be challenging—but they insist that it's a necessary part of the work of narrative inquiry: "The complex relationship between storytelling activities, resources, and conditions," they explain—that is, the relationship between stories and their scenes of production—"poses a serious challenge for narrative analysis." Holstein and Gubrium recommend a technique they call "analytical bracketing" to allow them to foreground particular dimensions of narrative practice while provisionally holding others in abeyance:

> We may focus, for example, on how a story is being told, while temporarily deferring our concern for the various whats that are involved—for example, the substance, structure, or plot of the story, the context within which it is told, or the

audience to which it is accountable. We can later return to these issues, in turn analytically bracketing how the story is told in order to focus on the substance of the story and the conditions that shape its construction. (165)

What Holstein and Gubrium are describing, in effect, is a strategic way of looking and not-looking, hearing and not-hearing. This "analytical bracketing" gets at the opportunities that we see for regarding student life stories, once rendered, as sources of storytelling data. By analytically bracketing off the integrity of the story as a whole, students may locate, within the text of a story they have written, any number of indicators of their storytelling decisions—especially when compared to other similarly, analytically bracketed stories they have rendered.

John Dewey describes the "tendency" of teachers to justify the value of their curricula by virtue of "miraculous potencies ... powers inherently residing in the subject, whether they operate or not ... If they do not operate, the blame is put not on the subject as taught, but on the indifference and recalcitrancy of pupils" (287–88). Similarly, we must caution that interview-solicited narratives are not imbued with "miraculous potencies ... inherently residing in" them. If they were, there would be no need to say anything more about them. Their miracles would be potent all on their own. Holstein and Gubrium's "analytical bracketing" is a curricular move that improves the likelihood of realizing potencies in their interview-solicited narratives. The secret is not in the narratives, *per se*, important as they are to the entire endeavor. The secret is in the interviewers' expectation and preparation for eventual bracketing. The interviewer / author / researcher / editor is always expecting and preparing to render a third-voice version of what she encounters in the scene of interview.

Goodson and Gill write, "Narrative encounter and elaboration involve the crafting and re-crafting of a personalized vision of life linked to a course of action, which is then invested with personal commitment, ownership, and agency. Thus narrative is an ideal pedagogic site for facilitating learning and personal development" (151). In Dewey's language, a narrative encounter "has these values if and when it accomplishes these results, and not otherwise" (287). We see the "re-crafting" of narrative—the re-storying of students' literate experiences—to be particularly potent, especially when given time and additional pedagogic intervention. But the value we see is not in re-crafting a *better* narrative—that is, a more well-crafted version of the same story (a hallmark of portfolio-based writing instruction, for example). Rather, we see the value in the former story's ability to give students, peers, and teachers a common text for further analytical bracketing. These texts become sources of storytelling data, if students are led to regard them as such. The operations we offer—both methodological and pedagogical—aim to ameliorate the qualitative spectrum that Goodson and Gill identify. Whether or not students tell *good stories* that emerge from their *individual narrative capacities*, their stories will yield *useful data* to inform their subsequent reflective activities, *as long as that is how the subject is taught.*

Shifting the Blame to the Subject as Taught

Following from these inquiries about the diagnostic and legitimizing power of stories, we see students' life-writing stories to have the following miraculous potencies that may operate within a reflective storytelling curriculum. Students' life-writing stories may

1. Surface what students claim to know
   - Provide opportunity to establish points on the fringe of what students "know"
   - Provide uniform opportunities for students to learn on the fringe of what they "know"
2. Provide opportunity to claim authority and experience legitimacy
   - Place students in subject position
   - Provide opportunity for readers to witness, not correct
   - Engender student interest/investment: in other words, stave off indifference and recalcitrance
   - Include/position all experiences as viable material for future learning
   - Provide topics/categories for inquiry
3. Make available vernacular rhetorical practices for future learning
4. Surface multiple selves—in space and time
   - Create possible selves
   - Archive versions of each developing student as storyteller
5. Provide opportunities for revision
   - Provide opportunities for peer interaction
   - Provide multiple points of access for appreciation/success
   - Provide multiple points of access for critique/failure
   - Provide opportunities for students to read their own writing
   - Provide opportunities for students to see possibilities for improvement
   - Provide opportunities for identification of the features of a compelling story

- Provide opportunities for identification of the features of compelling storytelling

6. Highlight the productive use of/need for challenges/failure—often in the story structure itself

7. Create inherently sharable texts: i.e., stories are to be told

8. Inspire risk taking if the excellence of any given story—as a story—is valued less than the story's ability to deliver scaffolded, analytically bracketable data. In other words, what is most necessary is that the storyteller *attempts* to make the moves most relevant to the learning objectives for the particular instance of storytelling: e.g., the story offers concrete examples from the author's lived experiences. Whether or not the student is successful, the student will be able to return to the presences and/or absences of such examples and enter into dialogue with the effects of her decisions.

How these miraculous potencies are realized depends, of course, on the scene in which they are created, licensed, engaged, and assessed—how, that is, the subject is taught.

Before we imagine how a successful *writing* curriculum may operate, let's imagine a scenario in which stories are invited and shared, with no curricular support for their subsequent, inquiry-directed analytical bracketing. Let's imagine, in this scenario, that students are invited, as a first move, to write a learning narrative (an assignment that exists in our own FYW curriculum). This is positioned as a first writing experience. Students do some brainstorming, draft their papers, revise them, and are given grades according to the success of these narratives in relation to the assessment criteria. Then students move on to the next assignments, following a similar approach. Let's call this a *one-and-done* curriculum, where performance-directed texts are pursued, finished, and then more-or-less abandoned. Imagine, for example, that each assignment is like a glass of water: once it's been consumed, it has no more use—if you're still thirsty, you will need either to find a new glass of water or find some new water to refill the glass, because that old water is ... done.

What kind of learning might this storytelling experience be likely to facilitate for students? Well, it would likely make them feel invited to use as resources materials over which they felt some ownership—that is, the resources of their own remembered experiences. It may or may not reveal to the teacher information about her students useful for diagnostic purposes, information that may help her make decisions about other pedagogical moves or strategies (perhaps the class turns out to comprise a critical mass of musicians; now the teacher can be confident that analogies to composing and performance may be productive for this group. Or perhaps the class contains several first-generation students, leading the teacher to conclude that she cannot assume privileged histories of schooling, and that she will need to work from the assumption that the codes and routines of higher education may be not be entirely intelligible to many of her students). It may help students feel welcomed into this community of learners—to feel a sense of belonging and confidence in their ability to engage with the learning experience of the class.

These are all important benefits for students and teachers, both—especially if these stories contain things that we may think of as truths. And yet, this curriculum—one that we believe to be common—does not, we believe, fully address the opportunities presented to us by the pedagogical potential of story. Recognizing that any given story is likely to be available for subsequent analytical bracketing—reinterpretation, reframing, repositioning, revising—treating any given storied account of a lived experience as *the* account misses the pedagogical potential of regarding the story as a record of a specific time and perspective in the life of the storyteller. The particular story is a record of an instance of storytelling rendered by a storyteller in development: a learner. Furthermore, what if these stories do not contain things that we may think of as truths? What if the things they report are fabrications? What if some of the students claim to be musicians because they want to fit in with the other musicians in the class? What if the first-generation students are afraid to "out" themselves to their new classmates during the first weeks of class? What if the miraculous diagnostic potencies of these stories fail to operate in week three of the fifteen-week semester? Where should we put the blame? Who is at fault? Certainly this would indicate a moral failure of these charlatan students, if not their indifference and recalcitrancy, *per se.*

Let's consider what the *one-and-done* curriculum described above will likely *not* do: it will not likely help students to see how their learning may change over time or to see that incomplete or partial stories have value as part of a learning journey; it's not likely to invite them to call upon the multiple selves implicated in single or multiple storytelling encounters or to engage with other storytellers as listeners and collaborators who have similarly engaged in solving rhetorical problems of their own; it's not likely to direct students to enter into dialogue with rhetorical decisions that were in some ways successful and in other ways unsuccessful. We are reminded of a student whose first learning narrative we recently encountered. The storyteller was an international student from Africa who had chosen to talk about things he had learned in Africa about being accepted or rejected and that he then encountered anew in the U.S. The story seemed to be dripping with miraculous potencies inherently residing in the subject itself. What could go wrong? Well, quite a bit went wrong. The story, as it unfolded, became a confusion of analogies and analyses of other stories. The story seemed to veer in so many directions that it became tempting to put the blame on the indifference and recalcitrancy of the student for the story's shortcomings. After all, the student had been given and had participated in opportunities for peer-revision and revision.

We were also given the opportunity to review the student's reflection that followed—this one, not peer-reviewed. In the reflection, the author directly acknowledged the story's misdirections and confusions. However, the author also revealed something that dashed putting the blame for the story's missteps on his indifference and recalcitrancy. The author had sought additional review of his work by two of his family members who had read right through his *non sequiturs* and logical counter-punches. They read his story to be about how he had been emotionally crushed by the death of his grandmother shortly after he had moved to the U.S. and how he had been bullied, primarily for being an international student of color, in his school in the U.S. He had been motivated to reveal these details in his story; however, he had been unable to risk revealing these aspects of his life to his brand new classmates for fear that they, too, may turn on him as his previous classmates had done. He was able to reveal these details subsequently—and only to his teacher—in his reflection due to his need to explain why his story had gone so awry. The story's failures had yielded some rhetorical successes for the author—ones that were revealed not in the story itself, but in the act of subsequent analytical (and rhetorical) bracketing. What may this student and his teacher not have learned if the production of the story itself—and not the subsequent story of its production—had been the primary or sole goal of the assignment?

Let's imagine, for a moment, that our primary concern is not helping student writers to learn about their writing processes by way of life writing activities. Instead, let's imagine that our primary concern is helping a gymnast learn from his (in this case) routines at a gymnastics competition. Bump's son, Sawyer, is a gymnast—and a pretty good one, at that. In his gymnastics competitions, Sawyer competes, is evaluated by qualified judges, and is awarded the results of his performance as evaluated. In many ways, his gymnastics performances are one and done. Sawyer, like all the other competitors, gets only one shot at being evaluated. One and done. But that's only in any particular competition. There are many competitions. There are many, many practice sessions. And there are hours and hours of accumulated video recordings of Sawyer's performed routines.

Suddenly, in these video recordings, *one-and-done* performances live on and on. Some do so because they are truly "awesome"! Others because they

BUMP HALBRITTER AND JULIE LINDQUIST

are ... not. It's often the failures—the footage of falling off the pommel horse, the missed hand holds, the dismounts that were over-rotated, the handstands that were not held—that yield the most valuable footage. That footage does not facilitate the "everything is awesome" story of a gymnast at the very top of his game. That footage facilitates a different story: one of a developing gymnast, an excellent gymnast who is still learning, a gymnast whose greatest lessons live in the spaces where his best one-and-done attempts can be reconsidered as evidence of learning that remains in process.

Informed by the record of this performance, Sawyer (and his coaches) can learn from the performance by analytically bracketing off some of his lived experiences in favor of what the video record may reveal. Sometimes that means he will cut a move, change a sequence of moves, practice harder, develop more specific strength or more general stamina, or simply set his mind more squarely on pulling off a specific move next time. Sometimes, Sawyer uses what he learns to improve his performance on that specific routine. Other times, he uses what he learns to see possibilities for other routines or for his general development. The point is that the record of the performance is not simply a record of his triumph or failure; it is a record of one attempt by one gymnast. Importantly, that gymnast in the video is *not* Sawyer. It's a video recording of Sawyer's *former self*. Sawyer is no longer that gymnast—the one who was doing that routine at that time. Sawyer is now the gymnast who has done that routine. He's a different gymnast: one who can study what that other, former gymnast did in order to inform what his present and future selves may do similarly and/or differently. That video recording is stable. The gymnast in that video can't learn; he's trapped in time. But Sawyer's present self can learn. And, combined with the excellent instruction that he gets from his coaches and peers, that's one of the ways he does so. The videos allow him to regard his former self's experience of having performed the routine from a different, present-self perspective. The video enables subsequent analytical bracketing by a different, emerging, learning version of himself.

Here's a real question: why on earth would we ever ask our developing, learning writing students to write one-and-done stories?

Learning to Listen: Listening to Learn

In the spirit of revisiting something our former selves have written, let's revisit and apply some analytical bracketing to something *your* former self read and that our former selves wrote just a few pages ago. Here's what our former selves read/wrote:

Viewing narratives as "an ongoing process of composition rather than the more-or-less coherent reporting of stories," point out Holstein and Gubrium, "opens to view the developing construction of personal stories, revealing the process by which narratives are connected, assembled, rearranged, and revised, but under the auspices of decidedly practical circumstances" (166).

When our former selves first encountered these ideas, our former selves were being asked to consider them as an expression of wisdom about interviews—about exchanges between the corporeally different selves of interviewers and interviewees. We now ask that our present selves reconsider these ideas (by way of an act of analytical bracketing) as an expression of wisdom about a different form of interaction—about exchanges between the temporally different selves of individual authors' former and present selves. What might happen if we regard this as the most important miraculous potency of acts of life writing for developing writers?

Of course, whenever we are considering pedagogic potentials, it seems wise to begin with a premise about how learning occurs. So here is a premise upon which all that follows is founded: *We learn on the fringe of what we know.* That is, we distrust—as have many researchers and theorists of cognition—that new knowledge is simply added to existing knowledge. Rather, it is assimilated; it is formed. Consequently, we are unlikely to make cognitive leaps. As instructors of writing, this should come as no surprise to any of us. In fact, evidence suggesting cognitive leaps in the writing of any student is bound to raise suspicion more immediately than recognition of the miraculous potency of our teaching. *Wait a minute, how did THAT first draft become THIS final draft?*

Rather than embrace our summative suspicions, let's, instead, imagine some formative possibilities. Let's accept that students, being human beings and all, learn on the fringe of what they know. If we are to observe their learning, if we are to construct pedagogic operations for their learning, we will need to learn first what they already know. That is, our first moves need to be moves that will enable us, much like Seidman's active interviewer, to do more listening and note taking than leading and directing. Again, here's what our former selves encountered a few pages ago: "On a third level, interviewers—like good teachers in a classroom—must listen while remaining aware of the process as well as the substance" (Seidman 79). Seidman asked us to think of interviewers as "good teachers." Let's shift our analytic bracketing to think of teachers as good interviewers—as those who are interested not only in having good conversations, but who are expecting *and preparing all along* to return to those conversations to see what else we can learn from them. As good interviewers, teachers should not only expect to learn more from the express content of the conversations, but, through careful study of the record of the conversations, to study the interactions between the participants, to search for signs of missed opportunities, to seek evidence not only to explain what happened, but to make informed decisions about how better to move forward. As good interviewers, teachers should expect *and prepare* to be informed learners. And, because the students' learning is the primary focus of the experience, the teachers must prepare experiences for students to be informed learners.

So how do writing teachers prepare for all of this informed learning?

Our former selves, all those many pages ago, began by asking your former self to consider Pandora's miraculous potencies to deliver a suitable soundtrack for your soirée. Our former selves promised that we were not interested so much in Pandora's algorithm as an algorithm, but in its algorithm as a curriculum. Most folks would likely think of Pandora's service as a *playing* service—that is, we open our Pandora apps when we want Pandora to *play* music for us. According to that analytical bracketing, *we* would be the listeners: Pandora plays; we listen. But, our present selves want to regard Pandora as a *listening* service. However, Pandora cannot simply listen; as an algorithm, it must be designed to listen. That is, the designers of Pandora's algorithm needed to prepare Pandora to always be prepared to listen even as it is playing (and preparing to play what it will play next). How does Pandora accomplish its magic? How does Pandora practice active listening? How does Pandora simultaneously deliver and participate in analytical bracketing? Who should we credit when it makes choices we like? Who should we blame when it makes choices we ... don't like?

Writing for the *New York Times Magazine* in 2009 ("The Song Decoders"), Rob Walker describes the Music Genome Project, the inspiration and infrastructure of Pandora, and explains the analytical bracketing that Pandora's listening app uses:

> Pandora's approach more or less ignores the crowd. It is indifferent to the possibility that any given piece of music in its system might become a hit. The idea is to figure out what *you* like, not what a market might like. More interesting, the idea is that the taste of your cool friends, your peers, the traditional music critics, big-label talent scouts and the latest influential music blog are all equally irrelevant. That's all cultural information, not musical information. And theoretically at least, Pandora's approach distances music-liking from the cultural information that generally attaches to it.

> First every piece is broken down into large-scale aspects of music: melody, harmony, rhythm, form, sound (meaning instrumentation and, if necessary, voice), and in many cases the text, meaning lyrics. Each of these broader categories might have 10, 30, 50 elements.

[Pandora programmer, Nolan Gasser, explains,] "We have a number of characteristics for vocals ... Is it a smooth voice, is it a rough, gravelly voice, is it a nasally voice?" Similar questions are evaluated for every instrument. The upshot was about 250 "genes" for every song in the original pop-rock version of the "genome."

The key to Pandora's *curriculum* is in its preparation to make informed decisions about what to do next based upon how we have reacted in the past and how we are reacting in the present. Pandora doesn't listen to our music. Pandora listens for the presences and absences of hundreds of pre-determined indicators in the music we say we like and the music we say we don't like: while we've been listening to Pandora, Pandora's been listening to us. It not only noticed when we skipped over Air Supply on our ABBA station, it made a note of it. It not only noticed when we gave a thumbs down to "Super 8 [Motel]" on our Jason Isbell station, it made a note of it. It not only noticed that we gave a thumbs up to that song we just heard for the first time by Leon Bridges, it made a note that we may like other tracks with "modern R & B stylings, jazz influences, mild rhythmic syncopation, repetitive melodic phrasing [Can you feel me?], extensive vamping, a busy horn section, major key tonality, a smooth male lead vocalist [Let me come through!], electric rhythm guitars, electric pianos, vocal harmonies [A'ight!]," and a few hundred other attributes of Bridges' song, "Bad Bad News." Pandora has heard our hearing by way of very different analytical bracketing than the way we heard Pandora's music selections.

Here's another thing about Pandora's curriculum: it's not one and done. That is, it's not designed to pick a song we love and call it a day. Pandora is designed to continue picking songs for us. Pandora's task is Sisyphean. That rock (and roll) will never reach the top of the hill. Furthermore, and consequently, Pandora is built to take risks and to have some of its risks fail. Its algorithm may decide that what we liked about Michael Jackson's "Billy Jean" was its prominent bass line. Consequently, it may offer us The Beatles' "Come Together"—a song we *love,* but *not* on our Michael Jackson station. Duh! Pandora has anticipated that it may blow it and has prepared for just such an occasion (or two) by both listening for our response and by giving us a means to communicate our response in a form that Pandora can use to not only make more effective choices for us in the future, but to take additional risks in the future as well. Pandora is designed to not only make mistakes; it is designed to keep on making them and to keep on *making the most of its mistakes.* Pandora's curriculum participates in a pedagogy of ongoing risk taking and informed decision making. It cannot make the most of its mistakes if it doesn't make mistakes. And if it doesn't make the most of its mistakes, we won't go on listening to Pandora. In Pandora's curriculum, everyone's a learner. We learn new music to like (or not) and Pandora learns how better to learn from what (we tell it) we like and dislike.

Collecting and Coding Synecdochic Selves: A Curriculum for Making the Most of the Pedagogical Potentials of Life Writers

So what would be the features of a story-selecting curriculum—one that makes good on the data-listening potentials of Pandora, and of the story facilitation potentials of phenomenological interview-based research? First of all, it would have to be designed to regard students both as collections of present, former, and potential selves, and as persons already in possession of assets for the inventive work of storytelling. It would have to be strategic about scaffolding that might allow these selves to emerge and come into conversation with each other. It would have to include, as part of the pedagogical apparatus, the means by which the stories of these learning selves could be documented and archived for future use—that is, the means by which they might be available as *data* for students to assess as evidence of new stories of learning. It would need to have opportunities for students to encounter, hear, learn from, and facilitate the stories of other students.

Most of all, it would need to be directed by an approach to assessment that would allow for students to tell stories that are partial, unfinished, flawed, experimental—stories in need, in other words, of intervention. This would have to be an approach to assessment that, as Bump likes to say, "makes your best lessons gifts and not penalties." This storytelling curriculum will need to look beyond the one-and-done nature of its assignments to see its assignments as formative means for continued development and not summative ends of development. This storytelling curriculum must be designed to not only tolerate student risk taking and the inevitable mistakes that may follow from it, but to make the most of those mistakes once they inevitably happen—because they, inevitably, will happen. This storytelling curriculum will need to be directed by an assessment model that will encourage students to take risks even as it does not punish the failed efforts that inevitably emerge from risk taking—because they, inevitably, will emerge. This storytelling curriculum must be designed—must be prepared—not only to solicit stories that represent students' best storytelling efforts, but to subsequently put those told stories to different work in the service of discovering signs of learning by their developing storytellers. This storytelling curriculum must be designed to facilitate its student storytellers (and their teachers) to learn on the fringe of what they know.

We have offered details of just such a storytelling curriculum elsewhere. In "It's Never About What It's About," we detail the final reflective act of the semester—a project we call the "experiential-learning documentary" (ELD) and how to set up a coordinating assessment structure. In "Documenting and Discovering Learning," we detail a process that we call "preflection": a method for generating and archiving materials that students will use to inform their always expected, inevitable, reflective activities and ELDs. Those are things our former selves have written. Here, our present selves want to discuss the three critical moves—projection, collection, recollection—that serve as the foundation for the ongoing scaffolding of a storytelling curriculum. Our present selves have been informed by our former selves' discussions of preflection, ELDs, and the assessment of ELDs. Consequently, our present selves will reference, but not detail, preflections and ELDs and their assessment. For detailed descriptions of these concepts and the assessment models that they have led us to create, please, see our other referenced texts.

There are six foundational, Sisyphean ideas about learning at work here:

1. We learn on the fringe of what we know.
2. To discover what we have learned (not just what we know), we must visit with our former selves (by way of a record of something that represents our knowledge) to demonstrate that our former selves must NOT have known something that we now know.
3. We never have been, nor ever will be, able to get student writers all learned up.
4. To make the most of our mistakes, we need to (determine that it's not a mistake to) make mistakes.
5. Identifying mistakes can help us identify goals for our learning.
6. We learn to identify mistakes on the fringe of what we know.

These Sisyphean ideas about learning are never satisfied. As we like to say, we never get all learned up. Our learning is ongoing. We never get that boulder to the top of that hill. We can, consequently, never sit back and say that we always knew what we know now. If we are to identify our ongoing learning, we will always need to weigh our current knowledge against demonstrations of our former knowledge. This work, being described as *Sisyphean* and all, may imply that we believe it to be futile. Nothing could be further from our intention. This work is *not* futile. This work is *ongoing*. Our hearts do not beat in futility. They beat in order to continue beating. Our hearts beat because that's what hearts do. Writers learn to write in order to continue learning to write. Writers continue to learn because that's what writers do.

Sometimes, however, they do not appear to do so. When that appears to happen, one way to shift the blame away from the indifference and recalcitrancy of the students and toward the subject as taught is to design a curriculum where it is nearly impossible for students *not* to be able to identify evidence of their ongoing learning. In short, such a curriculum shifts what it values most from evidence of good writing to evidence of writers' learning (made evident in their acts of writing). As we say in "It's Never About What It's About," the ongoing, scaffolded process is one of projection, collection, and recollection. Let's consider each in turn.

Students *project* what they imagine will be necessary to pursue any writing project. The important thing is not for them to be correct in their predictions. As we like to say, when it comes to student projections/proposals, they don't need to be right, they just need to be written. Projections may or may not lead students to courses of action that follow from them directly toward successful outcomes. Most, in our experience, do not. However, written projections may give our students' future selves a window into the knowledge of their former selves. What do those projections tell us, at the end of the project, about what students did and did not yet know about the sort of project they were about to undertake? What can those projections do to help students demonstrate what they have learned by way of their experience(s) of writing the project? How may this learning inform both our students' subsequent projections and what they may expect to do with those future projections in the subsequent writing projects inevitably pursued by their future selves?

Of course, for our students' future selves to be able to enter into meaningful conversation with their present and former selves, we will need to *collect and archive* the works our students produce. Even as Pandora prepares not only to deliver music to us, but to solicit our feedback and learn from our reactions to its choices, we must prepare to collect and keep artifacts of students' ongoing development so that they may refer to it and put it to different subsequent use. In other words, it's not enough to ask students to think about how they will go about pursuing a project, or even to write down their plans; we must keep those documents available for subsequent consideration. This is equally true for initial drafts, peer-reviews, revision plans, revised drafts, consultations with the teacher, final drafts, reflections, and any other steps in the process of pursuing the projects. As such, the projects themselves become less of the goal of the activity than the means for the subsequent study of how the work was managed. We cannot simply ask students to do this work.

We must keep it available for later use. All of it—because we can't know, as it's happening, what will be most relevant as evidence of our students' learning, because if it's ongoing learning that we want to make evident, we don't yet know what it will be. We need to be like Pandora: prepared, always, to reflect. We need to do so all throughout the class—not just within projects, but across projects. That way we can track short-term and longer-term gains (and losses). We highly recommend keeping these works available in an electronic environment, such as a course management system or in a system of cloud-based folders shared with (and only with) the entire class. What makes electronic environments ideal is their ability to both archive many large texts and render them searchable. Furthermore, they may be accessed instantly by multiple users at once, and elements of large texts may be copied and pasted into the works produced in the next move: *recollection.*

Finally, we will need to be guided by opportunities for our students to revisit their collected works in order to perform different analytical bracketing to the contents. We call this process *recollection*: students collect, again, evidence from their previous works in order to support specific sorts of subsequent analysis. Let's consider a few examples of prompts for subsequent analytical bracketing:

- Now that you have completed your project, let's go back and look at your project proposal. In what ways does it forecast the final version of the project? In what ways does it not? What might this suggest about what we can expect to learn about our projects while we are writing them versus things we (may think we) know about our projects before we begin writing?
- Go find a piece of advice you were given that you are glad you did NOT take. Why did you not take this advice? What text does this advice correspond to in your project? In retrospect would you reconsider taking this advice now? Why or why not? What does this suggest about the role of peer review and/or your relationship to or your regard for it?
- How have your titles been reflective of the projects they have named? How, specifically, do your titles relate to your projects? What do they name? How do they forecast the work of your projects or topics within them or your attitudes toward these works? What has changed about the titles you give to your works? What does that suggest?
- Find a piece of advice that you have given a peer that surprises you. What is surprising about this piece of advice? How might this surprise inform how you continue to offer advice to peers or to yourself?

- Find a section of any piece of your writing—a paragraph, a few sentences—that you think represents either your best work or work that makes you particularly proud to have written it. What elements of this work stand out as identifiers of excellence and/or of improvement? How do they compare to other similar but less successful portions of your writings? What goals may you identify for your future writing efforts based upon your consideration of this evidence?

It should be obvious how the work of *recollection* is utterly dependent upon the work of both *projection* and *collection*. And it should be equally obvious that none of this work inherently resides in any single assignment that may ask students to write a story about something from their lives. While we may be able to identify things we may learn from our immediate experience(s) of writing a story about a challenge that we overcame or about a time when we felt scared or about something that we learned outside of school, there's no guarantee that we will. Furthermore, if we are asked to do so, and if our grade depends upon our doing it well, and if we are writing a personal narrative for the first or second time in our lives, we will likely determine that the most important thing to do is to turn in a good story—one that we either write according to what we know to have been successful in the past or one that we … acquire. We may determine, in fact, that it is more important to hand in a good story than to have written it. We may determine that it is too risky to even attempt to write such a thing (I mean, how could *we* ever write a piece as good as Amy Tan's "Mother Tongue"?!?).

However, if we shift the burden from excellent stories to identification of student learning, then there's not only less incentive for students to find— and not write—stories, but there *is* incentive to undertake the potentially risky business of actually writing the stories. If students do not write the stories, completing the work of the highly valued *recollections* will be nearly impossible to do. What makes this possible is the shifting of analytical bracketing from telling/writing stories about events that are important to us to pursuing projects of inquiry *on* those writings as artifacts of our students' learning.

Collecting and Coding Synecdochic Selves: Identifying Learning Across Life-Writing Texts

We offer a violation of subordination to help frame our closing remarks. We close with a subsection that shares the title of the work to which it is subordinate. Why? Because we are no longer the same people who first encountered the title. The subordinated title of the same name does not do the same work now as it did when our former selves encountered it at the beginning. When we first encountered the title we had not yet listened to Pandora listening to us. We had not yet considered that successful interviewers were like successful teachers, and vice versa, in that much of their success can be credited to their deliberate, systematic, documented, and strategically deferred approaches to listening. We had not yet considered that the subject of the collection in which this title appears, *story*, would emerge as the *means* of the pedagogical potential we would pursue and not the *goal* of it. But that was then. That was our former selves.

Our present selves can read the identical title anew. Our present selves are in possession of different analytical brackets for filtering the ideas that we have collected. Our present selves can see new opportunities for the stories that our future students may tell in our classes and for the work that our future selves may direct our future students to do with those stories they write. Our present selves can see that the persons that we name as our selves are not so synecdochically us. Our selves do not necessarily name all of the complicated and changing aspects of our learning selves. The parts do not necessarily name the whole. The whole does not necessarily name the parts. But the various namings—past, present, and future—may lead us to more or less productive work at different times. They may help us see that our efforts and the efforts of our students are not simply repetitive, they are meaningfully iterative. They are not obviously futile; they are necessarily ongoing.

Our present selves can see, too, that our future selves have some planning to do. And that our even more distant future selves can expect to learn from that planning to project improvements on the results of that planning—for as long as our future selves remain present. Our present selves can expect that our future selves will not get all learned up. Our present selves can see the miraculous potencies that inherently reside in the promises of this new storytelling curriculum. And our present selves can immediately distrust that those miraculous potencies will operate unless that is how the subject is taught—by *our* selves.

Enjoy your selves.

Note

1. Bump Halbritter, Associate Professor, Michigan State University. drbump@msu.edu; Julie Lindquist, Professor, Michigan State University. lindqu11@msu.edu

References

Bauman, Richard. *Story, Performance, and Event: Contextual Studies of Oral Narrative.* Cambridge: Cambridge UP, 1986.

Bourdieu, Pierre. R. Nice, Trans. *Distinction: A Social Critique of the Judgement of Taste.* Cambridge: Harvard UP, 1984.

Britzman, Deborah. *After-Education: Anna Freud, Melanie Klein, and Psychoanalytic Histories of Learning.* Albany: SUNY Press, 2003.

———. *Practice Makes Practice: A Critical Study of Leaning to Teach.* Albany: SUNY Press, 2003.

Bruner, Jerome. *Acts of Meaning: Four Essays on Mind and Culture.* Cambridge: Harvard U Press, 1993.

———. *Making Stories: Law, Literature, Life.* Cambridge: Harvard U Press, 2003.

Clandenin, D. Jean, and Michael Connelly. *Narrative Inquiry: Experience and Story in Qualitative Research.* San Francisco: Jossey Bass, 2004.

Denzin, Norman K. *Interpretive Biography.* Newbury Park: Sage, 1989.

Dewey, John. *Democracy and Education.* New York: Macmillan, 1916.

Goodson, Ivor F., and Sherto R. Gill. *Narrative Pedagogy: Life History and Learning.* New York: Peter Lang, 2011.

Graff, Gerald. "Hidden Intellectualism." *Pedagogy: Critical Approaches to Teaching Literature, Language, Composition, and Culture* 1.1 (Spring 2001): 21–36.

Grumet, Madeleine. "The Politics of Personal Knowledge." *Curriculum Inquiry.* 17.3 (1987): 319–29.

Gunn, Janet. *Autobiography: Toward a Poetics of Experience.* Philadelphia: U of Pennsylvania Press, 1982.

Halbritter, Bump, and Julie Lindquist. "It's Never About What It's About: Audio-Visual Writing, Experiential-Learning Documentary, and the Forensic Art of Assessment." *The Routledge Handbook of Digital Writing and Rhetoric.* Ed. Jonathan Alexander and Jacqueline Rhodes. New York: Routledge Press, 2018. 317–27. Print.

———. "Sleight of Ear: Voice, Voices, and the Ethics of Voicing." *Soundwriting Pedagogies.* Ed. Courtney Danforth and Kyle Stedman. Computers and Composition Digital Press, 2018. Forthcoming.

———. "Time, Lives, and Videotape: Operationalizing Discovery in Scenes of Literacy Sponsorship." *College English* 75.2 (2012): 171–98.

———. "Witness Learning: Building Relationships between Present, Future, and Former Selves." *Writing for Engagement: Responsive Practice for Social Action.* Ed. Mary Sheridan, Megan Bardolph, Megan Hartline, and Drew Holladay., Lanham: Lexington Books, 43–60.

Hesse, Douglas. "The Place of Creative Writing in Composition Studies." *College Composition and Communication* 62.1 (2010): 31–52.

Holstein, James A., and Jaber F. Gubrium. *The Active Interview.* Thousand Oaks: Sage, 1995.

Lindquist, Julie. *A Place to Stand: Politics and Persuasion in a Working-Class Bar.* New York: Oxford UP, 2002.

———. "Hoods in the Polis." *Pedagogy: Critical Approaches to Teaching Literature, Composition and Culture* 1.2 (Spring 2001).

Lindquist, Julie, and Bump Halbritter. "Documenting and Discovering Learning: Reimagining the Work of the Literacy Narrative." *College Composition and Communication* 70.3 (2019): 413–445.

Mishler, Elliot G. "Meaning in Context: Is There any Other Kind?" *Harvard Educational Review,* 49.1 (1979): 1–19.

Rose, Nikolas S. *Governing the Soul: The Shaping of the Private Self.* New York: Routledge, 1990.

Schleifer, Ronald, and Jerry Vannatta. "The Logic of Diagnosis: Peirce, Literary Narrative, and the History of Present Illness." *Journal of Medicine and Philosophy* 31.4 (2006): 363–84.

Schuman, David. *Policy Analysis, Education, and Everyday Life: An Empirical Reevaluation of Higher Education in America.* Lexington: D.C. Heath, 1982.

Scott, Joan W. "Multiculturalism and the Politics of Identity." *The Identity in Question.* Ed. John Rajchman. New York: Routledge, 1995: 3–14.

Seidman, Irving. *Interviewing as Qualitative Research: A Guide for Researchers in Education and the Social Sciences.* 3rd ed. New York: Teachers College P, 2006.

Stewart, Kathleen. *A Space on the Side of the Road: Cultural Poetics in an "Other" America.* Princeton: Princeton U Press, 1996.

Thomson, Rachel. *Unfolding Lives: Youth, Gender, and Change.* Bristol: Policy P, 2009.

Walker, Rob. "The Song Decoders." *The New York Times Magazine.* Online. 14 October 2009.

Wortham, Stanton. *Narratives in Action: A Strategy for Research and Analysis.* New York: Teachers College Press, 2001.

4. *Writing Backwards: Adventures With Time and Structure in Life Writing*

SAM MEEKINGS[1]

It was on an unusually sunny day in June that my brother died. Luke was 24 years old, two years younger than me. And as soon as the shock of his death began to sharpen into grief, I decided I had to write his story. I would set down the facts and memories of our time together, I thought, and in that way I would keep something of him alive.

However, the task of writing my brother's life was not as simple as I had assumed. I had thought about writing it chronologically, covering each of his twenty-four years one by one and so leaving out nothing. Yet soon I found myself going off topic, veering away from chronology. I could not bear to start a story that would finish with his death, that would reach a final full stop at his funeral. To do so would be to commit to an enclosed narrative, one that had a neat beginning, middle, and end, and I could not do that to Luke. Our lives do not end at our death, and I was adamant that I would not close my narrative there. I resisted a directly autobiographical approach because I wanted to avoid a text leading to death, since that would be somewhat predictable for any reader, and predictable is something my brother never was. But more importantly, I felt that a chronological and biographical structure running from birth to death had to be eschewed, because our conception of lives in writing (and indeed the way we imagine our own lives) often resists such a restrictive structure. The more I read and the more I wrote, the more I was forced to reconsider traditional notions of narrative structure and linearity.

This was somewhat ironic. In my writing classes, as a prompt I have asked students to imagine that they are time-travellers from the future commenting on the strangeness of the present day. Such exercises were based on the fact that Luke and I spent many weeks of our childhood planning, discussing, and contemplating the construction of a time machine. The options were myriad and equally impossible. Creating a wormhole to fold time back on itself like a Mobius strip, surfing through the heart of a black hole, borrowing a Tardis, building a DeLorean to rip past the speed of light. It occurred to me only much later that time-travel is something that comes to us much more naturally than these outlandish options. It is endemic to humans; we do it every day. Wallow in nostalgia or pick apart the past; plan for tomorrow and plot our hopes, ambitions, future lives. It can sometimes seem as though most of us spend very little time in the present at all. Writing about my brother, therefore, would mean travelling in time.

Memories, after all, are not bound by order. They are bound by association. The text of association, therefore, is one that more accurately reflects how we conceptualize our own lives, how we tell our own stories, and how we organize our inner narratives. Life writing has always prioritized following the paths of memory over those of strict chronology. Consider Proust, who in *À la recherche du temps perdu,* in one of the most famous passages in twentieth-century literature, described how after experiencing a familiar taste, that of madeleine biscuits dipped in a drink of boiled lime-blossom, suddenly "the old grey house upon the street, where her room was, rose up like a stage set… and with the house the town, from morning to night and in all weathers, the square where I used to be sent before lunch, the streets along which I used to run errands, the country roads we took when it was fine" (54). A whole universe of detailed memory is vividly conjured up by the accidental stimulation of a memory. Proust too was a time traveller, and it is now a common ploy of fiction to employ songs, sights, tastes, and sensations to elicit an unexpected turn toward the past. Indeed, the device of the involuntary memory is arguably overused and over-familiar. Furthermore, it highlights some of the issues around writing without the skeleton outline of chronological structure; namely, how a writer might organize and construct such a narrative.

This issue first manifested itself in my own writing in the question of where to begin. After all, central to the creation of any story is the selection of a meaningful point in time at which to start the narrative. Should a history of the Second World War, for instance, begin with the invasion of Poland in September 1939, the annexation of Austria the previous year, the militarization of the Rhineland in the mid-1930s, Hitler becoming Fuhrer in 1933, or even the humiliating penalties enacted on Germany by the Treaty of Versailles in 1919? The question is never a simple one—each cause is itself caused by a preceding event, and so on back through time.

Furthermore, the starting point of a narrative fixes it within a specific period and so announces its borders and limitations. One logical starting point for the history of Luke and me would be the day of his birth, on the Eve of Saint Agnes; another would be the day of his death; yet another would be his funeral. However, none of these seemed right, since the first would commit me to a chronological structure I had already rejected, while both the latter options represented a focus on Luke's death which went against the project's purpose of recounting his life and demonstrating ways in which he lived on. I could not help but remember the words of Edwin Muir who, in his seminal *An Autobiography*, writes "It is clear that no autobiography can begin with a man's birth, that we extend far beyond any boundary line that we set for ourselves" (39). In the same way, we extend far beyond the boundary line of our death, so long as we are remembered, so long as our influence and effect on the world remains. I therefore settled upon beginning my story months after the giddy whirr and raw shock of the funeral, when all distractions are stripped away and there is nothing left to do but remember and reflect. This opened up the possibility of travelling both backward and forward in time, thereby foregrounding the loss of my brother without making it the single focal point of the narrative.

In addition, by beginning after the funeral had already taken place, I was also able to utilize two structuring devices more common to fiction: namely, a quest narrative in which the protagonist pursues understanding, and a slow revealing of information to the reader. For instance, I made a deliberate choice to build up slowly to the reveal of Luke's cause of death, while keeping the details of his last days mysterious until the very end of the book, in mimicry of the traditional structure of detective fiction. After all, the writing of a life is itself an active process of exploration and discovery, and not just a static form of memorialization.

One of the forerunners of the modern memoir, Edmund Gosse, also structured his work to reflect the progress of a quest. His *Father and Son* was a key influence on my writing since, despite being very much a product of the late Victorian era, its purposes appeared to be identical to my own—namely, to give a portrait of childhood and adolescence, and also to ensure that the narrator, the traditional subject of autobiography, is considered only in relation to another key character. For Gosse, this is the overbearing and somewhat puritanical figure of his father, and for myself it is of course my brother.

Gosse suggests then that one's identity can often be very much dependent on one significant other—for me that was Luke and for him that was, I believe, me. Like Gosse and his father, we were fundamentally dissimilar characters, and yet for that very reason increasingly came to define each other.

For Gosse, the world of his father—the world of the church, religion, and unquestionable moral standards—was profoundly alien; though his father and he occupy the same living space, their ideas, beliefs and values splinter to such a degree that by the end of the book they might as well be living in different countries. This affected my choice of material: I therefore decided to present a similar splitting by writing about the different situations Luke and I found ourselves in as we grew up—for instance, by focusing in one section on his hockey matches and the raucous and legendary celebrations that followed, and in another on my time in the school choir, in order to demonstrate how we each came to define ourselves by contrast with the other.

However, no matter how different we grew from one another, my brother's life remained intertwined with my own, and we remained bound by a common history. This was another reason why it seemed a false choice to begin any biographical writing at a person's birth. Had I chosen to start my own memoir with Luke being born, and then shown us steadily growing apart from one another, this would not have satisfactorily represented the complex ebb and flow of our relationship; the arguments and disagreements, but also the reconciliations and rapprochements. For me, that most important action of my narrative—my brother's death—does not send us off in different directions but rather initiates the movement of the structure that spirals between past and present. In this way, writing a life also might reflect through its form the fact than in grief it is time that had become disordered, rather than our relationship.

In order to build towards his own narrative climax, Gosse reworks many of the moments of the past so that they prefigure the future. Gosse creates a clear momentum towards one important action: the crucial break with his father that allows the narrator at last to seize hold of "a human being's privilege to fashion his inner life for himself" (178). Events are chosen for detailed description in his memoir because they foreshadow this break. For instance, the writer dwells on many intense moments when he becomes enraptured by books, thus foreshadowing the climactic choice he makes to turn to literature instead of religion. He describes, for example, reading a dramatic novel in the attic, discovering *The Tempest*, hearing his father read Virgil, and being transported by the poetry of death and grief in the garden. Gosse's purpose is clear: his narrative is one of learning and self-development, in line with the Victorian concept of continual progress. As in academic writing, therefore, it is beneficial for the life writer to identify this fundamental purpose at the start of writing. My own was somewhat antithetical to Gosse's; instead of showing the self learning and developing to become independent, in my writing I wanted to show how the self is dependent on others for meaning and identity, by focusing on how Luke made me who I am, and vice versa. This would also fit better with the historical situation under which the writing is carried out, for biographical composition in the age of Trump ought surely to reflect the changed cultural context in which the twists and turns of history do not suggest progress and evolution so much as coincidence and contingency.

In fact, it is the strange coincidences that suggest both the originality of the life and therefore the text that proceeds from it. One model for an approach to structure dependent upon such coincidental associations is Nabokov's modernist and "fictional memoir," *Speak, Memory*. In a chapter of *Speak, Memory* written in the form of a review of the book itself, Nabokov notes that "Nabokov's method is to explore the remotest regions of his past life for what may be termed thematic trails or currents. Once found, this or that theme is followed…it guides the author into new regions of life" (238). By sorting and grouping according to motif and subject matter rather than strict chronology, Nabokov's memoir is taken in new and unexpected directions. The thematic approach allows the writer to surprise both the reader (by upending traditional expectations concerning chronology) and themselves. Nabokov fosters a sense of being led by chance and caprice, which suggests that the past has its own peculiar gravity. Eschewing a linear progression in favour of allowing a narrative to be led by various coincidences of place, time, memory, and association can increase the dramatic unpredictability of a text.

Speak, Memory also demonstrates that writers have a duty to be selective in gathering and presenting their material. In this respect, the work of the memoirist is that of a curator: deciding which memories aid the narrative and which might detract, distract, or dilute. In this way, I was inspired to make the choice, early on, to focus very strictly only on the relationship between Luke and myself. I would travel in time strictly to those moments that involved just the two of us, and so organize my writing around those occasions and events when we were not surrounded by others. This act of curating allows for the life writer to focus in on one specific narrative strand and to edit out potentially distracting extraneous background in order to develop an intensity of theme and purpose.

Nabokov's theme and purpose are similarly single-minded; in *Speak, Memory*, he slowly builds a multi-faceted portrait of his family's life in St. Petersburg in pre-revolutionary Russia. In other words, like me, he works to reconstruct a time now lost forever—and central to that lost time is childhood: "The nostalgia I have been cherishing all these years is a hypertrophied sense of lost childhood, not sorrow for lost banknotes" (49). Nostalgia for a lost time was also part of the driving force of my narrative, and a key reminder that one of the functions of life writing is to preserve and recreate the past.

Moreover, it is interesting to note that during my research I discovered that the word "nostalgia" itself was coined in the seventeenth century by the physician Johannes Hofer to describe the feeling of extreme homesickness suffered by Swiss mercenaries gone to war far from their homelands. Many of us are homesick for a home we cannot return to—except through writing and reading. Hofer suggested that the Swiss were particularly susceptible to nostalgia because when they left the Alps and descended to fight in the wars of the European plains, the change in atmosphere caused blood to rush from the heart to the brain. The nostalgic can be noted, Hofer went on, by his melancholy air, and by the general wasting away of his person. These are also, without a doubt, some of the physical manifestations of grief. The strong pull of nostalgia (as a function of grief) was one of the key reasons why I moved away from a chronological structure and chose instead to ensure that each of my chapters "returns" to the childhood that Luke and I shared. This shared past is the center of much life writing, and so for me was the center of gravity: the place of solace and wonder that the narrative is consistently drawn back to. I could not, for instance, write about the woods behind the house I grew up in without picturing the military games and battles that Luke and I enacted there, and could not describe driving along the South coast without feeling as though I was being drawn back—back to the ancient pier and promenade where as children we had walked almost every morning, back to the grey terrace where we once lived. I wanted to make clear that my memory of childhood, hypertrophied by grief, cannot be escaped. Time does not proceed always forward, away from childhood; on the contrary, many of us return to the past as often as we can.

Finally, Nabokov's thematic structuring suggests that meaning rarely inheres in any particular moment but often flickers or plays through the connections *between* moments. Finding these connections thus became part of the primary objective of my life writing, and so dictated the ensuing organization of the text. After all, narrative frequently works by association. The best metaphors, and some of the most interesting plots, are those which send us off in unexpected directions. A structure based upon thematic associations and connections, therefore, not only guides much life writing, but also in my case specifically reproduces something of the movement of a grieving mind, searching for meaning in endless associations.

A thematic and associative structure will necessarily send the life writer travelling back and forth through time, and it is also likely to lead to an increased engagement with what Mikhail Bakhtin terms a "heteroglossia": namely the cacophony of overlapping codes and discourses that is human language. In my case this meant including all the codes associated with Luke and our shared childhood, from pop culture, West coast Hip Hop, and children's books about goblins through to etymology and the Bible. The mixture of different forms of discourse and genre markers is intended to suggest that life and character cannot be easily pinned down and constrained within one "type" or genre. To put this another way, and to echo Whitman, people contain multitudes. Bakhtin argues that we speak with many voices, which means we are made up of voices that are not (only) our own; language operates, he argues, on "the borderline between oneself and the other...the word does not exist in a neutral and impersonal language (it is not, after all, out of the dictionary that the speaker gets his words!), but rather it exists in other people's mouths, in other people's contexts, serving other people's intentions" (293-4). A portrait of one person's life ought, therefore, to encompass not only their own words but their sources or intertexts—for example, the books they treasured, the movies they quoted, the songs they sang along to, the beliefs they mocked, the stories they told. After all, according to Freud the self is driven by (and indeed composed of) many unconscious forces. The self is therefore not fixed, but fluid. It is not singular, but multiple. A person is made up of a range of urges, memories, ideas, and other internal forces that we often little understand. Indeed, Freud notes examples of unconscious forces that spill out into our daily life, such as the effects of dreams, the "forgetting of familiar words and names...slips of the tongue...certain errors... tunes hummed thoughtlessly and so on" (346). By including some of these unconscious forces in my writing (such as the songs my brother hummed, the things he forgot, the silly slips of the tongue), I sought to hint at the unknowable and unpredictable aspects of my subject. We exist within a tangled web of references that, once again, suggests the life writer must proceed on a journey of associations that does not always fit with chronological thinking.

For instance, in my life writing, I found myself writing of how:

> As a teenager, Luke would often retreat to his room and play his favourite songs so loudly that he made the floor shudder. Though he usually stuck with one of the latest West Coast hip hop releases, his taste ranged from reggae through to metal, the only common theme being that the songs he played at maximum volume had to be either raging vehemently against the world or else telling everyone in it to go to hell. Extra points were awarded, it seemed, for the number of expletives a song contained. His music came pounding out while he bench-pressed in the small corner of his bedroom that had been converted into a mini-gym, or practised throwing darts with such violence that he often later found it impossible to pull them out from where they had stuck deep in the dartboard or surrounding wall. None of this would have mattered very much, were it not for the fact that once he found a tune he liked he would play it on repeat, listening to the same track again and again, sometimes for hours. When this happened, the rest of us

would have to resort to earplugs or rival music to prevent ourselves from being driven mad. I suspect that half the time he played the same track repeatedly just to make absolutely sure the world knew it should go to hell.

Just as I found his habit of playing the same few songs again and again to be a form of torture, so Luke would often grow enraged when he heard any melody that was placid or calm, as if he could not quite fathom why anyone would listen to music to relax rather than to rouse or stir them. Among the CDs of his that I come across after the funeral are *The Last Meal, Fuck It, Lucky Star, Deeper Shades of Euphoria, Back to the Old Skool, A Grand Don't Come for Free, Confessions, Born Again, Death Row Greatest Hits, Rhythm & Gangsta, Shock Value, The Big Dawg* and *Execute.*

As I search through his bags and boxes, these titles remind me that his idea of a great song was one that had a relentless fist-thumping beat, wall-shaking bass, and lyrics that were either brag or slam. I cannot confirm this impression though, since I have no intention to listen to any of them. Indeed, the first batch I find fills me with such anger that I decide to smash them to smithereens. At first I try to snap a few between my hands, but it proves almost impossible. Next I stamp on a handful as hard as I can, but CDs turn out to be remarkably resilient and so I have to take a rolling pin from the kitchen to break them into pieces. It is slow and methodical work, and by the end I feel ridiculous, not least because I have to find the dustpan and brush to sweep away the destruction before Mum and Dad see it. Once again, I feel like Luke has deliberately made me look stupid. But even those I haven't destroyed will not be played—not because I am worried that the songs will bring back emotions that I cannot control but because I have come to believe that songs themselves are different each time we hear them. They are sponges that soak up our personal histories, those private moments when we first listened to them and the feelings contained within those moments. There comes, in fact, a point when we no longer hear the music at all.

As is no doubt clear, I never enjoyed his music. I called it repetitive, contrived, fake—all swagger and no substance; and he repaid the insults by lashing out at everything I listened to. I could not understand how anyone could enjoy listening to those same mindless songs again and again. It is only now, looking back, that it occurs to me that he probably could not have cared less about the music. It was not the melody, the lyrics, the catchy hook, the shouty chorus, the violent beat, the stomach-churning bass, the sly rhymes or anything else about the songs themselves that he enjoyed. It was the attitude. *Fuck It. Fuck It. Fuck It.*

It was the same with his intense bodybuilding and preference for dark glasses and aggressive poses. For his tenth birthday he begged for a black leather jacket. Every day for a month he pleaded with my parents to buy one for him. There was nothing else he wanted, nothing. Every mealtime, without fail, the conversation would be turned to the leather jacket. *Think how good I'll look in it. Think how impressed everyone who sees me will be. I'll clean my room every day, and never tease anyone again.* Pause. Silence. Then: *If you don't get me one I'll wait until everyone's asleep and then throw ice-cold water on the lot of you!* In the end, Mum and Dad had no choice but to give in. The one he chose was a tough, hardy biker jacket, black as octopus ink, and with an oil-slick sheen and a musky animal smell. Whenever I now catch the scent of new leather I see him prancing up and down the living room, flexing and snarling as though it had made him suddenly more animal than man. He wore it all the time, and it became difficult to take him anywhere since he could not pass a mirror without stopping in his tracks to admire himself, either nodding his head approvingly or else raising an imaginary gun towards the assailant he saw in the reflection, the enemy who might or might not have been just a figment of his imagination. He imagined himself more Schwarzenegger in *Terminator* than a slight, freckly, red-headed boy from Sussex.

When he played his music as loud as he could I would do my best to compete by turning my own stereo up to maximum volume. But there's no easy way to drown out *Death Row*.

In writing this, I was once again strongly influenced by Edwin Muir—this time his dictat that "no autobiography can confine itself to conscious life… In themselves our conscious lives may not be particularly interesting. But what we are not and can never be, our fable, seems to me inconceivably interesting" (39). I decided to attempt to reproduce this "fable"—my brother's fable, that is—through the many subtexts and intertexts of his life. However, these could only be seen in retrospect, and thus there was no better beginning for me than the days after Luke's funeral, allowing me write backwards, into the past. In other words: in the beginning, death.

Death, of course, is the engine of the events I describe, their motivation and spur. Part of the impetus of my project was, after all, to recover something of my brother from death's grasp. Moreover, death is the key to the book's very form with each chapter setting out to expose how close death is to life. Furthermore, it is death or, more precisely, mourning that dictates the spiral-shaped structure of much life writing. Mourning, it seems, will always destabilize a linear concept of time since it constantly brings the past into the present. This is demonstrated most explicitly in the work of W. G. Sebald, where adherence to the usual rules of temporality is questioned and where the past is shown to be ever present. In *Austerlitz*, the title character states "I feel more and more as if time did not exist at all, only various spaces interlocking…between which the living and the dead can move back and forth as they like, and the longer I think about it the more it seems to me that we who are still alive are unreal in the eyes of the dead" (359). Within any life writing about someone no longer living, the text becomes an interlocking space, one in which the lost person being represented is simultaneously alive and dead. The success of such projects frequently depends on representing scenes from the past with as much force as scenes from the present. In other words, the task of such works is to make the dead as real as the living.

One way of achieving this is a fluid structure that might move freely between different periods. Similarly, in Sebald's *The Rings of Saturn*, a nonfiction narrative in which a walking tour of the coastline of East Anglia becomes a profound meditation on loss, ruin, and destruction, each chapter proceeds from a place, theme, or action in the present that leads back into the past. It thus provides a clear thematic model for life writing that wants to emphasize the fact that in memory as on the page all times coexist alongside one another. Speaking of a house in Suffolk, for instance, the narrator remarks upon how difficult it is to "say what decade or century it is, for many ages are superimposed here and coexist" (36). A written life is a palimpsest of memories, where many ages run simultaneously within the text. Ages, memories, events overlap, since each one is connected to another. My own life writing was guided by this concept of time overlapping: I set out each of my twenty-four chapters as a journey between the past and the present, in order to show how intimately the two remain connected.

However, such a focus on time and chronology can lead to a number of problems. One issue in particular is getting bogged down in time. I myself became fixated on my brother's time. For instance, I obsessed over trying to piece together Luke's last days, trying to find out every detail, no matter how much they might bother me. But there was not much to go on. Most of our working days follow the same pattern, and are easily forgotten. There are few among us, for example, who can recall what happened on each day of the final week of January last year, or can recollect with clarity the minutiae of every Tuesday in April. Almost as soon as each day is finished it is cast aside and lost forever. Songwriters tell us that time is an ocean, and if this is true then it is one we plough with broken and tattered fishing nets, catching only a few fleeting moments. Of the tens of thousands of days that make up our lives, we remember only the tiniest fraction, and the few days we can recall are outnumbered thousands to one by the shadowy mass of the weeks, months, years, even decades that we have forgotten.

I sat at my desk and attempted to total up my brother's allotted time. I estimated that his life amounted to only 8,923 days. Of these I could account for perhaps two or three hundred at best, though admittedly most of these are woefully incomplete and full of holes. I tried to add to this deranged arithmetic the new experiences he never got a chance to try, the places he never visited, the hours wasted on sleep, the lost opportunities, and even the percentage of his life the two of us spent fighting, arguing or simply ignoring each other. Soon I felt as though I was standing at the edge of an arithmetical abyss, with nothing below but an infinity of lunatic calculations.

It therefore became clear to me that limits are vital. No life writing can cover the entirety of a life; no book can contain the entire world. Once again, a comparison with academic writing is apt: the life writer must set out the limitations of their methodology in order to guide the structure and constraints of their writing (or risk a text that might become sprawling and thus unfocused). I therefore decided to construct a text of twenty-four chapters, reflecting the twenty-four years of my brother's life, each focused on a particular day or event, in order to limit the urge to attempt an impossible task of setting down every detail about the past within my writing.

Yet this was not the only issue with focusing on time and chronology. Another key difficulty was the challenge of reconciling my brother's own childhood fear of talking about the past with my project of constructing our shared personal history. I know a surprising number of people who are afraid of clowns. Countless more who cannot even look at spiders or mice without screaming. A few who have an unhealthy fear of dwarves. I myself have a fear of snakes. I have even met one or two writers who claim to feel physically sick at the use of adverbs. But I have never met anyone besides my brother who suffered from a phobia of the past tense.

More specifically, it was the years before he was born that seemed to drive him mad. I would sometimes tell him stories about things that had happened before his birth, but he could not bear to hear. As a child he simply would not accept that the world had existed, almost exactly as it was now, before he arrived.

There was no rational way to explain it, yet that did not deter him. He agreed that since he was seven and I was nine that I was, therefore, two years older than him. He was also happy to agree that he had not been around forever. He would not, however, accept that anything had really happened before his birth—the Second World War or dinosaurs or Henry VIII were no more real, in his opinion, than Rumpelstiltskin or the Tooth Fairy. They were stories adults made up to keep us kids confused. No matter what evidence we produced he would not believe it, and any photos of times before 1984 made him so mad that he would chase me round the house threatening me with blue murder if I didn't throw them in the bin that minute.

I therefore faced a dilemma: how to reconcile this childhood chronophobia with the main facet of my project: constructing a history. How to write a history of someone who refused history? In my work, I dealt with this by trying to limit myself to the quirks of local history and events (from the great storm of 1987 to the hockey matches, the holidays, the school trips, and so on) that had occurred within Luke's lifetime, in the belief that this brief span of time (from 1984 through to 2008) was now marked out as his. I did not dare step outside of it, since I remembered so vividly his hatred of talking about things that had happened before his own life. I assumed that I could construct my creative history in such a way that the news and events of those years, both international and local, would take on particular meaning and significance in relation to my brother. However, when drafting and re-drafting the first chapter, I soon realised that this temporal organization revealed a basic falsehood in my logic: just because things occur concurrently does not mean their relationship is any more significant than any other two events. I therefore revised my plan and structure in order to demonstrate how meaning could arise from any historic events or ideas that provided a point of connection with Luke's life. Walter Benjamin notes that the historian can use such connections to create a "constellation in which his own epoch comes into contact with that of an earlier one" (265). For the life writer, these points of contact between different historical epochs can be used to show that the present is composed of splinters of the past. In my own writing, this would serve to re-cast my brother not as a product of only those twenty-four years but as a human composed of and inseparable from the unending text of human history. We are, in a sense, composed of time.

This, therefore, leads us to another problem. For just as science fiction tells us that travelling in the past might irrevocably alter the present (should we happen, perchance, to crush a prehistoric butterfly beneath our boot or to accidentally kill our own grandparent), writing about the past might have a similar effect. Paul de Man in his essay "Autobiography as De-facement" suggests that we may have the whole idea the wrong way around, since "We assume the life produces the autobiography as an act produces its consequences, but can we not suggest, with equal justice, that the autobiographical project may itself produce and determine the life" (920). My life is therefore a product of the act of writing about it; my memories of my brother become fixed in text, and therefore beyond both myself and my control. I worried frequently during my writing that the narrative I was working to create would therefore in some ways come to replace, obscure or obfuscate the memories, until all that was left of Luke was words. However, this anxiety was offset by the alternative possibility: that by not writing, nothing at all would be left of my brother besides memory. Furthermore, Sprinkler acutely notes that "No autobiography can take place except within the boundaries of a writing where concepts of subject, self, and author collapse into the act of producing a text" (342). Both the process and the product of writing suggest the mixing together of subject, self, and author within the text, so that the narrative comes to contain both the narrator and the world of which the narrator is both composed and composing. The ensuing text might therefore be seen as a type of map; the reflective life writing becomes a record of its own journey. For myself, it suggested a path through the messy landscape of bereavement. As I wrote, I remembered, reassembled and so reclaimed the past.

Attempting to write about Luke in my book *The Jester and the Ape* revealed the multiple problems with utilizing strictly chronological structures in life writing. Any life writing that proceeds in this way has to logically end with death; yet the act of writing is itself some proof of success in the battle against death. Moreover, since our inner narratives are frequently defined by association and heteroglossia, any biographical project that seeks to represent an active consciousness must extend beyond the boundaries of the time-bound story. In the end, I found then that despite my earliest fantasies with Luke, I did not need a Tardis, DeLorean, black hole, wormhole or magic portal to return to the past. Yet time travel is clearly tricky. A guide is required. And it was here that I found the comparison with academic writing most profitable: the life writer moving fluidly through time must identify both their purpose and set out the limitations of their methodology in order to guide the structure and constraints of their writing. By researching, analyzing and responding to previous texts in the same field, new avenues for exploration might be revealed, and new organizational models revealed. For through such fluid journeys the past might come into contact with the present, and my little brother remain alive.

Note

1. Sam Meekings, Assistant Professor, Northwestern University in Qatar. sam.meekings@ northwestern.edu

References

Bakhtin, Mikhail M. *The Dialogic Imagination.* Ed. Michael Holquist. Austin: University of Texas Press, 1981.

Benjamin, Walter, "Theses on The Philosophy of History." *Illuminations.* Trans. Harry Zohn. New York: Schocken Books, 1968.

De Man, Paul. "Autobiography as De-facement." *Comparative Literature* 94.5 (1979): 919–30.

Freud, Sigmund, "Character and Culture." *Readings on Human Nature.* Ed. Peter Loptson. Hadleigh: Broadview Press, 1998, 343–52.

Gosse, Edmund, *Father and Son.* Oxford: Oxford University Press, 1907; Oxford World's Classics edition, 2009.

Muir, Edwin. *An Autobiography.* Edinburgh: Canongate Classics, 1954.

Nabokov, Vladimir. *Speak, Memory.* London: Penguin, 1969.

Proust, Marcel. *In Search of Lost Time Vol 1: Swann's Way.* Trans. Moncrieff, C. K. Scott, D. J. Enright and Terence Kilmartin. London: Vintage Classics, 1996.

Sebald, W. G. *Austerlitz.* Trans. Anthea Bell. London: The Harvill Press, 2001.

———. *The Rings of Saturn.* Trans. Michael Hulse. London: The Harvill Press, 1998.

Sprinkler, Michael. "Fictions of the Self: The End of Autobiography." *Autobiography: Essays Theoretical and Critical.* Ed. James Olney. Princeton: Princeton University Press, 1980.

II

How We Revise Our Lives

5. *Moving Literacies: A Need to Tell Transnational Stories*

Lisya Seloni[1]

A Confession: Oh No, I've Been Hiding Behind Academic Writing!

As a transnational[2] woman who has lived her life as an ethnic minority both in my home and adopted country, *moving* has been an unremarkable fact of my life. To me, moving never simply meant a geographical displacement from one location to another. It also meant an ongoing sense of in-betweenness, otherness/otheredness—being on the move among languages, literacies, cultures, narratives, identities, and stories. As people move across borders, they not only take their languages with them, but also strategically appropriate and change them in order to make sense of their new contexts, communities, and social relationships. This act of moving also brings with it a wide range of human experiences and actions such as reflecting, doubting, negotiating, conforming, breaking, disrupting, and finally creating something new, something foreign even to oneself. While this in-betweenness can be unsettling at times, it is also what feeds us as thinkers, writers, and teachers bringing complex understandings to our individual and collective narratives about who we are as humans, how we evolve, and how we interact with the world around us. The stories transnational bodies tell as they *move* are always situated in their ever-changing social, cultural, and political realities, which constantly shape their assumed and self-ascribed identities and fluid literacy histories. While the experiences in these transnational spaces contribute to cosmopolitan identities, this back and forth mobility between different places harbors both fluidity and fixity within the stories we construct (Leonard, "Traveling" 13). Telling personal stories is messy regardless of the language(s) we use, but through my own transnational *becoming* I came to believe that it can be even more complex and non-translatable when the languages and dialects we use while telling those stories are not equally recognized as a valued human capital in the spaces we occupy. Just like the languages we perform, stories we choose to share or narratives shared about us might not always capture the complex picture of our experiences or might even take away our right to be heard, recognized, or exist in certain spaces. This essay is about the stories I choose to share about what it means to live unique experiences of multiliterate lives and what it means to write about them in a way that puts *self* and *narrative memory* back in writing, back in our scholarship. More specifically, this essay is about my relationship with academic writing and my plea for blended scholarship (and teaching) that bring forth human experience, especially during major life transitions.

Writing certain parts of this essay, such as the first draft of the introduction paragraph above, came easily to me while part of me felt betrayed as a transnational woman academic who is aching to share writing that articulates stories rather than theories. In academia, we tend to hide the real peopled stories behind the theories we like to re-tell perhaps for all the right reasons. Because I have been conditioned to write academically for more than a decade, the first version of this introduction included theories on geopolitics of language use across communities, the deeply embodied nature of language and cultures, and my own scholarly quest in understanding how multilingual writers like myself negotiate, create, conform, resist certain discourses in the literature, and how they reframe themselves as writers while navigating larger discursive systems. While all of these sounded important and relevant to what I wanted to write, my fingers kept typing big words—words that usually feel like rocks in my mouth when I try to say them out loud. My heart wanted to go deeper to dig the stories that I ignored, using the words that speak to my heart.

I cannot deny the fact that *academic* writing has been a safe harbor that helped me equalize my *accented* voice as a minority scholar while shielding me from prejudices, covering most of the linguistic differences that I bring as a non-native English writer due to its structure and predictability. Certain rhetorical moves that I learned to make in my academic training enable me to participate, be recognized and even taken up by people in my disciplinary community. Academic writing with its mostly predictable routine and definable audience has been my calm waters—perhaps not a deep blue ocean, but a well-maintained community pool in an affluent neighborhood where newcomers are disciplined to learn the values and the codes. While I owe part of my journey in my adopted home in the U.S. to being able to successfully enagage in academic writing and its relevant activities, the more I think about my literate journey across time and space, the more I realize that I have also been comfortably and perhaps willingly hiding behind academic writing. And, the more I navigate my way in academia, the more I realize telling stories in *one* way steals our right to tell alternative stories—stories that could perhaps better capture the full complexity of migrant lives, stories that carry affective aspects of human experiences.

The stories that I chose to tell in this essay frame my own transnational literate experiences with movement and writing through a lens of *rhetorical attunement*—an ear for or tuning toward difference and multiplicity. As Rebecca Leonard puts it, rhetorical attunement "seeks to account for lived literate experiences that rely on discursive and provisional truths," and "aims to account for a sensibility fostered over time, across a spectrum of language and geographic boundaries" ("Multilingual Writing" 230). As someone who leads her life in multiple literate and linguistic traditions (shuttling between Turkey, my birth country, and the United States, my adopted home), the stories I choose to share in this essay revolve around three Turkish words that do not directly translate to the English language. Instead of feeling lost in translation, these stories will ask the readers to tune towards difference and be okay with being lost for a while, a daily experience in a migrant life. These foreign words might be far from some realities, yet so close to our common human experiences. The words, *nazar* (evil-eye), *kısmet* (fate) and *hasret* (nostalgia, longing), represent the narrative vignettes in which I write how life unfolds as I move from one space to another and capture my feelings of nostalgia about my birth country and experiences of unexpected traumatic events lived in between.

A Need to Tell Transnational Stories: Mundaneness of Mobility and Translingualism

Translingualism is not as eccentric as it sounds in migrant lives. As a transnational woman, my use of multiple languages and literacies is a fact of ordinary life. It is unremarkable (Otsuji and Pennycook), ordinary (Dovchin), and by no means a new language phenomenon (Canagarajah). Some days the way I want to describe the scent of rain comes to me in English, and some days it is the Turkish language that captures my longing for the homeland and some of my childhood memories. Perhaps rather than romanticizing this notion, what needs to be discussed is the stories behind the translingual experience—the disappointments, joys, fears, resistances, challenges within our day-to-day lives.

There is an ongoing discussion of *translingual activity* in various academic disciplines including rhetoric and composition and my own home field of second language writing. This approach to language and writing encourages an open-minded attitude towards language difference and encourages us to look at writing activities outside our own contexts. It conceives of language difference as a resource that produces new meanings, rhetorics, and functions rather than interference on the way to reach some sort of a "Standard written English." In an era where mobility of people is faster than ever, translingualism underlines the fluidity of our literacies and languages and moves beyond the normative understandings of languages as discrete and compartmentalized codes. While all of this sounds promising when it comes to recognizing language difference within different speech communities, the mobility and fluidity of our multiliterate lives usually remains hidden behind numerous scholarly debates we read and theories we re/produce. The linguistic multiplicity that we passionately advocate in scholarship is rarely reflected through stories and lived experiences of newcomer or old-timer immigrants which in essence could better capture the human face of *movement* and bring a higher degree of agency to our writing and perhaps a more honest representation of translingual lives.

Social Space, Memories, Nostalgia: Stories That Connect Us

Nazar (noun): Curse. Omen. Insidious look. As a nation, we are anxious and fearful of nazar. One can protect oneself from nazar by wearing an amulet that is believed to guard one from negative energy. If any Turkish word characterizes part of my childhood, it is the word nazar.

Fourth grade. I'm skipping rope in the backyard with my friends during recess in what I seem to remember as an old building in a Jewish primary school near Galata Tower in Şişhane, a historic neighborhood in the old town part of Istanbul. A few of my relatives from my dad's side were visiting my school during the noon recess. I cannot remember why they were there or if they were there for me, but all I remember is that they gifted me with some of my favorite candies and chocolate bars. I really wanted to eat them all, but something inside me stopped me that day. There is this supernatural belief in my community that some people have powers to cast spells on objects—especially people who might not like you or with whom you have some sort of a conflict. The pictures of uneaten candies are still vivid in my memory. Instead of joyfully ripping the papers off the goodies, I gave them to friends, and threw the rest of them in the trash can amidst feelings of disappointment and relief. Taking a deep sigh, I whispered to myself "I just protected myself from *nazar.*" *Casting curses on things* was a statement that I heard many times in the presence of family conflict. It was the fear of *nazar* that prevented me from enjoying those candies. I must have naively thought that the candies were cursed, and I was the target of the curse. In my child mind, I was terrified to eat them and just drop dead in the middle of school. And, no one would know why my 9-year-old body had collapsed in the middle of school-yard. In my child mind, trashing those candies seemed like a wise move.

Even though the deceased loved ones always watch your back, one has to carry evil-eye beads in her pocket to shield against *nazar.* As the symbol of protection from all things evil, many mothers sew *nazar beads* into the undershirts of their kids to protect them from calamities; bus drivers hang it on their front mirrors while navigating their way in the bustling streets of Istanbul; women wear it as jewelry to protect their health. *Ojos Maloz!*[3] said my grandmother at times, who is a believer of all things supernatural, slightly spitting on my forehead and licking it, testing the amount of *nazar.* If one's forehead was salty, it was due not to the sweat of their body, but *nazar* to which they were exposed. And, as a kid, I had a lot of *nazar* according to my grandmother. These were the everyday practices in superstitious families such as mine. They intrigued me, but also scared me. This is why I must have been a cautious kid, and am a cautious adult today—usually uneasy, thinking that something dooming might happen soon, and that I would not know what kind of evil is coming my way. In fact, the 1980s were full of superstitions, fears, and anxieties for many in the nation. The third military coup d'état of 1980, less than a year after I was born, brought all kinds of uncertainties to the Turkish society. Military overthrew the government as a response to "domestic political anarchy" of the time. Many people got persecuted. The daily life was filled with street clashes. Thirty-six years later back in Istanbul, I witnessed the second military coup of my life. This time it was more vivid in my memory. This time I wished that I were a baby again soundly sleeping while the F-16 planes flew over our rooftop and the Parliament were bombed.

Narrative memory intrigues me. What intrigues me the most is what we choose to remember in the narrative memory of ours. Marya Hornbacher writes "Facts and memory share an edge, they overlap; they are not, of course, the same. They are, nevertheless, the raw materials with which the nonfiction-ist works, and each acts as a check on the other; memory inflects fact with sensory and associative detail—what Henry James called 'felt-life.'" Non-fiction is more than reporting the memory; it is also about shaping it by the languages we rely on. And, the languages we rely on could be multiple, reflecting multiple subjectivities and realities. While the concept of *nazar* cannot quite be encountered in mainstream American English, it is the telling of this felt life (and our stories attached to it) that makes the unfamiliar familiar. As foreign as these words might sound to some ears, transnational stories attached to foreign words could encourage openness to difference and patience to construct meaning and at some level willingness to connect with the felt sense of a foreign word/world.

The more I navigate through narrative memory, the more I pay attention to my current perceptions and representation of the world. There is something soothing in the kind of memory that is now a distant past—distant, but not foreign. The social spaces migrants occupy shape their everyday practices, including memories and experiences in these spaces. And, some of these memories are too vivid to forget even after some time. They are vivid because the incidents are simply too painful, frightening, worrisome or even joyful to forget. They continue to exert their influence in present time especially if present time constantly crosses geographical boundaries. Narrative memory in migrant life has been an important tool to understand social life in diaspora and to make sense of past experiences. It is not only the languages migrants leave behind, but also the images of past places and the sensory experiences we felt in those spaces. Jennifer Sinor in her essay "Writing Place" writes, "without narrative, a place is merely space, a geographical entity without any emotional resonance. In many ways, stories of place work like sculpture, defining a way for us to see and experience what was formerly invisible and formless. Story transforms space into place first in memory" (9–10). Our memories are experiences attached to the various places that we travel, both actual and imaginary ones. Yet, I always wonder why as academics we tend to divorce these memories from our writing, which carry so much of our lived sensory experiences, those that make us human. At the end, stories break down the imaginary dualities, fears we have towards other(ed) cultures and languages, bringing sensory experiences to life and connecting us to one another.

I grew up shuttling between two different kinds of communities: Turkish-Jews and Muslim-Turks. And none of these have been static communities. Growing up in a Turkish-Jewish community in Istanbul in the 1980s and 1990s was filled with contradictions coupled with a mixture of cultural and linguistic clashes. As an ethnic minority living in a Muslim majority secular country, these contradictions translated into unexpected actions in daily life such as changing your name to a Turkish name while playing with neighborhood kids on the street, making sure that you are not too visible in a crowd, constantly downplaying who you are, and keeping close relationships only with peers from your community. These covering acts also translated to developing all kinds of fears. You are fearful of your neighbors. You are fearful of the space you occupy. You are fearful of stories you hear from parents and grandparents about assimilation and discrimination. Living your life as an ethnic minority in the city of Istanbul also meant having to harbor a multitude of lives and having to make sense of a multitude of histories and literate traditions. Defining identity through the lenses of national and ethnic borders, people both at my homeland and adopted country question the extent of my Turkish-ness, Jewish-ness, American-ness as if those are the only labels that define who I am and who I become.

In his memoir, *Out of Place*, Edward Said writes about his identity confusion, cultural dislocation, and various conflicting affiliations of his Arab and Christian identities during the time he was growing up in Palestine, Cairo and then in the U.S. He recalls his identity confusions with, as he writes, an "acute memory of the despairing feeling that I wish we could have been all-Arab, or all-European and American, or all–orthodox Christian, or all-Muslim, or all-Egyptian" (5). Similar feelings of in-betweenness defined most parts of my childhood and young adult days in Turkey. However, while out-of-place-ness can make one feel restless at times, it can also be liberating, empowering and freeing in some unexpected ways. It is the personal stories that could communicate these experiences with the world. In this regard, storytelling and narrative emerge not only as trans-disciplinary exercise, but also as a way to bring agency and voice to one's writing through sensory experiences of personal story. Whether it is a story about the need to believe in *nazar* to protect oneself against the evils of the world or a story about the desire to observe fruits hanging from greengrocer stalls in the streets of Istanbul, it is the told sensory experiences that connect us to one another. It is the desire to connect with our individual stories that give a "human face" to our literate activities on the move. It is the desire to tell our unique stories that gives life to the feeling of out-of-place-ness. As bell hooks puts it eloquently: "Though I write about the healing process as an individual, the insights shared are collective" (15).

Kısmet (noun): Kısmet comes from Arabic word kısmat meaning fate. This word means that one does not have much say in how the future will get shaped. It is also used to describe a good prospect, whether this prospect is related to a job or a future lover. I grew up in a culture that believed that there is always a divine destiny that predicts your future and one cannot do much to change it.

If you asked my grandma, it was kısmet that brought me all the way to the beautiful prairies of central Illinois. I fondly remember the coffee reading[4] rituals in her sun-room overlooking a small garden in Istanbul. She always saw a peacock in my coffee grains, which translated to good karma, and winding roads, which meant travels to foreign lands. I did not leave my home country due to some catastrophe, discrimination or violence, although those are the very reasons that many of my family members and friends are now leaving Turkey due to its political turbulences. I came to the United States to pursue my graduate degree and had serious intentions to go back to my homeland. Yet, my two-year Master's program in central Missouri turned into a five-year doctoral study in Ohio, which turned into an academic job in the hilly outskirts of rural Pennsylvania, and then central Illinois, where the endless cornfields meet the wide blue sky. There I was: an accidental immigrant, who spent most of her adult years in her adopted home country, having no intentions of going back even though she once had dreams of settling in one of the Prince Islands of Istanbul. On the days when my Istanbulite self melancholically longs for the scent of the Marmara Sea or the sight of the slowly sailing ferry boats in Bosphorus, the Illinois prairie and its down-to-earth people bring me deep peace and stability.

It was exactly a month before the horrific day of September 11 that I arrived in the United States, without having an intention of one day making it my permanent home. It took me a while to explain to my grandmother that I was not physically hurt by the terrorist attacks of 9/11 or that where I lived was not near the World Trade Center. After all, she only knew two facts: Her beloved granddaughter boarded a big plane a few weeks prior to the horrific incident to fly to "America," and two big planes had just crashed into some skyscrapers in "America."

My mother wanted to buy me a huge hat and a flowery dress for my descent from the plane which took me to the dreamland for pursuit of graduate studies. "Don't be ridiculous, mom. I'm not a movie actress," I said without grasping perhaps the deep pain she must have felt for sending away her daughter to a foreign land located thousands of miles away from motherland. My arrival day to the new land and the months that followed were quite unlike feel-good movies, although part of me felt deep relief to finally have left the homeland. I had missed my connection to Kansas and was put in the Hilton at the Chicago's O'Hare Airport. To this day, I still remember the joy I felt while lying on the white sheets of my hotel room. During my plane ride, I had met a fellow Turkish student who wanted to be a mathematician. She seemed fearful of her future and kept saying that leaving home and coming to the U.S. was a bad decision. Trying to console her during our dinner was harder than I thought. My words were of no help. We silently ate our dinner and talked about the schools each of us were going to for our graduate studies. Grunting unhappily, she went to her hotel room, and I never saw her again. To this day, I wonder how her journey ended up.

The next day, I caught my plane to Kansas, and was picked up from the airport by Stacy, a tall, blue-eyed blonde American woman with the kindest smile—just like the American actresses I watched on TV in Turkey. She reminded me of Cybill Sheperd from *Moonlighting*, an American detective sitcom that my family used to watch every Sunday evening. Finding twins of people in the new land was an amusing game that I played almost on a daily basis when I met a new person. To forget my homesickness, I matched the new people I met with those that I know from home. It was the scent of the person or the way they walked that reminded me of someone I knew, a distant cousin, a high school friend, a shopkeeper. All of a sudden, I felt close to that person as if I knew her already from another lifetime. Unfamiliar was made familiar. And, I was not alone anymore.

It was shacks after shacks that I saw while driving to the small town called Warrensburg in central Missouri. I was certainly not in Istanbul anymore. I knew that *kısmet* brought me to this strange land called Kansas City and I was going to embrace it with open arms. I remember being asked all sorts of strange questions when I met locals in my small college town. "*No, we don't ride camels in Turkey. Uhmm, yes, Midnight Express sounds like a horrific movie, but I haven't watched it. Oh, yes, I heard of the Four Lad's song Constantinople. Istanbul was Constantinople. Now it's Istanbul, not Constantinople. Been a long time gone, Oh Constantinople. Now it's Turkish delight on a moonlit night.*"

It was true that my exuberant 21-year-old self from the Middle East disliked those questions, and secretly envied my blonde-haired, blue-eyed Swedish friends who were not subject to as many questions as I was. Each of my encounters in the new land was precious to me no matter how Orientalizing the questions got. I knew the western gaze was there since I stepped on this strange land, and my naïve self looked back in the eye, and just winked at it not knowing what else to do.

Talking about movement requires us to talk about space. Going beyond a Kantian version of space as fixed and immutable, Alastair Pennycook defines space as encompassing a notion of time and change: "A sense of place is related to a sense of movement" (26). When we discuss migrants' literacy practices across spaces, we think about how migrants see different aspects of their separation from their home country and relocation to the new country. In my field of applied linguistics, the inclusion of the personal through narrative writing is a relatively newly embraced endeavor. Narrative research has recently been used as an important tool to elicit and analyze stories, yielding a wealth of insights about experiences of migration and identity struggles. Most scholarship on migrant lives centers around issues of identity, right to speak, in-group and out-group belonging, positioning and self-presentation, through the use of ethnographic observations and interview data where the researcher tries to get to know the lived experiences of the migrant, focusing on the narratives constructed about migrant identity (e.g., Norton, Pavlenko). Yet, we usually read these accounts from the "researcher's perspective" forgetting the bodies and the stories those bodies chose to tell. Arguing for the need to include the personal in academic texts, Dorothy E. Smith writes: "Inquiry starts with the knower who is actually located; she is active; she is at work; she is connected up with other people in various ways; she thinks, eats, sleeps, laughs, desires, sorrows, sings, curses, loves, just here; she reads here; she watches television." (4) In migrant stories, language is embodied in bodies that travel across cultures. The familiar feelings of the past occur in the present just like how your present is intertwined with the nostalgic past.

Hasret (noun): Nostalgia, longing. The word hasret is derived from the Arabic word hasra, and refers to a deep longing and a melancholic desire felt towards a place or a person. One might feel hasret for the long lost homeland or a loved one who is physically or spiritually far. The word hasret is usually coupled with verbs such as "stay," "hear," "feel," so one either hears longing (hasret duymak) or stays in the state of longing (hasret kalmak).

Exactly 15 years after my immigration to the United States, I was getting ready to leave for Istanbul for a year-long stay for my sabbatical. I was newly tenured, and was quite ready to do the research that I had dreamed of for a long time, in the place I dreamed of re-experiencing, and with the people I dreamed of living with again in my beloved city of Istanbul. Yet, to my dismay, things had been extremely violent and chaotic in the months prior to my upcoming visit with my spouse and then two-year-old. During the first half of that year, Turkey had experienced seven terrorist attacks in Istanbul and Ankara alone, and around seventeen in other major cities in Turkey. All of them resulted in multiple casualties. Every time I scrolled down the heartbreaking news in my quiet office in our house located on a quiet street of Normal, Illinois, I felt both an urgency to be in Istanbul with my loved ones and also, selfishly, the relief of being far from it all. Little did I know that my sabbatical year would experience one of the rockiest times in Turkish history, and that I would get my share of political trauma. This was certainly not the kind of Turkey I was hoping to return to when I was fantasizing about my sabbatical year where we would have rented a small house in one of the Prince Islands overlooking Marmara Sea. There I would have worked on my writing while sipping tea and smelling the sweet scent of Judas trees blooming out of my window. I *stayed* in *hasret* for a long time in the U.S., and this was the year I was going to make up for all the lost times with the people and the places I missed all these years. Despite my aspirations, our return to our homeland this time was traumatic.

The night we stepped into our rental apartment with five suitcases and big aspirations Turkey was battling with a bloody coup attempt. When everyone thought the political role of the military was curtailed more than ever in the past years, a group of officers plotted a coup that would end with a state of emergency declared by the government. Only a couple of hours after our arrival, I was curled up like a ball in our bathroom holding my husband's hand, exchanging messages with my family, who were only ten minutes away from me this time, instead of thousands of miles apart. "If something happens to us tonight, please know that I love you all," I texted to my family. While texting, these lines sounded so clichéd but so unreal at the same time, just like the personal survival stories I used to read in the news. "I sure hope we don't make it to the news the next day," I said to myself as I was thinking about my daughter who was sleeping in the next room. I thought about all the sweet dreams a child should have at night. I was only hoping that she wouldn't wake up to the horrid sounds of F-16s that were flying right above our rooftop, gunshots and callings of muezzin[5]. We had no TV in the apartment, so social media was the only place we were able to get our information and follow the horrific events unfolding right in front of our eyes. It was the scariest night of my life. I was trapped in my beloved homeland.

The next day various media channels reported that the country turned from the edge of a disaster. It sure felt like we went through disaster itself. That night over 300 people lost their lives and more than 2,100 were injured, when civilians used themselves as a shield against tanks and gunshots to protect the regime. Yet, the weeks that followed July 15, the longest night for many Turks, were tense, unpredictable, and full of horror. As a response to the failed coup attempt, the government declared a state of emergency, initially for three months, then renewed continuously, and still in place after almost two years. The government also undertook a huge crackdown against coup plotters and other dissidents. More than 130 media outlets have been shut down; over a hundred journalists are imprisoned; 15 magazines were shut down; 29 publishing houses were closed; 2,346 academics were dismissed from their academic positions with a single governmental decree; 15 private universities were closed down and around 600 schools were shut down.

After long discussions with my spouse about whether we should stay or go back, we decided to stay in the country and stick with our plans—in the end this was our homeland. My husband said "At least we were fortunate to be mobile enough to move back if we wanted to." His words made sense, yet were not enough to ease the horrific scenarios I played in my head every day. I spent the initial months that followed the coup attempt in fear. My sabbatical year was passing me by. Nights were especially difficult to bear. I grew to be

more and more fearful of the many sounds of the city: a fast motorbike that
passed our street, fireworks on special days, or street send-off parties for military conscripts were enough to take me back to that horrific night. I couldn't
stop reading the news day and night. I couldn't wrap my mind around all
the people who live in neighboring war-torn countries. How did they sleep
at night? How did they go on? I distracted myself with research and writing.

It was certainly not the kind of Turkey that I was hoping to introduce to
my daughter. I had dreams of feeding the pigeons in Sultan Ahmet with her,
taking the ferry boat to Karaköy, visiting the bohemian cafes of my youth in
Taksim. I had dreams of going to Kadıköy with her, breathing in the odor
of old pictures and dusty books in Sahaflar, a famous historic book bazaar in
the city. Susan Brison talks about violence and the remaking of self after her
own traumatic experiences with an almost fatal sexual assault in her book
titled *Aftermath*: "Narrative memory is not passively endured; rather, it is an
act on the part of the narrator, a speech act that defuses traumatic memory,
giving shape and a temporal order to the events recalled, establishing more
control over the recalling, and helping the survivor to remake a self" (71). As
a transnational migrant, bringing narrative memories to present is important
to survive and to remake myself. Yet, at times, part of me feels a little ashamed
that I call some of my experiences traumatic. After all, I am not one of the
many who were imprisoned or got fired from my academic job during post-
coup crackdown. I survived. Regardless, the aftermath of the coup attempt
left me with paralysis and hidden depression, and in constant fear for and
from my own homeland. Eventually telling *my* story paved the way for healing. Brison also writes "trauma testimonies do purport to describe events that
actually occurred. And, what they do, or accomplish, if successful, is undo the
effects of the very violence they describe" (72). Many of the people I met in
the university where I conducted my sabbatical research, many of my family
members, neighbors close and far, also wanted to tell their stories of the traumatic months that followed the coup. So, we did. We exchanged stories.
We discussed politics, shared our fears of the future while reconfiguring our
past and present lives. Remembering and externalizing our collective stories
helped us remake ourselves.

I've come to believe that this is what it means to live transnational lives
and to navigate life with our multiple stories: You can't fully go back. You
can't fully stay. Perhaps the best thing one can do in between is to tell one's
stories to remake herself, to survive and hope to thrive in the meantime.
While the nostalgic sense of place slowly disappears in transnational stories,
the remaking of self is ongoing during changing life situations. I realize today
that writing stories matters to me more than reporting the facts. Telling our

stories and self-reflections earnestly to others not only helps us make sense of traumatic events, but also communicates the *felt sense* one feels through those events. Transnational stories are grounded in the wider histories of places and people. They can be unstable, messy, and even incomprehensible to some ears. Yet, we need to think about how to cultivate the stories that illustrate the complexity of everyday translingual practices so that we invite the listeners/readers to better understand other(ed) identities and languages and develop "rhetorical attunement" to difference.

A Plea for Blended Scholarship: Putting Stories Back in Writing and Teaching

Writing personal stories used to be my rescue while growing up in Istanbul in the 80s and 90s. Like many children of dysfunctional families living in those times, I turned to personal writing about the thoughts that haunted me, including traumatic memories and the unpredictable future awaiting me. In a way, writing personal stories was self-therapy. It was in my stories that I was able to control and make sense of my reality. Yet, my young self somewhat foolishly believed that personal writing was something to be done in the secrecy of a locked room in a locked journal, which would then be locked in a drawer. No one was supposed to read that; no one was supposed to respond to that.

I always knew that the academic writing that I was trained to do in my adopted country seemed to create space for me to join in ongoing disciplinary conversations. I wanted to be part of those conversations by chiming in and saying something smart and insightful. Personal writing didn't seem like a well-accepted move, especially for newcomers in my discipline. My love of storytelling took blows by the kinds of feedback I received during my earlier years in graduate school. I was usually asked to cut down my stories and tell the readers my arguments right up front using assertive and clear language. In fact, my very first writing in graduate school received a big red cross on its first page, like a big scar that needed to be healed. I had to write an academic essay with an appropriate "thesis." I always thought to myself "But, why ruin the movie by telling the readers what happens at the end?" I missed the flowery language of Turkish and writing from the heart even though I knew I didn't have the fancy moves in writing nonfiction. It is also true that academic writing at times came to my rescue as it was structural enough to mimic and predictable enough to be understood. As a second language writer, certain moves such as occupying a research niche and creating a research space seemed like the most important skills to have as an emerging scholar. There wasn't much space for variation and innovation that can transform the academic genres I was asked to produce to make scholarship. Ken Hyland discusses academic writing as creation of a text that "the writer assumes the reader will recognize and expect" (557). The hedging practices, use of citations, self-mentions, argumentation, and various other rhetorical moves and genre knowledge were there for me with the purpose of making the values and identities that relate to our discipline visible. I was sold early on that academic writing without storytelling was my ticket to success.

Today, I am drawn to personal writing more than ever in my life. I came to believe that doing research on transnational literacies cannot be done solely with academic prose. I like that personal writing helps me understand the complex realities of our lives. I like the connecting sensory experiences and the subjective moments shared with readers who might not share the same mother tongue with you. More importantly, I like that it actually helps make the unfamiliar familiar, showing the world that perhaps we are more the same than different. As a transnational woman in my field of applied linguistics, I have developed a conviction about storytelling in academic writing, especially when I am trying to make sense of my own lived experiences across languages, cultures, and identities.

Academic writing, void of stories, creates an artificial distance between our sensory and intellectual worlds, a distance that I wish to shorten both as a teacher and a scholar. I used to frequently have this feeling that readers will probably understand me more if I take the *me/self* out of my writing. I am beginning to see now that it might actually be the other way around. When the self, with all of its complicated intersectionalities, emotions, and experiences, is at the center of our quest and when we own our subjectivity, the information we uncover about the world becomes more accessible, and we can be more receptive of and empathetic to the new knowledge being created.

To better make sense of the multitude of my students' voices and stories behind their academic texts, I open up possibilities both for myself and for my students for productively blending scholarship with stories: stories we fear to tell; stories that move across time and space; stories that reconstruct our lives. Vivian Gornick eloquently writes that story is the "emotional experience that preoccupies the writer: the insight, the wisdom, the thing one has come to say" (13). In nonfiction writing, the writer is the truth speaker who reorganizes her experiences and reinvents the self in a way that creates oneness, empathy, connectedness between the reader and the narrator. My hope is that a similar empathy and connectedness can be established even when the reader and the narrator do not share the same cultural and linguistic backgrounds. Telling our transnational stories by embedding personal stories help make the intersectionality of our identities and languages visible. I find myself telling my students about different stories of *nazar, hasret* and *kismet*. I find myself telling them all about my language and its unique and beautiful features. I find myself making space for stories in academic writing, disrupting the conventions and playfully manipulating academic genres. We are always more connected at the end of those stories.

Today, as a transnational academic woman, I have been rediscovering the power of storytelling both in my writing and teaching. I understand the world around me at a deeper level and feel more connected to it when I turn research experiences into narratives. I often assign autobiographies, life writing, and narrative writing to my teacher candidates in the undergraduate and graduate classes I teach about language diversity to help them understand how their personal stories and reflections on their lived experiences can help them navigate and understand the teaching profession on which they are about to embark. Through stories, I want them to move their future students, to make a change in their communities and allow themselves to be changed. I also tell them that even though we might initially feel clumsy or uncomfortable in the way we tell our stories through experience-based prose, we all have the "right" to speak from our hearts and the "right" to do academic work through personal stories, and that the experiential discourse we create in personal writing is as meaningful and legitimate as conventional writing. If along the way I have encouraged students or readers to undertake the task of creating knowledge or teaching through blending personal stories, I have more than done my job here.

Notes

1. Lisya Seloni, Associate Professor, Illinois State University. lseloni@ilstu.edu
2. It is important to note here that my use of transnationalism is not the same as international or global. The concept of transnationalism is used by scholars in diaspora studies and migration studies to emphasize fluid ongoing-ness and mobility of migrants, and indicate cross-border connections of everyday individuals across real or perceived borders.
3. Evil eye in Judeo-Spanish, a heritage language used among Turkish-Jews.
4. Coffee reading is a common cultural practice in Turkey. It is believed that some people are gifted with a fortune-telling skills and can see the future by "reading" the coffe grains at the bottom of a Turkish coffee cup.
5. Muezzin is a religious official who prays from the minaret of a mosque, often with loudspeakers, to call Muslims to perform prayers several times a day.

References

Brison, Susan J. *Aftermath: Violence and the Remaking of a Self.* Princeton: Princeton University Press, 2002.

Canagarajah, A. Suresh. "Toward a Writing Pedagogy of Shuttling Between Languages: Learning from Multilingual Writers." *College English* 68.6 (2006): 589–604.

Dovchin, Sender. "The Ordinariness of Youth Linguascapes in Mongolia." *International Journal of Multilingualism* 14.2 (2017): 144–159.

Gornick, Vivian. *The Situation and the Story: The Art of Personal Narrative.* New York: Farrar, Straus and Giroux, 2001.

hooks, bell. *Sisters of the Yam: Black Women and Self-Recovery.* Boston: South End Press, 1993.

Hornbacher, Marya. "The World Is Not Vague": Nonfiction and the Urgency of Fact. *Assay: A Journal of Nonfiction Studies* 5.1. www.assayjournal.com/marya-hornbach er-the-world-is-not-vague-nonfiction-and-the-urgency-of-fact-51.html

Hyland, Ken. "Genre and Academic Writing in the Disciplines." *Language Teaching* 41.4 (2008): 543–62.

Leonard, Rebecca Lorimer. "Traveling Literacies: Multilingual Writing on the Move." *Research in the Teaching of English* (2013). 13–39.

———. "Multilingual Writing as Rhetorical Attunement." *College English* 76.3 (2014): 227–47.

Norton, Bonny. "Language, Identity, and the Ownership of English." *TESOL Quarterly* 31.3 (1997): 409–429.

Otsuji, Emi, and Alastair Pennycook. "Metrolingualism: Fixity, Fluidity and Language in Flux." *International Journal of Multilingualism* 7.3 (2010): 240–54.

Pavlenko, Aneta. "'In the World of the Tradition, I was Unimagined': Negotiation of Identities in Cross-Cultural Autobiographies." *International Journal of Bilingualism* 5.3 (2001): 317–344.

Pennycook, Alastair. *Language and Mobility: Unexpected Places.* Vol. 15. Bristol: Multilingual Matters, 2012.

Said, Edward W. *Out of Place: A Memoir.* New York: Vintage Books, 2012.

Sinor, Jennifer, and Rona Kaufman. *Placing the Academy: Essays on Landscape, Work, and Identity.* Logan: Utah State Press, 2007.

Smith, Dorothy E. *Writing the Social: Critique, Theory, and Investigations.* Toronto: University of Toronto Press, 1999.

6. (Dis)Arming With Stories: Power and Narrative Reconciliation in Retelling

Jessica L. Weber[1]

Stories I Tell at Networking Events

At 23, I landed my dream job: I was granted the opportunity to create a workplace writing center at a federal agency. It was the first of its kind, and it was an uphill battle—I was constantly justifying my position to older colleagues. But by 25, the service had become so successful locally that I had the opportunity to start expanding out to other branches across the country. On my 26th birthday, I gave a keynote speech at a regional conference. Before my 27th, I had been featured by *Harvard Business Review* and *Ragan*. I had been promoted twice. People from all over the world had started emailing me to ask if I could help them build a similar model in their own workplace. I loved every moment of my work; I was earning praise left and right that I had never imagined.

Stories I Tell in My Absence

Writing is a part of my everyday work life—conference proposals, budget requests, progress reports, training manuals. But the hardest piece that I have ever had to write was an away message in the summer of 2016—smack between that keynote and the *Harvard Business Review* article. I was asked to leave work for a week, though I had only requested one day off. After nearly twenty minutes of wrestling with my keyboard, I come up with a version so sterilized and standard that even I second-guessed my leave of absence: *Hello, I'll be out of the office without access to email through the week of July*

17th. I will respond to your email as soon as possible when I return. Thank you! It feels strange to say the week of the 17th, because that's a Sunday; I'm someone who usually counts weeks as beginning on a Monday. But Sunday is the reason why I'm leaving. Sunday the 17th is the date that is on all the medical paperwork. Sunday the 17th is what will find its way into my file at work. It's what will be on the police records.

It will always be the week of Sunday the 17th.

I imagine myself making casual elevator conversation when I'm cleared to return. Our workplace culture is conservative and politically neutral—it's not uncommon to never hear more about someone's weekend than *Great, I got a lot done.* And that's what I'll have to say when I get back, too: *Great, I got a lot of rest.* Or: *It was fine, how was yours?*

Stories I Am Told: Part I

July 17: When the EMT walks over, I start screaming again. I don't hear myself. In fact, for a moment I wish that the person screaming would stop. I know I'm supposed to feel pain, but I just feel light. Light, like I might float away from the ground entirely. And wet—and sticky as the thick trickles of blood dry on my arms. I am touching my head over and over, scared the back of it may not be there anymore. It's nothing but wet.

I am screaming only two things, in rapid succession—my boyfriend's name, and *I don't need to go.* The EMT is older than I am, and he's gruff as he grips my arm and leads me toward the ambulance. "You need to go," he says, and so I settle for just screaming the same name over and over.

His face shifts as though he suddenly understands. "Seth?" he parrots back. "Is that who did this to you?"

I stop screaming. I purse my lips and start crying more quietly. A new mantra: *No. No, he didn't do anything. No-no-no-n—*

"Seth is the one who did this to you," he says, making it a statement, and I start howling over and over that it wasn't his fault.

Stories Told in Print

The medical forms that I turn in at the end of my leave say only one thing: *Assault.*

That's it. That's all it says.

Stories Told Softly

When I am home healing, my coworker Chantel comes by my apartment with a card. "I'm not quite as creative as you," she says, "but I tried." She's pulled together the only two pieces of colored construction paper that have probably ever existed in our department. She's printed out a picture of a dog with an ice pack on its head, and has written "Feel Better!" in ballpoint pen, but thickly, as if it were a nice marker. Inside are signatures from my boss, the head of the department, people that I didn't even realize would recognize me.

"What did you tell them?" I ask cautiously.

"Uhh...I mean, I told Minnie that you got into a small accident but were going to be just fine."

I smile and thank her. Some people have a work husband. I have a work grandma: Minnie. She orders me the bonus colors of Expo markers because she likes what I draw on the whiteboard in my office. She can't know. Not the whole story.

I've already been doling out different versions of Sunday night to different people. Bite-sized pieces for coworkers. A few morsels more for friends. I come up empty-handed for my parents. And at home, I'm left swallowing the whole truth, too scared to ask Seth what story is in his head.

Stories I Told in My Interview

When my position was posted, I wasn't even quite sure they were looking for me. And maybe they weren't—but somehow, I managed to win over my current boss through a series of stories. I talked about the writing centers that I had worked in as an undergraduate and then as a graduate assistant. I asked them to tell me stories about the struggles that they had experienced with their staff's writing quality. I asked them to tell me what they had tried. And then I shared stories of the writing centers I had worked in—the international students who were so grateful for the opportunity to practice their English, they brought us homemade kimchi that we felt obligated to eat at eight a.m.; the writers in the community who would call in and make up fake student ID numbers because they wanted our feedback, too. The students whose trust I earned, whether they were 18 or 60. The interview went on for two hours, and I stepped out glowing.

My boss admitted later that the reason I got my job was that I seemed *disarming*. It was the first time that anyone had ever said that to me, so I looked up the definition just to make sure it meant everything I imagined. But the definition itself was me at my core—something that makes other people lay down their weapons. Something that strives to earn trust, make a connection, de-escalate danger.

At first, my coworkers don't seem to understand why I'm there. They insist, "I know how to write." They tell me how much more time they've been in the workforce. It takes me a long time to start to convince them that their job isn't to write reports. Their job is to make their reader understand what they've uncovered, to write and rewrite that message until it's abundantly clear to the readers that there is a problem, but a solution can be found. Their job is to protect our relationship with our readers, to deliver difficult information respectfully and to keep them reading on. It's our job to correct their narrative, to make them see things from a different point of view. To present them with a different version, one that's closer to the truth.

Stories I Am Told: Part II

After the ambulance ride, after the CAT scan, and *as* the doctor is switching between stitches and staples, a police officer walks in. "Are you Jessica Weber?" he asks, and I nod, scared. He produces handcuffs from behind his back and my eyes go wide. The cuffs click around my wrist as another staple sinks in to my head.

This is what I know: Seth started a fight. Drunk. Again. In the bad part of South Philadelphia. Over—of all things—a parking space. The man he was fighting threw him up against a wall and started getting more punches in, so I leapt forward and attempted to pull them apart. And that's when the man's partner ran out of their house with a kitchen knife. She jumped on top of me. I have been trying my hardest to recount the details in my head, because I watched the narrative split into several different threads the moment the neighbors started emerging out into the street to watch. Dizzy, losing blood, trying to remember details: how long the knife was, how many times she threw my head back against a set of concrete steps, what the neighbor screamed at me for bleeding on her stoop. Thinking, in the moment: *I could die here* and also *This isn't me.*

But one of the alternate narratives I feared has emerged.

The woman who attacked me has told the cops that we were breaking into her house. It's her word against mine. But she made the first accusation.

It's a lie, and I know it—but what's to say this story won't be accepted as the truth?

Stories of Redemption (or, a Near-Foolproof Lavender Shortbread Recipe)

When I return to work, I am carrying a tray of lavender shortbread. I had never made the recipe before, but they came out perfect—buttery, light, with a perfect crumb and just the right floral overtone. Despite my best effort at a distraction, my supervisor, Joanne, asks for a meeting with me later in the day. She sets the location as the third-floor porch. No one ever meets there. That's why I sneak away to work there all the time.

When we meet there, I choose a seat in the sun and let myself bake. I can feel my skin turning pink. If I get hot enough, I can't feel. I can't feel anything but hot. She tells me she understands more than I know. She says she has stories, and that she'll tell me if I want to hear. I don't know if I do. She asks me if I will go to therapy. I say I don't have time. She says I can go at lunch—she's already talked to my manager, Eric. She says everyone supports me. I can't say anything but ok.

I am fine. The stitches have been removed. I am handing out shortbread and smiling. I am fine.

Stories to Remember

With any good job, there are moments when you realize you are finally, at least professionally, right where you belong. For me, it wasn't the first time I had a positive performance review or the first time I was given a raise. It was the first time that a coworker stopped by my office and sighed heavily.

"Everything ok?" I asked, looking up from the report I was reviewing. I expect to hear the automatic, workplace-acceptable *Yes*, but instead, she says *No*, steps in, and closes the door behind her. Her voice drops to a whisper, and suddenly she has launched into a rant about how much her boss has been driving her crazy.

A big part of our writing center's success has been our ability to create a neutral, open space where people can talk through their concerns. It isn't my job to decide who is right and wrong in this scenario. It's my job to listen to different stories and to offer assistance where I can. And assistance is typically just asking questions—*why* or *how*. Asking them to step back through their thoughts and tell it again, a little more slowly, a little more thoughtfully. To help them shape the story, unwinding and retelling, over and over, like clay on a wheel. To bring the same sense of peace to their spinning.

At the end of her rant, she doesn't look at me for solutions or for judgment. She just takes in a big breath and thanks me. Everything may not be ok, but everything is a little bit better.

Stories We Make Room For

The first major meeting that I take when I am back at work is a virtual meeting for the biggest project I have tackled so far. I am developing writing training with a few content developers in St. Louis. I am used to working with highly analytical, highly critical bank examiners and economists, but in these meetings, I am sharing creative ideas with content developers who were formerly designers, English teachers, and bloggers. For that reason, my sanitized away message doesn't feel like enough to explain my sudden absence and my newfound quietness.

When I apologize for being out of the office without notice, they brush it off and ask if everything is okay. But in this group of individuals, whose focus is qualitative over quantitative, who value creativity over pure efficiency, I can't hold back. The real story—or at least one that's a little more real—comes spilling out on Skype. Even though I've pared it down to a more palatable version (*sans* handcuffs), I find myself crossing the boundaries of professional distance that I'm used to. I find myself laying down some of my defenses at their feet, still cautious, though humbled. But nobody balks. Everyone listens intently, reassures me, and then begins distracting me with work when I assure them that I don't want to step back from the project. They get it. They're storytellers, too.

Stories I Tell My "Followers"

Part of healing, part of moving away from that night, is purging my social media accounts. It feels strange to see alternating photos of Seth and me with photos from my prouder moments at work—my first workshop taught across the country, a conference brochure bearing my name in bigger type than usual. I watch two very different stories emerge: one trajectory moving onward and upward, the other spiraling down deep beneath the surface. It's like standing in an empty kitchen at midnight, rolling lavender shortbread into perfect balls between your clammy palms while your stomach churns in fear.

Here is a brief photo essay, courtesy of Instagram.

A: Seth is lying in a bathtub, laughing. His white cotton t-shirt clings to his muscular chest. His smile's so wide it's making his eyes crinkle up. I'm not in the picture because I've just climbed out of the shower to take it. Caption: *Sometimes kisses can't wait, so you climb in with your clothes on.*

B: A weathered wooden crate with dried flowers in it. Small things Seth bought for me so that I can craft some decorations for the walls of our new apartment. Caption: *Small pleasures.*

C: A box full of chocolates from my favorite little shop in Old City. Caption: *When your boyfriend bikes four miles in the rain to surprise you with chocolates, and an old man stops both of you on the street to tell you to never change.*

Stories I Can't Tell Myself Yet

Here is a brief photo essay, revised.

A: This photo was taken on a Tuesday night, and we're so drunk we can hardly stand. Seth is scared of eating. We go to the gym almost every single day, and if I eat before dinner, he'll find a way to tell me I'm weak. I'm getting skinny, probably too much so. One drink is never enough for me to have with him. He makes me match him drink for drink, no matter how much smaller I am. If I don't drink enough, I guess I'll realize anyway how sad I am. It's better to just fall into the tub and slosh water over the sides and just laugh and laugh and laugh.

B: The craft I am envisioning is a wall hanging to go above the kitchen sink. This should nicely disguise the pockmarks that the beer bottles left, after Seth threw them past my head and they shattered. I can't remember what I said that upset him. He tells me that if anyone threw bottles that night, it was probably me.

C: I am allowed to see fewer and fewer of my friends. Or rather—I'm allowed to, but Seth seems to become progressively more distressed about being left home alone, so I no longer feel safe leaving him behind. I will ask to stop by a happy hour and he will tell me that he'll probably be home when I get back, but he might also kill himself, or he might also pack up the dog and I'll never see either of them again. He casts these fabled threats as a way to reel me back home, as a way to prod me back behind a line he's drawn, to bind me there. The chocolates are an apology for me missing another party with my friends. The old man who approached us has a very different story in his head—the same story I am trying so hard to tell others. I try not to think of the three different anonymous women who have, on different nights, approached me and led me away from Seth when he starts to scream at me on the street and raise his hands or push me up against walls. I wish I hadn't brushed them off so quickly. I wish I knew their stories now.

Stories I Am Told: Part III

The female police officer guarding the door paces in and out of the room—if you can call a few sets of curtains a "room." She breezes in and out, and she's so expressionless that I assume she's angry at me. Maybe it was a slow night. Maybe she doesn't want to be here, keeping an eye on me. Maybe she thinks I'm as bad as I look right now. At one point, she stays out a little longer than usual. When she comes back in, her face has softened. "A young man out there was asking about you," she says. I blush, embarrassed that people can so easily see into the curtained area. I know what they must be thinking. She knows, too. And I even think she knows they're wrong. I think that she actually believes me.

"He was asking, 'What happened to the pretty girl in there?'" she says, looking almost pleased to have something so nice to tell me.

I can feel the blood drying against my face. It's making my skin feel tighter and tighter. They stitched up my head, pulled the wounds taut—and then as the blood dried, everything got tighter and tighter, as if it might all spring open any moment. But I know he wasn't looking at the blood coating my body. He was looking at the handcuffs on my skinny wrists.

"'What happened to the pretty girl in there?'" she repeats softly, smiling in a way that makes me believe she'd reach out and stroke my hair if it weren't crusty with blood.

At two a.m., the charges are dropped and I'm released.

Stories I Tell Myself

Seth doesn't open up often, but when he does, it's in stories that have me hanging on every word. They're origin stories. There's one he tells me when he's drunk: He wakes up in the middle of the night, just a child. His mother's crying in the hallway, dressed in a white nightgown. I can picture the hallway extending so tall above him, his mother crumpled on the floor. He assumes his father must be hitting her again, but on this night she reveals that his father has been cheating on her. He doesn't remember how old he was at the time, but he knows it wasn't old enough. A few years later she moved to some desert-sounding county out West, leaving behind three boys to take the blows, to stew quietly, to become a little more their father every day. "I would never hit a woman," Seth tells me, and I kiss him open-hearted, open-mouthed. His hands are rough like I imagine his father's, but they never grip belts or spoons. Just my wrists when I try to twist away from him, when I beg for five minutes alone in another room, when I'm sure I deserve it.

I think about his mother on nights that get bad. I think about a huddled white ghost in the hallway, a child tugging at her sleeve. I lock myself in the bathroom with the puppy that is trying to hide behind the toilet while Seth blows through the house, turning over chairs and throwing glasses and howling. I think about her on the nights that Seth lies down in bed, a sidewalk width between us, bodies cold like we're out on the ground. On the nights when he tells me that I'll never live up to the women he's known before.

I think about his mother on the sweltering July afternoon when I stand in our back garden, barefoot. It's not even a garden. It's a part of the alley we've smoothed over with soil. I've planted chrysanthemums and bitter parsley and cherry tomatoes that are bursting open, rotten, in the heat. We've grown more mosquitos on the watered pavement. I'm shifting from one foot to the other, summer dress swaying around my swollen, bug-bitten, blood-blooming knees. The staples are out but the wound is still itching. I call my mom and beg to come home.

Stories I Guard

My undergraduate university's writing center has a carefully worded confidentiality policy that allows tutors to acknowledge—with a student's consent—that they've been to the writing center, but not what they've worked on. The first few weeks of the semester are always jam-packed with freshman students who have been asked to write a personal narrative. It's amazing how many students anticipate a personal narrative prompt as: *Tell us the worst you've ever been through.* There's extra pressure on the writing center tutors during that first week, because these students are also nervous about turning in their first assignment of their post-secondary career.

Of course there are the typical essays—being cut from the cheerleading team, missing a goal in the championship game. But then there are students who come in with well-worn, loose-leaf paper in a hurry, begging the tutors not to read the piece aloud. These stories always caught me off guard—what it's like to bury your two-year-old brother when you're only eight, what it's like to hide an abortion at 15, what it's like to move to America in second grade when no one in your family speaks English. "You know, you don't have to turn this in if you're not comfortable sharing this with your professor," I always reminded them. But nobody ever leapt at the opportunity to change the topic and revise. These are their stories. They might be hurt by them, or ashamed, but they knew that it's the story that they had to tell in that moment. Instead, I asked them to consider themselves as a character, showing the same mercy they'd show to a friend going through the same thing. To put less of a burden on themselves to slay the beast before them, and more to find the beauty in it—and if none could be found, to find it in themselves. I made them reframe themselves as heroes, as survivors, as warriors, and in these ways, we would rewrite.

Stories That Heal

I've spent the last few years trying to seem older. I've had to prove to much older colleagues that I don't deserve to be called *kiddo* on conference calls. I've been playing house with someone who can hardly hold his own life together. And here I am, utterly infantilized, crying to my mom on the phone, asking for my childhood bedroom again. My younger brothers even now feel older as they help my dad clear room in the garage for whatever of my belongings are eventually recovered.

As soon as I move home—if you can call throwing an armload of wrinkled clothes into a plastic laundry bin moving—I tell Eric and Joanne that I'm willing to go on as many work trips as they want to send me on. I don't feel safe in the city yet, but my childhood home doesn't feel like home anymore, either. Both places feel too heavy, but work feels familiar, distracting. The workshops that I have been teaching at work have started being requested at other branches across the country, but I had turned down these opportunities because of how frequently Seth would call me to make sure I was in my hotel room, not out being tempted to talk to anyone else. He'd paint the world as too dangerous, urge me to stay home for my own safety. Now I go back through each previously declined request, and the more I accept, the more that come in. I book travel to Miami, Charlotte, San Francisco, Boston, Dallas, Cleveland, Atlanta, Chicago, St. Louis. I start getting comfortable with exploring new cities alone, with seeing places I never thought I'd reach, with sitting quietly at unfamiliar bars at night.

But one of the best parts of this series of travel is that I get to spread the message that initially drew me to this work. Throughout years of writing struggles, one maxim persisted for years through the department: *Tell the story*. The bulk of the writing tutoring that I do is helping analysts relay information clearly and succinctly to boards of directors and senior management of banks. Not exactly the most *exhilarating* writing, but it's important for our readers to understand the full context of the information, the impact that their actions can have on others, the ways that they got to where they are and how to change things. The analysts are initially resistant to the idea of "telling stories," until they realize that that's exactly what they're doing in conversations with their readers. And so now I'm jumping from city to city, in front of new faces, reminding them: *Tell the story. It's not enough to write it. You have to write it again.*

On the weeks between these work trips, I start to plan personal trips as well. Seth has spent the last two years very carefully removing me from each of my friends. And in a heartbreaking sweep of random events, the four closest to me have taken job offers in different cities in the span of only six weeks. Each out of the blue. Each knowing I don't deserve to tell them to stay, when it's as if we've been living worlds apart in the same city.

But now that I'm starting to see what happened more clearly, I need them to know. And I need to apologize for the way that things seemed, for the way that things are. One weekend I drive to Pittsburgh. Another, to Baltimore. To Washington, D.C. I take a long, sleepy, rainy bus ride to New York City. I drive to every neighborhood of Philadelphia where I still have friends. I fly to Phoenix, and my Phoenix friends drive me to Tucson. I tell my story over and over and over again.

This process takes about four months, and it is amazing to me that I can tell the truth each time, but the story is never identical. In the first few weeks, I'm defensive of Seth. I say he didn't know any better. I admit to some that I'm still paying for the apartment so that he can finish school. I choose to believe that maybe he was right—maybe he didn't throw me against a brick wall that night, and instead I just fell back against it. Maybe he laid a soft but sad, heavy hand against the cab I escaped in, not actually punching out the taillights. Maybe the orange-tipped gun that I pulled out of a box of my salvaged belongings really had fallen in by accident, and wasn't meant to flood me with fear when I reached in for nail polish but touched the cold trigger. I tell my friends I'm sorry that I didn't spend any time with them. I tell them how scared I was, how weak and how sick.

But over time, I don't feel as weak, as sick. I gain weight, muscle. In the hours when I'm traveling to see friends, I start listening to music again. My friends and I go to concerts and dance, we run through parks, we take out huge slices of pie to eat on the couch and cry and laugh into. I stop apologizing for Seth and defending his behavior. The narrative shifts from *he didn't mean it* to *he was evil* to *he is sick and I can't carry it all.*

And my own narrative shifts as well: from *I was so hurt* to *I am strong.* Each retelling feels like a wave pushing me toward a more solid shore. It leaves me fighting for breath but finally laid out in the sun, bleached clean and unhidden and new. Even when the old versions, the haunted thoughts, remain lapping at my tired feet.

Stories I've Fought For

When I began my job, my first order of business was creating a set of writing standards. I was surprised to find that the only existing guide was a good number of years older than I was, and nobody seemed to even recognize the copy that I had found buried in a cluttered supply closet. The goal was to make the guide as approachable as possible, so I went with a spiral-bound, pocket-sized, color-coded guide that wouldn't seem too clinical for people to want to use. I wanted it to mirror the approach I was trying to use in person—simply being friendly and approachable. And so, much to our editorial department's chagrin, I insisted on opening the writing guide with a narrative.

The narrative I chose to tell was about the first time I realized the influence that storytelling could hold. I was at a sleepover with several third-grade classmates, about half of whom were picking on others or whining to our host in a way I *never* would have gotten away with at home. In the middle of another round of bickering, I gripped my plastic flashlight beneath my chin and turned the beam upward—the eerie glow flickering in time with the batteries' rattle, paired like lightning and thunder. My classmates had gathered close for a ghost story, sitting cross-legged in a campfire-style circle. I started running through every scary story that my older neighbors had used before to frighten me: the Hook-Handed Man, the Ribbon-Round-the-Neck, the Babysitter and the Telephone. The kids who were my friends had already heard these stories before, and they delighted in the retelling. But the bullies who were hearing them for the first time were shrieking in terror, then calling home to be picked up early. The rest of us ate up all the extra birthday cake and had a pretty good time after they'd left.

Hearing those stories had frightened me so badly before, had sounded so far away until the lights went out. But in my own voice, with my eyes on my own goals, surrounded with my own allies listening—those stories were pure magic. It may have been the first time I'd ever felt powerful, watching their eyes shine, still tasting the frosting on my whispering lips.

We still print this story in each edition of the writing guide that we hand out to new employees. I want them to remember that the writing they do every day isn't about perfect grammar or even pleasing a particular manager. It's about making information powerful, about reaching your reader in the right way. It's hoping to set off a ripple of change when they've seen something that isn't quite right. It's taking a mess and making it a narrative. It's telling—and retelling—the story.[2]

Notes

1. Jessica L. Weber, Writing Center Director, Federal Reserve Bank of Philadelphia. jessicaleighweber@gmail.com
2. This piece contains descriptions of violence and domestic/intimate partner abuse. If you recognize these signs in your own life or in a loved one's, please visit thehotline.org for the National Domestic Violence Hotline, or seek out local resources in your area.

7. *In the Space Between Chaos and Shape: Reclaiming the Bound Exile Through Affect Study and Life Writing*

Karen-Elizabeth Moroski[1]

"*I told my version—faithful and invented, accurate and misremembered, shuffled in time. I told myself as hero like any shipwreck story. It was a shipwreck, and me thrown on the coastline of humankind, and finding it not altogether human, and rarely kind. And I suppose that the saddest thing for me, thinking about the cover version that is* Oranges, *is that I wrote a story I could live with.* <u>The other one was too painful. I could not survive it.</u>

I am often asked, in a tick-box kind of way, what is 'true' and what is not 'true' in Oranges. *Did I work in a funeral parlour? Did I drive an ice-cream van? Did we have a Gospel Tent? Did Mrs. Winterson build her own CB radio? Did she really stun tomcats with a catapult?*

I can't answer these questions. I can say that there is a character in Oranges *called Testifying Elsie who looks after the little Jeanette and acts as a soft wall against the hurt(ling) force of Mother.*

I wrote her in because I couldn't bear to leave her out. I wrote her in because I really wished it had been that way. When you are a solitary child you find an imaginary friend.

There was no Elsie. There was no one like Elsie. Things were much lonelier than that."

—Jeanette Winterson, Why Be Happy When You Could Be Normal?

Orphan. The word sounds anachronistic, Dickensian. *Orphan*—viscerally, the word evokes an understanding of violent (whether implicit or explicit) <u>loss</u> that requires no further shorthand: someone has lost their parents, their anchors *in* and *to* this world. If language can be repurposed—as Derrida suggests, and as ever-evolving dialects confirm—then the generative possibility of defining orphanhood expands: to be orphaned might mean the explosive loss of *any* optimistic attachment (Berlant) wherein the loss leaves us sans identity, sans home, set apart.

I am a gender orphan. I use the term deliberately and devoid of my usual cheeky, impish charm. I say "gender orphan" because traditionally conceived polarities of gender do not hold me, because "non-binary" suggests (to me) I think there *is* a binary and that it's just that I'm not part of it, and because I want to evoke that deeply felt sense of violation and loss that comes with losing core pillars of prescribed, cruelly optimistic identities. As many others have theorized, gender gels our attachments to most relational parts of our lives: we are someone's gendered child, gendered sibling, gendered friend; our earliest socializations have often been steeped in gendered activities and colors; we are so far removed from the Lacanian Real in this regard that it may well be impossible to trace our authentic, agentic selves back to where we might have begun—but, I'm going to try.

That's what this essay is about: who might we have been? Why aren't we that person? How can we tell? What does it mean, to me, to be a gender orphan—and how can I rebuild my sense of belonging? Most importantly, here: how does writing about and for my own life help me answer these questions—and how do interdisciplinary scholarship, life writing, and art combine to provide new pathways into ourselves and throughout one another's stories?

Writing about identity, for me, means tracing the events and stories and ideas that ecologically constitute "me." Pulling from Jane Bennett and Sara Ahmed combined, I see myself as a changeling constellation of light whose boundaries and borderlands are informed by an intellectual-come-physiological inheritance of queer trauma and queer joy: the body is a narrative, a place of interpellation, a place of possibility. The queered body is especially so, unmoored from the polarities and binaries that too often generate only liminal space in a human life. I have spent much of my adult life researching and writing about how my body came to tell this particular story—that of the joyful gender orphan, playfully and painfully creating the country of my own existence. *I am what I am,* sings Fierstein's Albin. Me too, Albin.

This story is cobbled together by hopestitch and dreamweave, thatch covering the places where trauma has struck like a fist, insulated with pages of novels and wired by critical theory. The result—what have I built, all this time? I don't know. It might not be a machine. It might not be a home. Then again, it might be. Life writing and scholarship are the process through which, like the famed Velveteen rabbit, I have become real. As the legend goes, you can only become real when you've been loved for a very long time. I am not so old, and have loved myself only a few years—but here, let my story itself tell you how incredibly alive I am. Let my story narrate the magic that happens when we dare to invent the language necessary to name ourselves.

The first radical act of life writing is to dispel wordlessness. I like to talk about my formative queer wordlessness through my collegiate experience of reading Patricia Highsmith's *The Price of Salt*. The novel's tracing of two women in love (with each other) illustrates the struggle against queered identity's quest to dispel wordlessness as well as the fight against what feels like a life of impossibility. Therese and Carol, the protagonists, are old friends to me: their story informed my earliest experiences of queerness and inform me still.

So much of my queered *becoming* has been the process of understanding and releasing what I am not, naming those losses, and grieving them. From my earliest years identifying as, at first, non-straight (later, a lesbian; later still, annoyed to be labeled at all; lately, proudly and defiantly queer), I struggled to connect with other people of queer experience—to find words or labels for myself (my experience is not unique, let me assure you). And without those things, I couldn't find my own context (also not unique). Patricia Highsmith's story helped me understand my own, and set me on a journey to *find the words and name myself.*

Protagonist Therese can't relate to butch-identified lesbians—to "people like that" (83), despite her relationship with Carol. Like me, Therese envies people who understand their own context: "She envied him. She envied him his faith that there would always be a place, a home, a job, someone else for him. She envied him that attitude. She almost resented him having it" (133). As a younger person (and even now,) I sometimes envied my straight and cisgender friends their movies, their love songs, their clearly defined places in the world, their goals of parenthood and marriage, the love of their extended families. The longer I openly loved women and the less I looked like one, the more firmly shut the doors around me felt—access points to pop culture, to beauty, to sociopolitical context, to my own future all slammed on my reaching fingers. Still, I found myself—or, ironically, the loss of myself—in Highsmith's text: "There are some people or some things people do that you can't salvage anything from, finally, because nothing connects with you … Everything's not as simple as a lot of combinations," Therese grieves (105).

I learned, through Therese and Carol's excision from their own lives, the queer inheritance of loss. I learned, too, that—as author Jeanette Winterson describes so beautifully—"In the space between chaos and shape, there was another chance."

As I read the novel and felt the cisgender, heterosexual world to which I once belonged getting farther and farther away, I relinquished my grasp of it.

There was peace in the letting go; there was possibility in it, too: "My little orphan,' Carol said. Therese smiled. There was nothing dismal, no sting in the word when Carol said it" (163). Years later, that line would echo in my mind the night I told my wife I was fairly sure I was a gender orphan. She loves me into possibility, journey and all. But even the first time I read the words, I felt comforted by them: you could walk away from yourself, from everything, I thought, and still be alright. My orphaning had begun. So had my desire to find my second chance.

Years later, and my work with affective neuroscience, trauma theory, affect theory, and memoir suggests that we can't really abscond from the past like my twenty-year-old post-structuralist self might have believed: we carry our stories within us wherever we go, even when we don't want to own them anymore. Even when they are heavy. Even when our baggage is filled with memories that no longer fit. While I was right to think: *You can leave. You don't have to be any of these things anymore,* I'd soon learn just how much weight you must take with you when you go. We are still, neurobiologically speaking, everything we've left behind—but like a kaleidoscope reflecting light, we become something new in our leaving. We also become something new in our coming back, and in our staying.

One of the things I became was *Scholar.* Specifically, *Queer and Queering Scholar.* I would spend the entirety of graduate school threading various disciplines together, queering them, trying to explain how it can be so that we never really leave ourselves behind. In truth, I did this work to thread myself together as I went along—my course papers, my work were all in the service of telling my own story: a flying trapeze act of self-discovery above the lion-jawed tensions of graduate study. I spent years researching the intersections of affective neuroscience, critical theory (specifically post-colonial, post-structural, and affect theories), trauma studies, and memoir writing: I developed a concept called Bound Exile, in which a person's ecological consumption of damaging social stimuli (Moroski) changes their actual physiology (Bennett)—not just their psychology—engendering lasting harm (Ahmed) despite eventual, seeming enfranchisement. I wrote, really, about myself: a gender orphan, restless, tired. It would take nearly a decade until that restlessness transformed into playful, flexible adventure.

But my pursuit of myself drained me, in those years. Affect theorist Lauren Berlant would attribute my life's third-degree burns to my Cruelly Optimistic pursuit of suburban happiness; neurophilosophers like Churchland would agree, suggesting our actual sense of moral order crumbles when we are excluded from communities we trusted. I have been orphaned by straightness, by gender, by Catholicism, by most things that would impose meaning and order on an ordinary life. This, alongside my academic work, taught me what it means to have moral order crumble: with no "internal structure" (Winterson) to reference, anymore, through my queerness I became a stranger and outside threat even to myself—Homeless, even when Home. The Exile within the Empire. My project didn't talk about me, but it talked about people *like* me, and in writing that book I also came to write myself. I want to write about that process. I want to explain how it came to be so, and how the rupture could heal. To quote Jeanette Winterson's *Weight*, "I wanted to tell the story again."

   I wanted to tell the story again.

   Winterson, an adoptee whose gorgeous prose and numerous novels (as well as her autobiography) are preoccupied with belonging, love, identity and loss, has written all her career about the flexibility of identity, the ways in which revising the self might reforecast the future, and the question of whether or not the facts are really the truth about our stories.
   I read Winterson throughout graduate school, as I worked through my ideas and through myself. Her autobiography, *Why Be Happy When You Could Be Normal?*, beautifully underscores the grief of inventing yourself by necessity: "Adopted children," she writes, "are self-invented because we have to be; there is an absence, a void, a question mark at the very beginning of our lives. A crucial part of our story is gone, and violently, like a bomb in the womb" (5)—evoking the necessary creative and amalgous process of traumatic memory's effort to reclaim a self.
   I read Jeanette Winterson's memoir over and over until I had pages of it memorized. I wanted to speak it out loud to people I knew; I wanted to answer questions about myself in its cadence. Winterson's *Why Be Happy When You Could Be Normal?* shared in thrilling, tender prose the things my scholarship has suggested for years: that writing can heal *not just memory* but also *physiology*, that "fact" is distinct from "truth," and that we learn ourselves as deeply through constructing our lives as imaginative narratives—"the faithful and the invented," as Winterson describes it—as we do through trying to brutally nailgun our skin to a static map of "the real." Winterson seems to believe as I believe: you tell your own story, and you choose what's true, and that is your power and that is your cross and that is where the learning lives. She also knows that to unlearn does not mean to unremember: "Written on the body is a secret code, visible only in certain lights; the accumulations of a lifetime gather there. In places, the palimpsest is so heavily worked that the letters feel like Braille. I like to keep my body away from prying eyes, never unfold too much, never tell the whole story" (*Written on the Body* 89).

Winterson understands the relationship between trauma, articulation, and identity development—indeed, she makes no qualms that much of her work, both her fiction and nonfiction, centers around her own quest to make sense of her past. She writes:

> Mental health and emotional continuity do not require us to stay in the same house or the same place, but they do require a sturdy structure on the inside—and that structure is built, in part, by what has happened on the outside. The inside and the outside of our lives are each the shell where we learn to live (*Why* 59).

I believe that our "structure on the inside" is shaped by things we intellectually and ecologically consume (and science does agree). For example: if you consume poison, you get sick. Common sense, right? The more interesting turn comes when exploring the work of neuroscientists like Jaak Panksepp and Lucy Biven (primary process emotions), Antonio Damasio (memory mapping), Stephen Porges (dysregulation of the vagal brake) and V. S. Ramachandran (mirror neurons) to answer *this* question: *Do we become the abstract/intellectual stimuli we consume?*

Of course, we are not all neuroscientists (I'm not one, myself)—but if I had to assemble the neurotheorists above into a sort of reductive (but informative!) linguistic flowchart (ah, the humanities…) it would look a little like this:

> *Panksepp and Biven's work tells us that our emotions are actually informed by activity in our brainstem, and that we tend to lay the foundation for cognition through very basic, instinct-based emotions (fear, panic/grief, play, rage, seeking, etc.).*

↓

> *Ramachandran's work on mirror neurons tells us that our most basic responses to stimuli (whether the impulse to run away from a Grizzly Bear chasing us or the impulse to hug a loved one) largely stem from neurons in our brain that perceive the actions of others and suggest we act accordingly in pursuit of survival. (We've cognitively evolved past "survival" a lot of the time, but that doesn't mean our brains abandon their ways.) This means that if we see someone, say, closeting themselves, we are likely to do a quick risk-analysis of that action and consider closeting ourselves. Similarly, if we see someone laugh at a joke or hide from a gunman, our same survival impulse kicks in.*

↓

> *Porges' work on the vagal brake system is complex and myriad, but here's the important takeaway for right now: when you experience danger or trauma, your body's heart is part of the vagal brake system that decides how much adrenaline or blood your body needs. If you experience trauma long enough or severe enough (and, for example, Claude Steele's work on stereotype threat suggests that underrepresented*

groups—including queer folks—are always under attack), that vagal brake system never really slows back down. You'll be easier to startle; you will feel anxiety easily; your body's "resting state" isn't very restful at all.

Damasio's work on mind-mapping suggests that our memories are (obviously) compiled of experiences we've had over time, and that those maps interact with our neurology to inform our bodies of what to do or how to feel. Further, his work—along with Panksepp and Biven's—suggests that that informing doesn't happen in the cognitive mind. It's deeper than that, which is why you can't say "Aw, everyone loves me, I'm okay!" or "Sheesh, what do I have to be anxious about?" Damasio believes maps can be changed, but only over much time and through much reconsidering of the past, present and future. In short, we need to re-learn our own lives.

All this taken together and put back into the context of this essay gives us a summary that goes: Queer people live in a world where they're under constant threat; their bodies and brainstem look to the actions of other queer people, as well as queer histories of trauma, to inform how to be "safe" and also how to relate to one's self and to others. Because, historically, so many of these queer relationalities have been traumatic, it is unsurprising that queer-identified folks inherit many of the symptoms of trauma: their bodies are trying to survive. The more cultural signifiers queer people consume, the more their bodies defer to the monolith of trauma... and become symptomatic of survival mechanisms borne of those traumas.

I've written elsewhere on the ways in which consuming traumatic social stimuli— homophobic slurs, communal memory of traumas ranging from the AIDS crisis to the Pulse massacre, ongoing and very public political debate about queer personhood and possibility—are consumed by the brain, and then performed as trauma within the body. Further, Claude Steele's work on stereotype threat suggests we can't just put those anxieties down simply because, cognitively, we perceive ourselves to be loved or at rest or in a safe place. We are ecologically constitutive of the public and social narratives constructed about us or about "people like us," and we inherit the trauma—or the privileged lack thereof—generated by those narratives. Bessel Van Der Kolk's watershed text, *The Body Keeps the Score,* has a title that pretty much says it all: even as we try to abandon our traumas, we carry them with us in our corporeal selves. We change shape and revise, but the process of physiologically unlearning our traumatic responses to a painful world does not include the process of unremembering trauma itself. Instead, we name it and dissemble the monolith (Herman). These ideas were the main thrust of my scholarship in graduate school—but the main push of my life, the life I am writing about when I am life writing, is that we can do the same with joyful experiences of queerness, too.

Judith Herman and Bessel Van Der Kolk, seminal voices in trauma studies and psychotherapy—as well as Jaak Panksepp and Lucy Biven and Antonio Damasio—taught me that the neural pathways we most often cultivate are the ones our hearts will most often travel, and that we can revise and reconstruct those pathways to lead us back to a better and happier version of ourselves.

Of course, this happy stuff has not yet—until now—made it into any published works. It's harder to write about. It requires a more personal, generative space. It requires the chance to tell a story.

I want to tell you about the first time I told one of my tutors (I coordinate a Writing Center) that I'm nonbinary. I was anxious and had never said the words out loud to anyone but my best friend and my wife. That "Havannah" song was playing on the radio. People kept jaywalking. We were already talking about gender and politics when I managed to stammer, "Did I ever mention I'm nonbinary?" Not missing a beat, the student smiled and said, "No! How didn't I know that? That's cool. She/her still okay, or…?"

I want to tell you about the time I was nineteen and sobbing in my parents' backyard, telling my Mom that I wished I wasn't a lesbian and that I wished I could be like everyone else. She hugged me tight, tight, tight and told me to never again wish myself away.

I want to tell you about the time I told my colleague and dear friend Jon Olson that I didn't think I really had a gender. His response? "I think you're perfect." I want to tell you about how when I first knew Jon nearly ten years ago, he invited my girlfriend and me to his semester cookout and I cried because until that point no adults except my parents had ever acknowledged my girlfriend at all.

I want to tell you about how when I told my high school Chorus teacher—Leanne Amabile, a woman I idolized—that I had a girlfriend, her response was to tell me she loved me no matter what, and that sometimes "Prince Charming turns out to be Princess Charming. If you're happy that's all that matters!"

I want to tell you about what happened when a group of young guys harassed my long-term high school boyfriend about me now being with women. His response, even at age eighteen, was that he loved me and was so happy that I am happy.

I want to tell you about the first Christmas I wore pants and a blazer instead of a dress and my Gram told me I looked beautiful.

I want to tell you about how patiently my wife listens and loves me through every iteration of myself. When I told her I was nonbinary, she said "Well, I love you. Whoever and whatever you are. You can talk to me about anything, and just let me know what to do." I want to tell you about how I married her, how I was able to marry her, about how all our families came to the wedding and we wore beautiful dresses (and incredible shoes) and how my uncle played the guitar and my Dad read from *The Little Prince* and how on our honeymoon we saw three Broadway shows with front row seats. I want to tell you about how I bought a house with her this year, and how we love it there, and how we have been making it our home and how good it feels to finally *be at rest* after so many years of moving and moving and moving. I want to tell you how proud I am to tell everyone I ever meet for the entire rest of my life that she is my wife, my heart, my love and that even if that sweet little house were to burn to the ground, *she* is my home. I want to tell you that I know how wildly ordinary that sounds and that there is still some deep and profound peace in having a part of my life that feels so abundantly human and so ordinary.

I want to tell you about how we go into New York City to see drag shows, and party with club kids, and kiss in the street, and dance at Boots and Saddle, and how good it feels to laugh and howl and share the night with other queer people.

I want to tell you, I want to tell you, I want to tell you, I want to tell you—

I want to tell you that queer people laugh and howl and share their nights and days and lives and that despite the monolithic hurt of our departure from the worlds we were born into, we are so often so full of joy.

I want to tell the story again.

It is harder to study these types of subjective, singular happinesses: they don't always belong to a whole community; they are harder to trace; they change—again, like a kaleidoscope—and reshape in memory's eye; they are sometimes moments so small it's hard to even write about them. Some moments are so tiny, they even slip out from the shape of a word. But they accumulate into a life, a full life, a rich life that defiantly dances and hollers and flaps its wings above whatever horizontal battleground any type of binary or polarity ever presented. They hover, glide, soar, transcend.

When I allow myself to accept that *joy* as part of my identity—when I use what I've learned about transfer, neuroscience, trauma, memory, and theory to not only talk about how I am ecologically constitutive of suffering but also of sunlight... well, henny, that's how you slay the house down boots! That's how you subvert the form. That's how you stop worrying about the master's house, and do what you can to build your own and build it big enough to shelter others until they can do the same.

And that, dear reader, is how the process of life writing and scholarship—when used in tandem—helped me transform myself from being simply a gender orphan with only traumatic loci for self-explanation and no

Wintersonian internal structure into being both an architect and *architext*. *Architext*, here, is a word I'm inventing on the fly (go, queerness, go!) to mean a master-text of one's own existence. Like an archangel or an architect, you become the driving force in charge of the creation of, defense of, curation of, and possibilities of yourself. Like Fierstein's Albin, *I am my own special creation*. Though I am orphaned by conventional identity standards and am ecologically constitutive of the trauma of that loss, I am equally comprised of layers upon layers of love—both the storybook kind, and the bell hooks kind: a political powerhouse of empathy and possibility. And the more I write about that, and the more other people read what I have written, the more real it becomes. And the more real it becomes, the more real I become and the more real others like me become. By bearing witness to this transdisciplinary approach to scholarship as an act of writing the self, you have afforded me an opportunity to reinforce to both my heart and my brain's dendrites that I can transform the traumas I have inherited and that I can commingle them with joys.

I am so many things—and of the glorious arthaus collection I call my life, I have curated a gender that reflects me in majesty and that *liberates me from seeing myself in terms of polarities or binaries I can't and won't fulfill...*

My gender is the Pulse massacre, and how for months after the color red would make my right eye twitch and I became afraid to go dancing. My gender is me, age four and in my mother's arms, as she smoothes my hair and calls me her sweetest girl. My gender is the scrolling bar on CNN, reporting the latest anti-LGBTQ legislation. My gender is the smell of men's cologne and the lightning streak of my Oil Slick lipstick when I laugh. My gender is the way old dudes in gay bars sometimes mistake me for a really cute younger man until they notice my breasts. My gender is combat boots and velvet John Fluevog heels. My gender is my first girlfriend's voice when she told me we could never be married, that she hated herself for loving me, and that she wished she were normal. My gender is my wife's warm hands and the way her eyes exploded into fireworks when she saw me on our wedding day. My gender is the tender way my brothers still call me "little sister," and how loved it makes me feel. My gender is thunder, Ginko trees, the way it sounds when my mother says my name, the nighttime drives with my Dad as he taught me stories about the constellations, gin & tonics, watermelon, the moment I became Dr. Moroski, the feeling of just-cut grass turning my feet green, the feeling of crossing a half-marathon finish line, the 10th Anniversary Royal Albert Hall cast of *Les Miserables* singing "One Day More" on repeat as I drive home in a snowstorm, the way the afternoon light catches the shine of my piano, the first sip of a Blue slushie, the way my favorite pair of Birkenstocks squishes when I walk in them.

I am *everything, everything, everything*—and through the process of using my scholarship as a form of life writing, and through learning the ways in which revision of the self is an act of reclaiming the self, I have come to realize that perhaps the monolith of queer trauma and queer gender need not be monolith at all.

When I radically queer my perception of queerness—when I revise the narrative and tell the story again—when I reconfigure the framework through which I experience myself—when I liberate myself from the belief that I have failed or transgressed the liminal spaces presented by cisgendered and heterosexual lives—*I come to realize that perhaps I was never an orphan.*

I can only be orphaned if the gender binary served as an anchor on the floor of a world whose subjectivities offer me endless, glistening sea.

I can only permanently experience queered trauma as my inheritance if I don't open myself up to the possibility of also inheriting queer joy—or creating my own.

I am not bound to any single version of my narrative, nor to my experience of narrating, nor to the way you might experience my narration. Still, I tell the story. I have to. I must. It keeps me alive. It makes me real. *I want to tell the story again.* Winterson understands:

> The stories of Arthur, of Lancelot and Guinevere, of Merlin, of Camelot and the Grail, docked into me like the missing molecule of a chemical compound. I have gone on working with the Grail stories all my life. They are stories of loss, of loyalty, of failure, of recognition, of second chances. I used to have to put the book down and run past the part where Perceval, searching for the Grail, is given a vision of it one day, and then, because he is unable to ask the crucial question, the Grail disappears. Perceval spends twenty years wandering in the woods, looking for the thing that he found that was given to him, that seemed so easy, that was not (*Why* 37).

My scholarship has been a way of life writing: I have been excavating myself, rebuilding myself, learning the tools I would need to complete the job. I have learned, too, that this way of theorizing affect study—and life writing—as storytelling methods and as sites for scholarly excavation offers horizons more expansive and more generative than single-disciplinary, isolated fields could ever allow. Though a gender orphan by conventional standards, I am my own architect and *architext*. A masterpiece. The kind of queer, flamboyant, joyful life-form that no one label and no one discipline could contain. I love to tell *that* story. Already, I want to tell it again.

Note

1. Karen-Elizabeth Moroski, Assistant Teaching Professor of English and Co-Curricular Programs Coordinator for Writing and Languages, Penn State University, University Park. kxm5044@psu.edu

References

Ahmed, Sara. *The Cultural Politics of Emotion*. New York: Routledge, 2004.

Bennett, Jane. *Vibrant Matter: A Political Ecology of Things*. Durham: Duke UP, 2010.

Berlant, Lauren Gail. *Cruel Optimism*. Durham: Duke UP, 2011.

Churchland, Patricia Smith. *Braintrust: What Neuroscience Tells Us about Morality*. Princeton: Princeton UP, 2011.

Damasio, Antonio. *Self Comes to Mind: Constructing the Conscious Brain*. London: Vintage, 2012.

Herman, Judith. *Trauma and Recovery: The Aftermath of Violence from Domestic Abuse to Political Terror*. New York: Basic Books, 1992.

Highsmith, Patricia. *The Price of Salt*. Mineola: Dover Publications, 2015.

Moroski, Karen-Elizabeth. "My Little Orphan": Tracing the Impact of Isolation and Invisibility Upon Queer Identity Development in American Women through the Lenses of History, Literature and Affective Neuroscience (Order No. 1543624). Available from ProQuest Dissertations & Theses A&I. (1431903182). 2013. Retrieved from http://ezaccess.libraries.psu.edu/login?url=https://search.proquest.com/docview/1431903182?accountid=13158

Panksepp, Jaak, and Lucy Biven. *The Archaeology of Mind: Neuroevolutionary Origins of Human Emotions*. New York: W.W. Norton, 2012.

Porges, S. W. *The Polyvagal Theory: Neurophysiological Foundations of Emotions, Attachment, Communication, and Self-Regulation*. New York: W.W. Norton, 2011.

Steele, Claude M. "A Threat in the Air: How Stereotypes Shape Intellectual Identity and Performance." *American Psychologist* 52. 6 (1997): 613–629. "https://psycnet.apa.org/doi/10.1037/0003-066X.52.6.613"http://dx.doi.org/10.1037/0003-066X.52.6.613

Ramachandran, V. S. *The Tell-Tale Brain: A Neuroscientist's Quest for What Makes Us Human*. New York: W.W. Norton, 2011.

Van Der Kolk, Bessel. *The Body Keeps the Score: Brain, Mind, and Body in the Healing of Trauma*. New York: Penguin Group, 2014.

Winterson, Jeanette. *Why Be Happy When You Could Be Normal?* New York: Grove Press, 2012.

———. *Written on the Body*. London: Vintage, 2014.

8. *The Me I Don't Meet* Unless: *Life Writing, Play Studies, and an Untested Story*

D. Shane Combs[1]

It was in my first graduate composition course—the course that led me to switch from creative writing to rhetoric and composition—that I read bell hooks' writing on how the offer of tenure induced in her dreams of running away—or *dying*—in order to escape it. I can't recall whether or not I had the capacity to understand such a provocative statement in my first semester as a graduate student, but what I did have were two creative writing friends in my cohort, both of whom likely believed I was setting myself up for a bell hooks *descent into death-wishing* by joining composition, but each handled the situation differently.

The first of the two waited until we were drinking at Christy's, a local bar in Greenville, North Carolina, to accost me and composition. He shouted to a table full of friends, while looking only at me, about how nobody in composition has ever contributed new ideas to the academy. I think I yelled back something about the circle-jerk nature of the writing workshop, and all that was accomplished on either side that night were hurt feelings and what I considered, then and now, to be an embarrassing public affair that I wish I hadn't taken part in.

The other friend, for his part, waited until I had some success in the composition program, until I had a conference completed, until I had a direction I was going—trying to make visible introverts and highly sensitive people in rhetoric and composition—before he spoke to me about the switch.

"You know," he said calmly, in another space at the same bar where I had the aforementioned dispute half a year prior, "when you joined composition,

I thought you were actively trying to destroy your soul. But now I see what you are doing, and I think you made the right move."

He probably doesn't know how much those words stay with me, as I found myself wishing, in the last month and a half, that I could rewind back to that moment, back to a time when my friend, Tim, saw clearly what I was doing in rhetoric and composition and, just the same, to when *I* saw clearly what I was doing in rhetoric and composition, a time when we both thought I was making the right move.

I write these words almost five years after those incidents. I write these words in the summer of 2018, as I begin my rhetoric and composition dissertation, so I can go on the rhetoric and composition job market, so I can cross my fingers and knock on wood for an eventual rhetoric and composition job. And yet, at the very same time, I find myself a month and a half behind writing word one of the dissertation, and not only do I find myself feeling what bell hooks felt, that it might be better to run away or die, I find my health failing, my identity fading, as well as a persistent fear that I've limited myself to the two worst-case scenarios for my life—that I won't find a job in rhetoric and composition and, equally scary, that I will.

As I put words to page, I find myself asking myself, *How do we trod so far down a lived-and-narrativized path only to find ourselves somehow shocked to be on it? How do we, the painfully aware academics that we are, find ourselves marching, wind at our backs, to places we don't know if we even want to go?* Towards how we do this, I offer a potential consideration: we divorce story from the frameworks it needs to do what it needs to do. For instance, for me, I have spent the last month and a half sitting on a couch that isn't mine, staring at a coffee table that isn't mine, thinking dark thoughts that, I'd like to think, aren't mine. With each second, each minute, each hour, each stare, I have found myself drifting further from myself and deeper into a depression that seeks to surround me. While story is, of course, present in the experience I just recounted, it's a lazy and shapeless kind of story, because I've long ceased testing my stories against the sharpened edge of the life writing pen.

Oh, never fear. I still *teach* life writing. I still *talk* life writing, even when (sometimes *especially* when) I feel like those around me in rhetoric and composition don't want to hear it. But, when it comes to practicing what I preach, I'm afraid I've been living a life writing *sin*: I've allowed myself to succumb to the pressure of a story *untested*. This untested story tells me that, in order to succeed in rhetoric and composition, I must separate myself from my more introverted self, from an identity that feels more inward than outward, and embrace an exclusively external position on what it means to be human. In fact, this untested story has stretched itself so wide that, under the cloud I've been living, my inability to start writing the dissertation coincides with my (and my doctor's) inability to figure out what is wrong with me which coincides with the fear that no favorable job could come to someone who can't write his dissertation or figure out his medical diagnosis which coincides with a nagging, persistent feeling that, somewhere and somehow, I've lost the me that I've always *most* considered myself to be, the introvert that lives within, fueled formerly by imagination and an intimate interiority, and that I will never again feel like the me that I've believed myself to be.

That is the story that has been shaping my life, my thoughts, and my imagination for almost two months. It's only now, while writing, that I remember what I would never have forgotten had I been writing: we must continually press story *against* a space like the page, where each felt sense has to publish itself, account for itself, where each idea has to meet the next idea, and each directional thought goes one-on-one with the previous and the next one coming. I haven't been doing that work. I've been a storyteller who has disrespected the story. I've been a storyteller who has been disrespected by the story. And neither I nor the story are better for this (lack of) exchange

As I write these words, however, I find myself finding myself. I find story and teller having to take a walk and iron out some overdue thinking, pressing out the *lazy* in return for the *lively*, trading an oppressive shapelessness in return for hard-pressed, hard-earned shape. Within these words, within these stories, as they press one against the other, it is obvious that I never truly believed the negative words I said about creative writing so long ago. I was drinking, in a bar, and I felt that not only my identity but the identity of my life choice were under attack. And, just the same, these five years later, I don't feel towards composition in a way that should make me freeze up, fold up, and cease to work. I only now realize that I have been feeling, once again, what it's like when identity and the identity of a life choice feel under attack.

But it's not composition I fear. Walking the page carefully, storyteller and story, (one hand on the lettered-keys and the other on "backspace"), I begin to see what a month and a half of casual glances never allowed. With creative writing, composition, or any other definable way of doing/being, if we think about that subject only by its most negative components then we've sentenced ourselves to live in that frame of mind, that frame of existence, no matter how true or untrue it all might be. In fact, if I were being accurate, it was creative writing that originally gave me liberty to live, move, and have my being on the page, and it was composition that gave me the framework to contain that identity, lest it slip away as soon as the typing ends. With creative writing alone, I am too loose, too prone to wander. With composition alone,

I find myself caged by the very ideas and identities that, if motion and liberty to change were granted, could help define my life for the better.

No, it's not composition that I fear. Nor is it a job that will ultimately define me. What I fear is any job that might *overly* define me. But, as I type these words, I find myself moving from a space that has contained me, at times making it difficult to think clearly or breathe easily, to a space that might at least feel *livable*.

This process begins, oddly enough, with the word *stretch*. The word pops in my head only after I'm writing again. I think about it. Type about it. I say things to myself like, "I want a pedagogy and lived experience with *stretch*. I want a pedagogy and lived experience that always allows for motion and evolution." Somehow these words lead me, felt-sense-first, to a Wikipedia page about Play-Doh, then to *Google*, where I type, faster than I can think, an onslaught of words that eventually reveal an intellectual space I didn't know existed: an interdisciplinary field called play studies, with a journal titled *The American Journal of Play Studies*.

I start to click links, and, as I begin reading past volumes, the words in my head that have locked me down for 45 days go from concrete to malleable, a kind of putty in my hands. The answers that confined and depressed me wink and say, "Surprise! We were really just questions all along."

The writing process, with its explorations and discoveries, has opened something in me, around me. I've created a space to play, *for* play, a space to wonder and wander, to make believe something better than I've known these last 45 days. But I'm not finished. I still need to tend to how my imagination became so dark, and I need to make a case for the ability to play, along with play studies, as a part of life writing. I also need to make the point that play studies in life writing should also be a part of rhetoric and composition. And I must make the point that play studies in life writing in rhetoric and composition must remain, ongoing and consistently, a part of my life and my work.

Thomas Henricks and a Nature of Play

Thomas Henricks met me playfully in the *Google* search. His article, "The Nature of Play: An Overview," sits at the intersection of *knowing nothing about play* and *knowing enough to get started playing*, and for this I will forever be thankful. In the article, Henricks highlights an incredible amount of work done in play studies, across academic concentrations, and from some of the foremost authors in play studies, including Brian Sutton-Smith, whose work will be focal in this essay.

It doesn't take more than two paragraphs before I realize play studies could be relevant to life writing and that it is relevant to the struggle I've been having these last 45 days. In paragraph one, Henricks provides an array of activities that most would consider play, from telling a joke to pulling a prank to building a castle. Yet, by paragraph two, Henricks is complicating all these supposed acts of play, including the one that caught my eye in my current immediacy: castle-building. In this regard, Henricks asks, "Is it still play if our castle-builder must follow the directions of some authority figure—say a bossy older child or an overly instructive adult—rather than pursue her own inspirations?" (158). I'm not sure Henricks ever gives a direct answer; I'm not sure he needs to. Whether we are talking play or life writing, I'd say, "No, it is not play—it is no longer play *or* life writing—if we are brought under the rule of an overly instructive authority figure." It would be too easy now to make a comparison between composition or academic systems and this imagined bossy instructor that bosses the life out of creativity, play, and question-wielding, access-granting life writing. It would be all too easy and, yes, sometimes fair to make this comparison. After all, I spent 45 days thinking about the overly structured nature of the dissertation, thinking about how my last attempt at publishing life writing went 0–4 in composition conferences and journals, while going 1–1 in creative writing studies. And on I would go, those 45 days, thinking, thinking, thinking, pitying, pitying, pitying, accusing, accusing, accusing. But writing? *Perish the thought.* Holding myself as accountable as those around me? *Pish.* I was locked inside an untested story and neither it nor I needed to do any work in order to justify our pitiful situation.

Now that I find myself writing, however, I quickly discover a different lesson: the first bossy instructor each of us needs to watch out for is the one within us, the one *as* us, who would rather disparage others than talk to the page about ourselves, who would rather imagine the world against us than write our way to ideas that we and the world might take up to better ourselves in relationship in-and-with the world. This is unfortunate, and ironic, since I teach life writing, in part, because I believe it is the best space for stories to be tested. It's not that there isn't a role for academic papers that set out a road map, lay out theory, and walk the reader through an exact application of prediction-through-process, but that role is not life writing. To do life writing is to reverse the role: as life writers, we can't set out a map, at least not initially, because the first direction of good life writing is to write yourself off the map you came to too easily. To do life writing, then, is to ask questions, rather than construct answers. To do life writing is to disrupt before you put back together, disrupt even if you can't yet put back together. To do life writing is to do more than paint a picture of the world as it is; it is to paint a picture of the world as it still might be.

It is here that we move to the idea of life writing and play. Play, according to Henricks, is described as "the freedom of human beings to express themselves openly and to render creatively the conditions of their lives" (159). It is play, as it is with life writing, that allows us to "create and then to inhabit a world of one's own making" (159). It is life writing, as it is with play, that allows writer and reader to do what I have done so far in this essay, "to be a barrier to the unremarked passing of ordinary events. Thus, [play and life writing] allows people to seize certain moments and then reconfigure them in fanciful ways" (160).

Though there are endless comparisons that can be made between play and life writing, with the space remaining, I will use one of Brian Sutton-Smith's seven rhetorics of play, from *The Ambiguity of Play*, to not only get more deeply into the situation I faced these last 45 days but also to demonstrate how it took life writing to test an untested story. While the reader may find interest in life writing and Sutton-Smith's remaining six rhetorics of play (progress, fate, power, community identity, self, frivolity), I will use the fifth—rhetorics of imagination—to attempt to open up passage, as it were, from not knowing my situation, not understanding it, not having say in it, to better knowing my situation, better understanding it, and *always* having say in it. In this way, we may come to find life writing, with its expanding genres (including written and nonwritten texts), to best be seen as *the playground* that allows for intentional framing and reframing of the *acts of play* we need to develop in our lives. These acts of play and the space we need to play them out become necessary as a response mechanism when our imaginations and lived situations seem turned against us. This process, I will argue, allows us to better "form, de-form, and re-form...in accordance with [our] own fascinations" (162).

The Imaginary

In the worst of the last 45 days, my crisis point, despite what it seemed, was never really about writing a dissertation or not writing a dissertation, seeking a job or not seeking a job. In fact, it was only in the final days, as I was turning (back) to the playground of life writing, that I realized my block hadn't been present-or-future-minded at all. My block, as it revealed itself, as if in a fleeting moment where it stood, back to me, face over shoulder, letting me catch a glimpse of it, was that I feared that I had long ago lost and would forever lose the me that I had most attributed to me.

This *me*, as mentioned briefly before, could be said many ways. He is the introverted me. He is the me who built his interiority as closely, specifically, and painstakingly patiently as my seven-year-old nephew currently builds Lego playsets. He is the me who turned to imagination as a child, when his parents turned to alcohol and domestic violence. He is the me who *played* to escape the house, *played*, then, as a matter of survival. Introverted, highly sensitive, and doused by trauma, he had to play to learn how to move, act, and be as a person. His identity in the world came secondly, because he first learned to lift his voice while playing as imaginary characters in the backyard, then as a writer of fiction, now as a life writer.

It was all of these former-and-somehow-current versions of me that the untested story played itself against these last 45 days. This story, untested, placed me back in an old familiar battle, pitting me against a world that I sometimes fear is so focused on the material and external that it will eventually mean full erasure of the introvert, of interiority, of the very applications that kept me alive long enough to make it to an educational system that sometimes taught me to belittle or deny these internal spaces.

When this conflict was located primarily in my mind, it played out in black-and-white. It was me, and the me I used to be, against rhetoric and composition. It was me, and the me I used to be, against any present and potential futures. In the darkened imagination of this untested story, a link bore out, emotionally if not rationally: I was failing at everything, from the dissertation to my health, because I had betrayed my former self in order to exist in the academic world and have a professional life.

Nowhere in my darkened imagination was there allowance for the nuanced reality that it was rhetoric and composition that actually tempered me, internally and externally, to prepare me to be who I am today. Rhetoric and composition, in focusing so much of the work we do outward, into the material and external, did for me what Elaine Aron says must be done for the highly sensitive person: "If an HSP is not forced to be practical, [they] will lose all touch with the rest of the world" (*The Highly Sensitive Person* 119). In this way, and maybe oddly to some, this was the inevitable reason I had to switch from creative writing to composition. Creative writing came too easy to me. Not the writing and mastering of writing, unfortunately, but, in creative writing, it was all too easy for me to get lost in an imagination that, having been a service to me as a child, was now demanding that I stay in it, at the cost of ever requiring myself to professionalize myself in new ways.

It was rhetoric and composition that finally introduced my interiority to the social world at large. It was rhetoric and composition that let me loose into the greatest public space of play and imagination that I have ever found—teaching in the college classroom. Already, in the last year, I have designed courses on "Bearing Witness through Life Writing" and "Joy Narratives and the *Harry Potter* series." Already I have seen students, at first glance, resist such play, such imaginings, but I have also seen those same students come to find comfort, hope, and agency in play, in imagining. I have seen the majority of these students, before the semesters conclude, finding themselves willfully and thankfully playing at an intermingling of vulnerability, risk, trauma, laughter, and joy. I have seen, in multiple semesters, a relational imagining—a playing, making, and remaking of identity—and I have counted these to be the most sacred secular spaces in which I have ever stepped foot.

It takes life writing, and the playground of the page, to remind me of *both* sides of this story. In thinking, in typing, in telling my story, I remember the me who was saved by interiority *and* the me who almost isolated himself from the public with this same interiority. I remember a rhetoric and composition that helped find me, helped me find me, and helped shape me, *and* I remember a rhetoric and composition that, to my estimation, has sometimes been downright cruel and dismissive to the pioneers of this concentration who focused on exploratory pedagogy, on interiority, on life writing, on pedagogies of surprise.

If, as Sutton-Smith writes, those who gather around a rhetoric of imagination are "all who believe that some kind of transformation is the most fundamental characteristic of play," (127) then, under the untested story, I had lost my space in that gathering. If, as Sutton-Smith continues, an "early preference was to call the overall rhetoric Proteus...as in Bakhtin...that there is in all our minds an internal dialogue of voices, just as in play and festivals there is a dialogue between the different characters, some of whom change their shape as the dialogue proceeds," (128) then, short of returning to the playground of life writing, I had lost the variety of voices, of perspectives, to a single, persistent, untested story.

Chimamanda Ngozi Adichie, in "The Danger of a Single Story," expounds upon how impressionable we are to a single story, and I have attempted to learn from this. A single-minded story flies in the face of everything I teach about life writing, namely that we escape our negative scripts and our untested stories by writing our lives, bearing witness to other writers and having them bear witness to us, as well as the *ongoing nature* of these interchanges. With Bakhtin, I emphasize the combination of the "radical variability in the... meanings that occur within the imagination as well as in the interactions between people" (qtd. in Sutton-Smith 145) as a two-fold bind that needs to be kept close. In the last two semesters, I have presented students with a pedagogy along these lines, one that I call *a living composition*, or, in short, "a composition that isn't based solely on text, but on composing ourselves" with each other (Combs, "Can I Be/Get a Witness?" 71).

In "Go Craft Yourself: Conflict, Meaning, and Immediacies through J. Cole's 'Let Nas Down,'" I elaborate:

> In teaching life writing, I've come to realize that my goal is often opposite of many in English Studies. Many are desperately seeking to lead students to the page, to the essay, begging them to craft something. I seek, conversely, to reveal to them that the potentials of the page are already with them in every moment of their lives, in every choice of thought and action they make. I am not asking, then, that they *do* life writing. I am asking that they *be* life writers. I am not asking them to simply craft the essay. I am asking them to craft their lives. (Combs)

And, yet. Throughout those 45 days, I was governed by a single, untested story, prompted by a difficult summer that triggered all the usual suspects of my darkest imaginings. In those 45 days, I wasn't a life writer, nor was I doing life writing. I was, instead, both stranded *and* stranding myself, separated from life writing, separated from a community of life writers, and separated from anything that wasn't a dark, governing imagination.

And, yet. We know that the imagination can be made up of more, of better, than what I was contending with. Sutton-Smith, pulling from Friedrich Nietzsche and Richard Schechner, writes that "there is abundant evidence that the human imagination can be used in quite diverse ways and can deal with the nonsensical, dark, and monstrous sides of thought as well as more poetic or scientific elaborations" (132).

Because the imagination is always active, for good or ill, here I'd like to move into the potentials of the "as well as" aspects of the imagination. "The playing mind," as Sutton-Smith puts it, "daydreams and fantasizes and cannot keep itself from doing so" (136). Which brings us back to life writing as playground. It is this continual push of the mind, of the imagination, that I argue should lead us to the page. Life writing as playground, then, becomes a space for seeing the internal externally, for using intentionality and pushback where there had once been confusion and surrender.

Here, with page-as-playground, we can admit that the darkest parts of our imagination have been at work longer than we might have been fully aware. Perhaps someone said something that stuck with us and, without much intentional thought, that comment has been working to frame an untested story around us. It is this way in the work of Denise Riley's *Impersonal Passion*, when, in chapter one, "Malediction," she begins by writing that "[t]he worst words revivify themselves within us, vampirically" (9). Here we witness words as "injurious speech....hurled like darts" (9) at and into us. In the second paragraph of her chapter, Riley pushes back against the "old playground chant of 'sticks and stones may break my bones, but words can never hurt me'" (9). What she does after this, however, is to create a playground on the page, full of more sophisticated ideas and approaches to language, in order to better address what is going on in the aftermath of aggressive speech. In her chapter, Riley (and the reader) turn over everything from language to accuser to accused, as we explore words that "indwell" and "ingrow" (11) in order to attempt to "dedramatize" and "sedate" (12) the words that otherwise seem stuck to us and ever moving through us. Riley's chapter, whipping through theories and approaches, serves something like a very sophisticated merry-go-round (though the word "merry" is a false capture of what is going on), where Riley and reader are, at once, spinning in circles, becoming dizzier, yet, somehow, inching towards pathways to feeling *less* the sting of words hurled while empowering approaches that might move us out of mental and affective paralysis.

These negotiations, for Riley and reader, occur on the page. To see life writing as playground, then, is to come to the page ready to negotiate rules to what has been going on, once external to us, and, for too long since, living within our own imaginations. On this playground there can be a new space for the ongoing negotiation of identity (rather than through incessant thoughts alone, the new space will be the page, will be scholarship that speaks to our situation, will be comments from people who we allow into the conversation, and, sometimes, will be comments from people we'd rather not allow in but who get in just the same). In this way, the rules have to be negotiated and renegotiated. ("Why am I awake at 3 a.m. thinking about this? Off to the playground I go.")

The important aspect here is that once we have staked out a turf to do the work of identity making and remaking, of imagining, we no longer have to sit passively in the happenings of our own lives. Now we have space to be players in this game. Now we can speak back to the thoughts, speak back to the comments of the day. Now we can attempt to do what I have attempted to do in this essay: to test an untested story.

Towards an Ongoing Play(fulness)

In this essay, I have attempted to demonstrate life writing as play and, in doing so, have cast the life writing page as a playground. To challenge untested stories that plague both imagination and external reality, I've proposed life writing as a site for renegotiation. To contend on this playground, above all else, we must be consistent in our visitations to this playground. This process, however, is no different than how many people, on days difficult or easy, won't so much as approach the grocery store without first making a list. Yet, when our imagination is turned over to its darkest form, when people say things that make us feel like they are colluding with the darkness or, worse, when people strive to help us but we've become so lost to an untested story that we can't even approach their voices, how instrumental it becomes to have a place to go where we can list what is going on, can divide thoughts where they need dividing, can separate narratives where separation is needed. How little our patience to walk the aisle of a grocery store more times than necessary, but how willing we are to endlessly walk the aisle of untested story, until we bear witness so deeply to the lies of a darkened imagination that it becomes absorbed within our beings and our *being*.

But, perhaps, there is a test to know when an untested story has taken over. Henricks says, of play, that it is "to see the world hypothetically" (175). In other words, it's to see the world as it is *and* as it might still be. In this regard, an untested story reigns when we have lost all options and potentials to see the hypotheticals outside a single, untested story. It is in this moment, whether our strength is great or diminished, that we must do one small and powerful thing that I believe us capable of doing: we must treat life writing with the reverence of a grocery-store list. We must come back to the page and assess. We must add what is needed, cross out what no longer applies. We must write back to the narratives that we know to be false. We must speak (and listen) to the parts of the imagination—the "as well as" parts— that would help us color against the darkness.

In his final page on rhetorics of imagination, Sutton-Smith begins to trouble the differences between *play* and *playful*, or a space given to rules versus a space more apt to toy with rules. In reading him, in writing this essay, I began to discover that what I needed to regain was never some *former me*, as the untested story suggested, but, rather, what I needed to regain was a lifeline back to the *playful* me.

I needed the playful in how Sutton-Smith defines it in the latter portion of this quote: "Perhaps...[these terms] are...the ends of some continuum, one end of which has play genres that are framed, follow the rules, and have relatively predictable expectations...and the other end of which doesn't play within the rules but with the rules, doesn't play within the frames but with the frames" (150).

Years ago, another cohort member told me something similar to this. It was her way of making me feel like I was needed in rhetoric and composition. She said, "We need those who will conduct the studies, of course, but we equally need people with the felt sense to figure out what we need to be studying next."

Next. The very concept I feared in the untested story is what I strive for on the page. *Next* is what continually illuminates play. *Next* is what makes life writing a necessary *vibrant* in the world of rhetoric and composition.

Rhetoric and composition, to its credit, fulfills the call to play as defined initially in the comparison above. Rhetoric and composition takes genre, takes rhetorical situation, takes frameworks, and structures them with rules and expectations that students can grasp, pull down, and use to infinity. But life writing, to its credit, reminds us that just because we have defined one idea doesn't mean we can ignore another. Life writing reminds us that just because we have defined a topic once doesn't mean we won't have to define it again, and differently. Life writing reminds us that just because we've packed an idea neatly, framed it, and made it ready to go, doesn't mean someone won't come along, eventually and playfully, to cut the smallest hole in the packaging, in order to let the idea, so cramped and contained, have a moment to escape, reshape, and breathe again.

The untested story wanted me unable to breathe. It wanted me to see myself as simply interior. It wanted me to see myself as who I used to be. But play calls *next.* Play disrupts the notion, and life writing shines a light on the folly of the idea.

Sure, I am my interior. I am my past. But I am also this present moment, and I am what comes next. I am rhetoric and composition, and I am life writing. I am the darkness of my imagination—the history that triggers the untested story. I am the brightness of my imagination—the "as well as" portion that will always write *me* towards redemption.

Like *play* and *playful,* which are the same continuum, like rhetoric and composition and life writing, too: I am part all these things, and I am part *of* all these things.

And here stumbles a truth too difficult for my past self to look upon. I cover his eyes even as I finally open mine. The past me, because his trauma came directly from the social world, because his escape was through the imagination, will always be fighting to keep me from the social world. It's the only story he knows how to tell. But present me, seeing from the vantage point of this playground page, understands a paradox that, until now, went unconsidered: just because the past me will always be with me doesn't mean I can't still go places he would never go.

I let these words roll out, partly as revelation, partly for accountability. They go something like this—I can be part of the greater social world and *still* retain the imaginative, intrinsic part of myself that I mourned for though it was never truly lost.

Note

1. D. Shane Combs, Ph.D. Candidate, Illinois State University. dcombs@ilstu.edu

References

Adichie, Chimamanda Ngozi. "The Danger of a Single Story." *YouTube*, uploaded by TED, 8 Oct. 2009, www.youtube.com/watch?v=D9Ihs241zeg.

Aron, Elaine. *The Highly Sensitive Person*. New York: Three Rivers Press, 1996.

Combs, D. Shane. "Can I Be/Get a Witness?: An Open Letter to the Life Writing Students I've Not Yet Met." *Writing on the Edge* 28.1 (2017): 63–73.

——, "Go Craft Yourself: Conflict, Meaning, and Immediacies through J. Cole's 'Let Nas Down.'" *Assay: A Journal of Nonfiction Studies* 3.2 (2017). www.assayjournal.com/d-shane-combs-go-craft-yourself-conflict-meaning-and-immediacies-through-8203j-colersquos-ldquolet-nas-downrdquo-32.html.

Henricks, Thomas. "The Nature of Play: An Overview." *The American Journal of Play* 1.2 (2008): 157–80.

Riley, Denise. *Impersonal Passion: Language as Affect*. Durham: Duke University Press, 2005.

Sutton-Smith, Brian. *The Ambiguity of Play*. Cambridge: Harvard University Press, 1997.

III

How We Survive Our Lives

9. *Hearing Voices*

Brooke Hessler[1]

Two years after I wrote this story, I quit my tenured professor job at Oklahoma City University and moved to the west coast to figure out what comes next:

Direction (2013)

Wherever I go, I hear Elaine's voice. When Lou Gehrig's disease stole her ability to talk she got a computer to talk for her. Everyone calls it Siri's voice but all I hear is Elaine and I keep asking her for direction just the same. The day Elaine had her feeding tube implanted the nurses visiting her hospital room mistook me for her twin sister. It was a common mistake. It happened at work all the time. We were English teachers at the same college aged 10 years apart in that vague span between 40 and 60 where women with long hair and glasses become virtually indistinguishable. We're the ones who always show up for committees, and win teaching awards—maybe because we're good or maybe because we care so damn much.

We were both writers who didn't write enough. Both divorced. Living in houses that needed fixing with rescue dogs who kept vigil as we graded papers late into the night. The departmental brochure featured a photo of her sitting in the grass with a small group of writers. Today I'm the one in the brochure and Elaine has faded into campus lore as our patron saint of selfless teaching.

During her eulogy on campus the new president spoke fervently about how much Elaine had meant to him during his 6 months or so of office. He read long excerpts from his email messages seeking her wisdom and editorial feedback. He made a point to describe how, during her final weeks, when she could barely manipulate her fingers, he had offered to grade papers for her if she would teach one more online class.

I'd been depending on Elaine to help me figure out how to work wholeheartedly without giving myself completely away. When her diagnosis came she'd been praying for a personal transformation.

She got one.

I don't know what to pray for anymore. So I'm trying to ask better questions and listen for better answers.

Elaine was a good listener. The moment I knew she really got me was at one of those parties where faculty sit around arguing conundrums.

The History professor asked, "Why do we even entertain that question about the life raft? It's not like anyone would allow themselves to be eaten to save the rest." Elaine said, "Brooke would."

And she was right. I'd have done that for Elaine because the world needed her more than it needed me. Needed her poetry, her composure, her wicked wit.

I wouldn't have done it for the History guy.

I wrote it as a piece of flash nonfiction for a digital storytelling workshop in California. I'd traveled there to practice using mobile phone apps for my new media writing classes. It wasn't the story I meant to write that day, but it had been haunting me for months and I had to get it down. Looking back, I can see how much I needed Elaine's narrative to begin making sense of my own—to confront parts of my life I'd been too timid to change.

Like many writing teachers, I spend a lot more time helping others tell their stories than telling my own. Even more so because outside my regular classroom I am also a story-worker, facilitating digital storytelling workshops in different parts of the world with people whose voices aren't usually heard—caregivers and behind-the-scenes mentors, youth and elders who've been overlooked or underrepresented, survivors of bullies and natural disasters. I help people reflect on pivotal moments in their lives and compose short videos in a collaborative, small group process that emphasizes mutual support and deep listening. The basis of each video is the voiceover track: the storyteller narrating a story only she can tell, in her own voice.

Much of what I learned from "Direction" arose during the process of making it, in the kind of environment I just described: the text above became my script; I assembled the rest into a video on my mobile phone with an editing app, incorporating photos taken during a lunch-hour stroll through a city and campus that weren't mine but were familiar in that way of college towns. The interchangeability of college campuses—in terms of their landscapes as well as their bureaucratic constraints—was a dimension of my story just hinted at in words but referenced more explicitly on the screen. Likewise, the urban context of the story—visually Berkeley but, in fact, Oklahoma

City—featured familiar markers of my everyday life: graffiti and prayer flags, gentrified enclaves and cooperative gardens.

It wasn't written into the essay, but both Elaine and I had re-homed ourselves in Oklahoma, buying houses there as single women in our 40s as a way to stake our claim in that place, to make our relationship with it official. We both did a lot of community outreach that enriched us but didn't fill all the gaps in our lives in the ways we'd hoped. Viewing the urban scenes, plunking images of Berkeley into my video about Oklahoma City, reminded me of the same-ness of places, how Berkeley is a place I could do good work just as I did in Oklahoma City, but that if I replicated my life in that new place, I'd probably feel very much the same, good and bad, enriched but under-fulfilled.

Because the story was composed rapidly, my snapshots and my visual compositions were done fairly intuitively, so in that regard they tapped into a non-discursive way of thinking and communicating my reflections. Everything converged and made new story, new meaning. As Suzanne Langer says, an image is the vessel as much as it is the cargo (Murray, 75). Images give us a way to convey meanings that we haven't yet (or may never) put into words.

In *The Faraway Nearby* Rebecca Solnit cautions that sometimes the stories we tell are actually telling us. We come to accept the inevitability of our roles and relationships. Mid-career academic women who teach first-year writing, for example, tend to both resist and resemble the sorority Susan Miller wryly canonized as "the sad women in the basement" (121). We know better than to empty ourselves into all the forms of institutional service that seem to require our competence and collegiality. We know it will make us sick and tired. We do it anyway. Because the work seems to matter. Because it's who we are. I walked the campus thinking about Elaine, a mentor and role model. Following in her footsteps had for a time seemed noble as well as inevitable. It seemed disrespectful for me to *not* want to end up like Elaine—so admired and beloved. It was something I was ashamed to admit and didn't know how to articulate.

Back at the digital storytelling workshop, when it came time to do my voiceover I thought I might cry so I decided to record it in my rental car. This took several tries because a flock of blackbirds had landed on my hood and kept squawking as they fought over a hunk of hamburger bun. I remember laughing and crying and finding that my multiple re-readings had moved me into a tranquil space. The story by then felt elegiac, as if I were bearing witness: to my friend's life, to my own, to our attempts at mattering.

Making Space

There's a topography to storytelling. You can see it digitally. If you view the audio track of a recorded story you see the wave file of the spoken words. Each is unique. Every instance of every utterance will be distinctive even if you re-record the same person speaking the same words in the same room later the same day. Behind the wave file you see negative space. This spaciousness is not emptiness; it is ambient sound, the invisible context of the spoken story. When I look at an audio track I see a micro cosmos of story. Every instance is as individual and as ephemeral as the memory being shared—and the space will affect what we tell, how we tell it, and whether we really mean it.

Viewed rhetorically, Berkeley was my *topos* for "Direction"—the place my story started. In his scholarly memoir *Yonder*, Jim Corder explains that physical places are rhetorical, they hold stories and evoke them. We map our memories and identities onto physical places even as we perpetually misremember them. Our fictionalizing of a place is part of its rhetorical power. "Direction" wasn't about Berkeley but I couldn't have written it anywhere else.

I wrote the story on a handful of Post-It notes in a boutique hotel across the street from the University of California campus. My room's decor was inspired by the 1960s coming-of-age film *The Graduate*. The blown-glass bedside lamp was a converted hashish bong. It was the week before classes began at my home campus in Oklahoma. I'd rented a car to drive between my hotel and the workshop and then to visit my father's family in Alameda, a few miles away. I'd lived in the area for a couple of years as a teenager, dropped out of high school at 16 by taking a pre-emptive GED, and moved alone to San Diego to enroll in a community college where classes were $5 a credit hour and I could study anything I wanted.

I'd always loved learning but had trouble staying focused. I pictured college as a place to get away from my family and think new thoughts. I remember fantasizing about UC Berkeley specifically as I sat in the girls' bathroom at Alameda High swapping stories and cigarettes, cutting class after class.

Thirty years later I was a college professor with all the things—Ph.D., tenure, full professor rank—and had spent over a decade mentoring youth who were navigating the sometimes rocky path into college life, just as I had. It felt like my karma, if not my calling.

Like Elaine, I got a first tenure-track job that was out-sized for a new assistant professor: she entered OCU as a department chair; I entered as an endowed chair with administrative expectations. It was flattering and challenging and made me feel valued. Grateful. Grateful in that way people in the Humanities are supposed to feel about getting any sort of tenure-track job. Grateful in that way that, over time, can make you feel stuck because surely you couldn't get this lucky again, especially after you've stayed long enough to become a fixture. Like a lamp. More serviceable than exotic. Like that lamp retrofitted onto a hashish bong, looping absurdly through the iconography of a university culture that both eluded and defined me. Story is complicated. But it's not.

Berkeley represented a life I wanted but didn't get; Elaine represented a life I got and no longer wanted. I wove those perceptions into a story about my friend that was really a story about me. And now I am telling my story about writing that story in an effort to pause and observe what that storytelling taught me—and how it taught me.

The pausing itself is how we prepare to learn from stories. For a story to teach us something we have to make a space for it, space for reflection and writing, space for reading and ruminating, space for listening. What I initially gained from sitting with "Direction" was the relief and relative mental clarity that came from stepping outside my normal routine to compose my thoughts. Then, in its own way, the narrative opened more space for deliberation. I carried it with me everywhere—as a three-minute video on my mobile phone—and whenever it felt safe to share my feelings about Elaine or about my evolving restlessness, I'd plug my earbuds into the phone and invite a friend to listen to my story.

Siri's Voice

As a digital story "Direction" begins with the synthesized voice of Siri, the iPhone robot, giving routing instructions down streets I hadn't walked since adolescence. Siri's voice was the "found sound" that inspired me to write about a friend who'd had to adopt that artificial voice as her own; it's also the first way that the story became an inquiry into vocation and authenticity.

As I worked on this essay I returned to my archive of emails with Elaine over the three years between her diagnosis and her death. For months, Elaine continued to attend department meetings and to serve on committees, using voice-synthesizing software on her laptop. I'd find myself observing her fingers, noting moments where she'd begin to type an opinion but refrain from hitting ENTER. She wasn't silent or silenced, but she was restrained. In contrast, I felt like I was talking too much in those meetings, over-compensating. Once I emailed her about that afterwards, asking about her selective communication, apologizing for talking too much—and then for my self-consciousness about it. She said she hadn't noticed herself holding back, but also that she was recognizing how in the old days, when she was able to speak up differently, the voice that was speaking was never her own.

When I read that passage now, I find myself thinking that actually, perhaps, they were all her voices. The artificial voice she recollected as her bureaucratic voice or diplomatic voice, was one of her voices. Siri's artificial voice was more jarring, its tone not her own, but maybe it was also more real because her roles were changing. She could be more blunt and honest. Or maybe I just want to believe that.

For a time I served as acting chair of the English department, occupying her former role, sitting across from her old bookshelves and file cabinets, having occasional out-of-body experiences as my voice recited policy and conciliation to colleagues. That voice was me and not me. Jim Corder would call that voice one of my rhetorics, my ways of composing and communicating a reality (167). Each voice, in a way, still my own.

In writing classes it's common to praise narrative voices that sound authentic, realistic, true. Even as we philosophically problematize such notions as Truth and Authenticity, we admire the prose that seems to be tapping into it, just as we admire everyday humans who seem genuine rather than fake. Elaine spoke a lot of truth through artificial voices. And my speaking about her became a way to speak more truly.

My Voice

What I gained most from "Direction" was courage. It may have been undetectable to everyone who read or heard the story, but I was angry at my boss and said so.

Approaching the text as testimony fortified me to give details that were awkward but true. Two years after her funeral, I was still angry at the president for urging Elaine to continue teaching during her final months of life. I believed he meant no harm, but assumed too much as he conscripted her (in life and in death) into whatever he needed her to be—a consigliere, an advocate, an editor, a muse, a saint. In retrospect I see that I was doing my own version of that. Still am.

Nonetheless, the day I recorded the story was a brave day. Because I knew the video would be public. I knew he might hear the frustration in my voice. I knew I was taking a risk. But I needed to hear myself do it.

After making "Direction" and posting it online I felt emboldened to read one of her poems on Facebook as a response to an ALS Bucket Challenge from a former student. Recording myself was still uncharacteristic and hard. That poetry reading was the first time I published a video of myself online. I taught social media methodologies and had published, by then, literally hundreds of posts on six different anonymous blogs, but I'd always used pseudonyms. I wanted to speak my truths without compromising my professional reputation or drawing attention to myself. I made a YouTube tribute channel to invite others to record themselves reading Elaine's poems. I posted "Direction" there, under my own name, and I performed another reading. I invited the president to perform one there too.

The Poet's Voice

I quote Elaine directly only once in my story—just a quip. It shows her way of sizing things up. It's the version of her I still miss the most. You can hear it in her poetry, which is where I imagine she would send you to find her real voice. When it came time for me to choose the poem I would read for her tribute channel, I picked "What Women Dance For." It's a poem about yearning and writing—things I wrote about anonymously for years but hadn't felt ready to claim on my own. Elaine's channel was my sequel to "Direction." I wanted to diversify the stories being told about Elaine and to give her another chance to speak for herself. The channel was a place where Elaine's stories could continue to be told and retold, heard and re-heard. Like a Tibetan prayer wheel. Having her friends, colleagues, and former students speak her words was a way to put more versions of her narrative in the world.

At the time, this project felt somewhat subversive because my motive was to revive her passionate poet persona as a contrast to the martyr. I remembered the ways she had worked to complicate those kinds of portraits, of women especially. She writes about her grandmother facing death, not as a "namby-pamby, saintly, sanctimonious" character but as "a tiger woman" with "fire and sky at war in her awful eyes" ("My Grandmother"). In life Elaine had resisted the mantle of Inspirational Figure. I was frustrated by the stereotype of the selfless teacher. And, of course, part of my problem was that I was still feeling somewhat disempowered in my own life, uncertain about how to put more versions of myself into the world. I could more easily rationalize promoting her life than mine. My body said her words and she enlivened me. I was hoping that happened for others too. The fierce poet's voice was Elaine's and it was ours. It was never only one voice anyway, and we all needed it.

Listening

One thing I'm still learning from Elaine's story is how to shut up and let my students do the talking. As she began losing her voice and mobility, Elaine restructured her classes into an online-hybrid format: students would meet face-to-face in a classroom; she would videoconference with them from her parents' home in Kansas, typing her comments on the screen as students took turns each week facilitating the discussion. *The Chronicle of Higher Education* heard about her story and sent out a technology reporter to cover it. Reflecting on her role, she explained, "I had in the past often confused listening with waiting for my students to stop talking so that I might resume the very important business of performing" (Young). She challenged professors to consider the extent to which our vocal dominance in the classroom might be a form of ego-gratification, and a way we keep students at a distance (Young and Smokewood). Trusting students to facilitate class became a way to trust so much else about them, sharing a new intimacy with their hearts and minds.

The process of hearing Elaine's voice through the spoken words of people who cared about her, including myself, reinforced my commitment to continue exploring ways to incorporate human voices into my teaching and community arts practice, whether I continued working in a conventional professor job or not. I invited my students to experiment with me, doing more voice work as oral history, verbatim theater, and vocal collage, and those became exercises in radical listening as well as alternative ways to articulate our own ideas.

In the classroom, if we listen carefully, we will hear different voices every day from our students. But sometimes we approach them as if they have just one—one way of composing and communicating their knowledge and creative vision. In my work as a writing and learning center director I've observed that, ironically, the students most often approached as monovocal are those who are multilingual. By prioritizing sentence-level correctness, for example, over other dimensions of communication, teachers and mentors risk becoming more attuned to students as grammarians than as critical thinkers with diverse sources of insight, as if accented English is its own category of expression and that it must be remediated before nuanced communication can happen.

As an academic story-worker, I integrate narrative into most every class I teach in an effort to help students activate prior knowledge, articulate insights, and make connections with assigned subjects and with one another. The best moments of this work, the instances when I hear dialogue bridging differences in language and culture, usually occur when I am able to turn the classroom into a makerspace lab with students sitting side by side, listening to each other's audio recordings as they help one another review and edit videos. Many students can do this work comfortably on their own, outside the classroom, but I require them to do much of it together in pairs so they can inquire into the stories behind the stories, bearing witness to a significant life event or insight. Sometimes we process stories collectively. We see a photograph on the screen, a snapshot of a man exiting a bus in San Francisco's Chinatown. We practice noticing deeply: the angle of his gait, the body language of the passersby, the signage on the street, and what it all seems to tell us. Then we ask the owner of the snapshot, "What are the things you can see that we cannot? What are the things you understand about this scene that we do not?" Composer John Cage observed that "everything is noise until you listen to it, then it becomes fascinating" (3). This is what I'm teaching now. To listen, to pay attention, to expect to be fascinated.

The digital story—the sliver of experience they have scripted and spoken and minutely edited—is a window to a personal experience that informs each student's perspective on life and learning in and beyond our class. If we treat it right, it becomes a threshold for learning and communicating so much else. These projects are often, of course, terrifically useful for engaging writers in the study of authorship, media literacy, intellectual property, appreciative inquiry, and so on. But even if they are not used that way, they matter because they do, because each person took the time to say something deliberately, in their own voice, and they were heard.

Embarking on this approach in my new job—having traded tenure for a new adventure and liminal status—brought to light some of the reasons more of us who believe in life writing are cautious about foregrounding it in traditional academic curricula, and why some are reluctant to replace lecturing with listening. Faculty who publish scholarly memoirs about disrupting conventional pedagogy often do so from positions of privilege: they have some degree of autonomy over their assignments and assessments; they may already have tenure or seniority or retirement. Or perhaps they feel they have nothing left to lose.

The latter may be me. After 20 years of this work I know that stories are how dialogue begins and that dialogue is what we are really preparing students to do as global citizens. Earlier this year my *topos* for re-assessing place/space/identity became storytelling itself. In a rushed meeting held shortly before spring classes began, a ranked colleague with good intentions and moderate influence announced that all instructors of composition for international students were expected to shift the emphasis of their courses

from an independently chosen theme and pedagogy that would surface critical thinking and writing about diversity, power, and privilege (the established
approach for all sections of the course and for all students) to an emphasis on
direct grammar instruction and vocabulary acquisition. In other words, at a
time when intercultural communication is more vital than ever, the general
education course with the most concrete intercultural communication learning outcome would foreground sentence-level correctness as a way to achieve
it. I tried speaking up, referencing scholarship, asking diplomatic questions
regarding best practices, and so on. I left the meeting feeling steamrolled.
Unheard. I retained storytelling as the theme and methodology of my course.
It was a minor act of rebellion. I didn't jettison grammar or vocabulary. I
just didn't make them my focus, because I knew I could do better than that.
I trusted my pedagogy to yield the desired outcomes. In such moments I
try very hard to discern whether my inner pedagogical guide is the voice of
wisdom or ego. From my new vantage point I see a lot of familiar institutional
behaviors—the circumspection, the back channel anxietizing, the silencing...
all in the name of good teaching. And I observe myself remaining a bit too
quiet as I translate the discourse. I recognize that I've moved from the rhetorics of relevance within the tenured caste to those of the unranked. But
then again, I came to my new institution to contribute and cultivate a more
authentic vocation, to be a better version of myself. Not a more timid one.

Story-work has taught me that every story matters and that something
important happens when a storyteller hears her own voice claiming and considering her experience (Hessler and Lambert). In an institution (like so many
others) where most faculty are adjuncts or unranked, and where nearly half of
the students are multilingual and over one-third are international, many of us
are trying on new voices every day, whether we are using accented Academic
American English or not. I honestly believe that an important part of my job
is to help more of us practice speaking up and out as well as listening. Stories
can help us do that. So I've begun capturing stories to promote and ponder
the diversity of meaning-making: first-person experiences recorded as short
multimedia narratives about what it looks and sounds like to learn something
new.

These days, no matter what else I do in my classes, I have everyone,
including myself and anyone who visits us, record our voice saying our own
name and post it to an online discussion board. We sometimes share the stories behind our names; sometimes we don't if we aren't ready, because those
stories can be charming but they can also hurt. In my class this summer I had
a student who goes by Alien. It's a name she got in middle school. She never
told us why. But I'm still listening for it. Because it may still come up, outside

of class—in the writing center, perhaps. I want to be there to catch her story and whatever comes with it.

Resonance

In one of his essays on voice, Peter Elbow talks about resonance—a quality deeper than clever verbalizing that binds us to someone's story, a quality that we too can cultivate over time. It begins by finding a single note that we can sing loud and clear, so that we can be heard, because until we've mastered that one we aren't likely to get an audience. Next, "if we are brave and persistent enough to sing our note at length—to develop our capacity for resonance—gradually we will be able to 'sing ourselves in'…to more frequencies…and make every note resound with rich power" (172). Elaine's disquieted narrator resonated with me from a place in my own memory until I could find her in images and in words. Writing about her story helped me find, if not my note, at least my key.

Note

1. Brooke Hessler, Director of Learning Resources, California College of the Arts. bhessler@cca.edu

References

Cage, John. *Silence: Lectures and Writings*. Lebanon, NH: University Press of New England, 2000.

Corder, Jim. "On the Way, Perhaps, to a New Rhetoric, but Not There Yet, and if We Do Get There, There Won't be There Anymore." *College English* 47.2 (1985): 162–70.

———. *Yonder: Life on the Far Side of Change*. Athens, GA: University of Georgia Press, 1992.

Elbow, Peter. "Voice in Writing Again: Embracing Contraries." *College English* 70.2 (2007): 168–88.

Hessler, Brooke. *Remembering Dr. Elaine Smokewood, Poet and Teacher*. 2013. https://www.youtube.com/channel/UC9GYkGrx9Cv1lFXCMf_3zRg

Hessler, Brooke, and Joe Lambert. "Threshold Concepts in Digital Storytelling: Naming What We Know About Storywork." *Digital Storytelling in Higher Education: International Perspectives*. Ed. Grete Jamissen, Pip Hardy, Yngve Nordkvelle and Heather Pleasants. Cambridge: Palgrave Macmillan, 2017, 19–35.

Miller, Susan. *Textual Carnivals: The Politics of Composition*. Carbondale, IL: Southern Illinois University Press, 1993.

Murray, Joddy. *Non-discursive Rhetoric: Image and Affect in Multimodal Composition.* State University of New York Press, 2010.

Smokewood, Elaine. "My Grandmother Wrestles the Angel of Death." *Southern Poetry Review* 35.2 (1995): 34–36.

—. "What Women Dance For." *Glassfire*, 1.1 (2006). Retrieved from http://www.pegleg publishing.com/glassfire/whatwomendancefor.htm.

Solnit, Rebecca. *The Faraway Nearby.* New York: Penguin, 2014.

Young, Jeffrey R. "Taught by a Terrible Disease." *Chronicle of Higher Education.* 3 Jan. 2010. *Technology,* www.chronicle.com/article/Taught-by-a-Terrible-Disease/63347; Accessed 22 May 2018.

Young, Jeffrey R., and Elaine Smokewood. Retrieved from *Chronicle of Higher Education,* website, https://youtu.be/9BhHsbx9aH4, 2010.

10. *Writing a Queer Life, or,* S-Town *in Five Rhetorical Situations*

Jonathan Alexander[1]

How does one write a life, and why would one do so in the first place? No communication modality can capture the complexity—ontologically or phenomenologically—of a lived life, but the effort to do so itself prompts reflection, the desire to shape more consciously the multiplicities we are as they move through time. So confronting any kind of life writing enacts opportunities for action (and being-in-action) that are simultaneously temporal and spatial, a timed shaping of the matter of ourselves in relation to the matter around us.

What matters around us?

So many, many things. And people, and experiences and encounters, and the inexplicable interplay of imagination, fantasy, reaction, reality. The limitations of this platform (writing on a laptop for a collection of essays) condition my choices, so I choose here to reflect on my experience, ongoing, of the podcast *S-Town*, itself a form of life writing that has prompted much discussion, some outrage, and even deep engagement as those of us interested in life writing consider what kind of life, and what kind of "writing," is on offer here. In the process of my own engagement, I have decided the only way I can approach *S-Town* meaningfully is to write alongside, or with, or in the phantasmatic vicinity of the experience of this podcast. Rhetorical analysis has become the technology through which I attempt here to give shape to thoughts, writing a part of my life in relation to a part of the life written in part in *S-Town*.

So, considering the importance of—

A Rhetorical Situation

—I begin my consideration of the podcast *S-Town* with my particular rhetorical situation, specifically with how I am listening to this podcast. I listen to nearly all podcasts while on the treadmill at the gym. I'm a 50-year-old, white, cis-gender-appearing (though not cis-identified) queer male, and I exercise less to maintain any kind of attractiveness (which I've never felt I had) than to keep the body moving, to forestall against all of the ways that a body seems to start to betray you as you age: creaking joints, a creeping stiffness, a decided turn toward immobility.

This scene is not irrelevant in my personal reception of this story, which has been recommended by numerous friends and colleagues who want to know what I, a cis-gender-appearing (though not cis-identified) queer male who also frequently writes about queerness, might think about this story about a gay male—one who, like me, also happened to be from the South and who (spoiler alert), if he had survived his life, would be about my age.

How have I survived my own life? Am I surviving it, and will I continue to do so? What does it mean to "survive" a life—a cis-gender-appearing queer male life—at this particular moment, and why does John B. not survive his?

Before I even begin listening to this podcast, I'm approaching it through the context of my own existence, my own seemingly parallel narrative, and I realize that there's already one story we could tell about *S-Town*, the story of the one who got away versus the one who didn't, the story of the queer who, born late mid-century, decides at some point that he won't survive if he stays in the deeply sexist and homophobic South; so he leaves, as I did, moving to Colorado, then Ohio, then settling in California, the land of fruits and nuts, the queerest home I've ever found.

I worry over the word "found." For I have found less than I have learned to make, and it has taken much of my lifetime to learn to make a queer life, a queer family, the queer connections that are sustaining, that enable me to sit here, writing my life, writing someone else's. I bring all of this to *S-Town* before even beginning the podcast—and this is not unimportant because it conditions my reception of the narrative, at least initially, but also maybe permanently bending it along a particular path.

I will return to this issue of reception in a moment, but first, some—

Genre Trouble

—for *S-Town* launches itself as one genre, the whole narrative initially revolving around the genre of journalistic investigation, a follow-up to its podcast (and corporate) predecessor *Serial,* but ends up being something very different. In broad sum, according to Wikipedia,

> In 2012, antiquarian horologist John B. McLemore sent an email to the staff of the show This American Life asking them to investigate an alleged murder in his hometown of Woodstock, Alabama, a place McLemore claimed to despise. After a year of exchanging emails and several months of conversation with McLemore, producer Brian Reed traveled to Woodstock to investigate.
>
> Reed investigated the crime and eventually found that no such murder took place, though he struck up a friendship with the depressed but colorful character of McLemore. He recorded conversations with McLemore and other people in Woodstock, which are played on the podcast.
>
> McLemore committed suicide by drinking potassium cyanide on June 22, 2015, while the podcast was still in production. In the narrative of the podcast, this occurs at the end of the second episode; subsequent episodes deal with the fallout from McLemore's death while exploring more of McLemore's life and character. (https://en.wikipedia.org/wiki/S-Town)

I quote from the Wikipedia description of the content or "plot" of *S-Town* because it renders succinctly the genre trouble of the podcast, which narratively swerves from the deep dive of journalism to sensational memoir-by-proxy, all the while recalling through its slick production, frequent plot twists, and sustained attention to "character" interiority the influence of "quality television." And what a character indeed. John B. is a polymath who lived his whole life in rural Alabama, in the town Woodstock, which he calls "shit town," owing likely to the relative "backwardness" of its inhabitants. For John B. is a true eccentric, often vibrant and larger than life, a horologist (a clock preserver) who cares for his mother while also constructing a massive hedge maze in his backyard. He's likely gay, without a "partner," but someone who has collected various stray young straight males, mentoring and guiding them, perhaps becoming a bit too invested—but what is meant by that "too" and that "invested" will become a point of contention in the post-mortem analysis of his life. He's also likely depressed, fed up with his life in particular and the larger culture in general, but his angry rants are pyrotechnic feats of verbal ingenuity as he castigates contemporary society for its ravaging of the planet and relative indifference to suffering humans inflict on each other. His is a complex life that begs for interpretation, analysis, at least discussion, and Brian Reed, the podcast producer, quickly switches focus from the earlier "murder" to John and his suicide, wanting to write this life—for reasons that aren't ever particularly clear beyond Reed's own fascination with a Southern gothic queer eccentric. But the drama of Reed's particular interest isn't written here, and the drama of John B.'s life is. And that's part of what makes *S-Town* so complex—and in need of some accounting.

Investigation, portrait, "high-quality" dramatic narrative— such hybridity (if that's what it is) has irked some commentators, such as Aja Romano, who writes that "it's important to be clear that despite its Serial roots and an investigative premise that initially seems like a journalistic jaunt into an unresolved murder, *S-Town* is not a true crime podcast." Romano begins her analysis of the podcast by stating that she is "not convinced it should have been made," worrying in particular over the inability of the producer to obtain consent from John B. to document, much less systematically analyze, his life: "[A]s powerful as it is, it would have been even more powerful had its subject been able to consent to its being shared with the world."

Why is such consent so important? The shift in genre focus—from the red herring of investigating one phantom death to exploring through portraiture how another individual came to his own end—swaps out one object of analysis for another while holding on to the investigative imperative to narrativize the causes of a death. The original genre of journalistic investigative reporting thus becomes troubled as its energies are transferred from one subject to another. Such genre trouble becomes ideologically significant, for, following Anis Bawarshi and Mary Jo Reiff, I also believe that "genre [is] less...a means of organizing kinds of texts and more...a powerful, ideologically active, and historically changing shaper of texts, meanings, and social actions. From this perspective, genres are understood as forms of cultural knowledge that conceptually frame and mediate how we understand and typically act within various situations" (4). So, if genre is a "[form] of cultural knowledge that conceptually frames and mediates how we understand," what cultural knowledge is produced in *S-Town*'s genre shift? A better question might even be this: what kinds of cultural knowledges are reproduced—unthinkingly and uncritically—in this hybrid genre? For *S-Town* starts to seem more and more like a case study of a troubled homosexual than anything else, one that transfers the energies of criminal investigation from one subject to another, carrying over a patina of pathology adhering in investigative journalism to its emerging portraiture of John's life. In the process, it actually replicates, however unwittingly, a hundred-plus-year-old narrative strategy for rendering visible the lives of queer people—

The Homosexual Case Study

—which was invented and practiced by sexologists at the end of the 19th century to catalogue and categorize varieties of sexual experience and practice.

Specifically, it mobilized narrative to discipline sexual behavior and, in the process, such narrativized behavior came to be conflated with emerging sexual identities. As Foucault famously argues in *The History of Sexuality, Volume 1*, the intense medical, psychiatric, and sexological scrutiny of inversion and homosexuality allowed some of those pathologized as homosexuals to create "reverse discourses" in which they recast their "illness" as positive identification. In *S-Town*, however, it is not possible for John B. to engage in such a discursive, rhetorical, and political practice. Instead, his life is rendered spectacularly for us to witness—and that rendering has a hard time escaping pathologizing rhetorics.

Even in Romano's sympathetic accounting of *S-Town*, the specter of mental health haunts descriptions of the podcast, which is about "the fallout of a missing will, failed romantic opportunities, barely articulable fantasies, untreated mental health," resulting in a potentially botched and unethical form of "journalism exploring the life of a private citizen who struggled intensely with mental health issues and never had a chance to consent to some of the facts that *S-Town* reveals about him." Again, there's much sympathy here, but also judgment: John B., a homosexual suicide, must be protected as someone diagnosable under the disciplinary regimes of psychology and psychopathology. His death is thus narratable, even for Romano, as the result of "barely articulable fantasies," as though a clearer articulation would have "saved" him; it's hard for me not to read in this formulation a demand that the sexual, erotic, and intimate be made narratively renderable, so as better to be diagnosed.

The cataloguing of John's deviation from normative health reaches a crescendo in the final episode's "reveal" of John's sadomasochistic practices with his friend Tyler, which, in the narrative arc of the podcast, are offered as the fullest proof of John's psychological instability. He's presented as essentially having lured his younger friend into what Romano describes as a "ritualistic pain fetish." The ritual, called "Church" by John and Tyler, involved various forms of whipping and tattooing (Tyler is a tattoo artist) that is grisly listening for some. Reed titles this episode, using John's own words, "You're beginning to figure it out now, aren't you?" But John isn't referring to the pain ritual, so Reed's use of this question is pointedly interpretive, John's own words used against him to situate the pain ritual as core and central to understanding this pathological homosexual. Romano calls Reed out on such narrative positioning of the pain ritual, arguing that the podcaster "presents John's ritual in an odd way—not as a known BDSM practice but as an alternative to cutting, something he implies could have been brought on by John's depression." In the process, Romano argues, Reed's "choice to put John's fetish on the record with so little contextualization feels irresponsible and out of sync with the rest of the podcast." But even Romano's descriptions can't quite escape the pathologizing rhetorics, already suggested by her use of the term "depression," and her conclusion that "John was attempting to practice an unhealthy, unsafe, and nonconsensual form of structured masochism, in isolation, outside of healthy established BDSM practice."

Romano is ultimately correct in pointing out that what we are missing is context, a fuller understanding of what the pain ritual meant to John, or to Tyler for that matter, who is depicted as an unwilling participant. As such, the practice is left described and diagnosed but not understood, except through psychological narratives that also (perhaps unconsciously) call up the troubling specter of pedophilia. For the absence of Tyler's understanding of what the two were doing leaves intact our culture's deep unease with intergenerational intimate engagement, which I understand as a pedophilic revulsion transferred to unconventional relationships between consenting adults of different ages. Such transference bolsters a particular vision of heteronormative family structures and desires.

In the process, *S-Town* becomes less portraiture than case study, another example in a long line of sexological narratives suggesting that documenting such "cases" remains one of the dominant paradigms through which we understand sexual nonnormativity (or perhaps sexuality in any form for that matter). Such rendering, however, cannot quite occlude—

Queer Life Writing

—for we can attempt to understand *S-Town* as a form of life story, of life writing, however botched in execution at points, and one that honors its object as opposed to diagnosing and disciplining it. John B.'s voice survives the podcast's many attempts to narrate his experiences for him. He rants and raves, the grain of his voice speaking to his sense of outrage, not just at the local circumstances surrounding his life but also about the global structures that render our planet increasingly toxic to human life. Reed rightly clears some space—but all too little ultimately—to listen to this gorgeously flamboyant pique:

> We ain't nothin but a nation of goddamn chicken-shit, horse-shit, tattle-tale, pissy-ass, whiney, fat, flabby, out-of-shape Facebook-lookin, damn twerk-fest peeking out the windows and slipping around, listening in on cell phones, spying in the peephole, peeping in the crack of the goddamn door, and listening to the fuckin sheetrock. You know Mr. Putin, please, show some fuckin mercy, I mean come on drop the fuckin bomb...won't you?!? Uhhhh I gotta have me some tea. (from episode 5)

Reed unwittingly offers us a rant that might justly be aimed at Reed himself, for the podcaster's "spying in the peephole, peeping in the crack of the god-damn door" of John's life itself. Indeed, John's rant raises questions of ethical relationality, of who gets to tell what stories about whom, of who in particular gets to tell queer stories. Such questions put me back—

On the Treadmill

—where I'm listening to this podcast and wondering about my own right to re-tell this story, but this time hoping to tell it a bit differently, perhaps filling in bits and pieces that seem left out, made opaque by the drive to interpret, cate-gorize, explain. But I must also acknowledge that I'm listening on a treadmill in a gym for which I pay a monthly membership fee in a city that's amongst the most expensive in which to live in this country, while the podcast episodes are periodically interrupted by ads encouraging me to build my own Squarespace website and appropriately brand my accumulated cultural and professional cap-ital, and to sign up for Blue Apron which will allow me the luxury of assem-bling curated food stuffs in the privacy of my own home without the bother of jostling others in a busy supermarket. Perhaps I too, as queer as I imagine myself, have become a citizen of the world that John B. (not unjustly) feared: I peep and spy, participating in this bit of Southern gothic tourism, returning only glancingly from the comforts of my precious environment to a place I left a long time ago, the Deep South. I am part of the problem.

I have moved into my own particular future, my life following a narrative of escape from the South to the relative (if costly) freedom of an urban coast. John, now dead, cannot move into his. But perhaps he's left us signs of what that future might have looked like, how his cut-off life might have devel-oped? Perhaps there are enough clues to suggest that John B. was already well along the path of crafting the future he wanted, even if such ended in suicide. We can only speculate, and in risking such speculation, like Reed and Romano, we risk insertion of ideological predispositions and the replication of presentist norms. Indeed, and in general, in rendering John's life, *S-Town* the podcast promulgates a very particular notion of—

Queer Futures

—that I want to note and critique as a way of thinking about queer futurity differently. While Lee Edelman says "no" to the future, and Jose Esteban Munoz wants to cruise utopia, many of us occupy time somewhere between these two poles—negation of hope for the future and belief that things will

necessarily "get better." At the very least, many of us recognize (and sometimes resist) what Elizabeth Freeman calls "chrononomativity," or the man-
agerial and biopolitical organizing of our (present and future) time to max-
imize our productivity in a consumerist and capitalist society. But we also
worry enough about where we are individually and collectively headed in
ways that don't quite feel sexy yet, that aren't attractive and desirable, that are
trying to think and feel beyond "productivity." We want to desire the future,
a form of hopefulness, but we struggle with what futures to desire, feeling the
dissatisfactions of the present but wondering how to change.

John B's life, to me at least, seems marked by this temporal predicament.
It's a quirk of metaphorical synchronicity that he was by trade a horologist,
someone devoted to maintaining time pieces, especially the preservation of
old clocks. What does one do with one's time? And what kind of future is
possible? John wasn't particularly sanguine about the latter question, worrying as he did over the apparent downward spiraling of our planet's ecological
systems and mass governmental waste and corruption. But he also worried
too much about the future to just say "no" to it, and, in his view, it's a future
that's far from sexy; nothing worth cruising yet.

Brian Reed, though, doesn't unpack John's preoccupation with time
along these lines—as a life spent, at least in part, attempting to call attention
to the warning signs all around us. Instead, the penultimate episode of the
podcast renders John B.'s life as a lesson in temporal—specifically chrononor-
mative—failure. Reed interviews at length another gay man, Olin, who is
about John's age and with whom John had had something of a romantic
affair. Told with great pathos from Olin's view, the story gives us a sense of
how difficult it was to maintain a gay relationship in rural Alabama, even in
the late 20th century. It's all very *Brokeback Mountain*, just set in Alabama in
the 1980s and 90s. Reed offers the story as an attempt at a romance but one
ultimately botched—and he largely lays the blame at John's feet; John B.'s
rants about climate change and the economy drove Olin away, who was left
wondering why John didn't just leave Shit Town and start over somewhere
else.

The force of the narrative here leads us to believe that John B. had a
chance at happiness, a chance offered through the heteronormative relationality of pair-bonding, but that he denied or sabotaged that chance and
thus failed to secure his future happiness. This narrative—that we should
find our "soul mate" and make a home together—is amongst the most
chrononormalizing narratives our culture offers; it prescribes not just how
we should manage our intimacies and desires (focusing them on an individual) but also lays down a temporal trajectory that invites us to imagine the

necessity of finding that individual who becomes the person with whom we face the future. John's failure to find or nurture that soul mate becomes one of Reed's primary explanations for why John likely turned to sadomasochistic practices, luring an inappropriate object of affection into assisting him with his pain rituals; it's also likely why he committed suicide when Tyler refused one evening to see him. The great rhetorical pathos of *S-Town* coheres around the denial of certain normative futures and the attempt to enact an impossible future—specifically, the relationship with Olin that never really fully developed, and the attention to a relationship with Tyler that could have no future.

I can't help but think, though, that *S-Town* ultimately privileges a particular narrative of love. And, in the process, it ignores the complexity of the relationship with Tyler, who clearly loved John, even if he didn't always know how to respond to him. But what about Tyler—the young man whom John employs and helps out, to whom he offers advice and acts as a confidant, and with whom he constructs an extraordinary backyard shrub maze—that maze serving perhaps as its own metaphor for the twists and turns of a relationship that didn't have a set path, a prescribed trajectory, a normative way of understanding itself? Reed variously tries to understand this relationship through the lens of mentoring, even using the word "shepherding" and noting John's previous "romantic friendships" with young men who thought of John's home as a "safe space." But John was too invested, perhaps too obsessive, in Reed's view. The relationship was doomed. Instead of dwelling for a moment in why it's so difficult to maintain and nurture such relationships, Reed suggests that a fight between the two men led to John's suicide—which it's all too easy to interpret as meaning that John's inappropriate investment in this young man killed him. John's relationship with Tyler had no future.

If I had been telling this story, I would have wanted to dwell a bit more with this friendship, thinking it through Michel Foucault's late interview, "Friendship as a Way of Life," in which the philosopher meditates on what it means to spend time together, particularly men spending time together: "How is it possible for men to be together? To live together, to share their time, their meals, their room, their leisure, their grief, their knowledge. their confidences? What is it to be 'naked' among men, outside of institutional relations, family, profession, and obligatory camaraderie? It's a desire, an uneasiness, a desire-in-uneasiness that exists among a lot of people" (136). This uneasiness intensifies, Foucault notes, if there's a substantial age difference between two men: "Between a man and a younger woman, the marriage institution makes it easier: she accepts it and makes it work. But two men of noticeably different ages—what code would allow them to communicate?

They face each other without terms or convenient words, with nothing to assure them about the meaning of the movement that carries them toward each other. They have to invent, from A to Z, a relationship that is still formless, which is friendship: that is to say, the sum of everything through which they can give each other pleasure" (136).

In so many ways, Tyler and John were having to invent their relationship, from A to Z, as it unfolded, and there should be no surprise that there were rough spots, difficult patches, misunderstandings. But they seemed to keep at it, even when its intimacies became... "complicated." Reed and even Romano want to understand their intimacy as unhealthy, with Romano characterizing Tyler as "the straight object of his sublimated attraction"; note the psychoanalytic and psychopathologizing interpretation. I think these formulas are too easy and dismissive, denying not just John's agency and interest but Tyler's as well. I won't argue that this friendship, a la Foucault's formula, offered a new and attractive model for human relations, but, in the words of Tom Roach glossing Foucault's thoughts on friendship, it certainly represented "a turning away from the identities dispensed by various biopolitical institutions, a turning away from established relational norms" (69). Moreover, as Roach puts it, "If friendship is 'the development towards which the problem of homosexuality tends,' a relationship that must be 'invented from A to Z,' then such friendship only comes into being when homosexuality as a sexological concept is annihilated" (69). That is, to see what a relationship like John and Tyler's offers, we need to set aside our heteronormative and pathologizing ways of thinking about such friendships. I think Reed, Romano, and even most of us, acculturated as we are to sexological narratives, all too easily diagnose the unhealthiness in such friendships and then miss some of their beauty, how the particular friendship John and Tyler had actually sustained both of these men for a long time and gave them both much pleasure. No friendship, no relationship, no family bond, no marriage can secure a future. But this friendship, like those Foucault thought worth exploring, opened up a not-quite-fully-glimpsed because still-always-in-process trajectory for imagining other kinds of relationality that exceed the normative bonds of family and heteronormativity. Those trajectories gesture toward future forms of relationality that, in attempting to shake off constraining expectations of what relationships should look like, can't quite yet be seen fully. They have to be made up as they unfold. So it's no wonder that Reed had a hard time seeing this relationship, not just for what it was, but for what it gestured toward. The future is, after all, opaque. But that doesn't mean we don't try to make—

Queer Possibilities

—and I'm thinking in particular of David, who is like my little brother, someone I met when he was a student nearly a decade ago, someone who ever since has become more and more a part of our lives. He lives now in Brooklyn, but we text weekly and visit when we can, me going there, him coming for dinner and coffee when he visits his family in SoCal. We sat together a few weeks ago on a recent visit, drinking wine and then whiskey, talking, commiserating, and then we took out the art supplies and started making collages. We filled small cardboard boxes with pictures and text that spoke to our desires for the future, creating little packages of wishes, time capsules that we can return to and meditate on. Corny, for sure. But friends with whom you can share the corny *are* your family.

Indeed, we see more of him than any "real" family member. Hence, little brother. But the familial metaphors seem insufficient. They can only be approximations for the kind of relationality that isn't blood but also more cherished precisely because it isn't blood; it has been carefully nurtured, cultivated, pruned at times, but also allowed to flourish wildly at others. It was not chosen for us; we have chosen it ourselves. I turn poetic trying to find the right vocabulary, the articulation that honors while not distorting. Our language doesn't have much in the way of a lexicon of friendship, for seeing in friendship the creative possibility for forming other kinds of relationships, for being with one another in ways that aren't already structured through family, marriage, law, and custom.

My husband, Mack, and I have been together for over twenty years now. Our relationship continues to grow, indeed, but it is also structured in at least some significant ways around legal obligations and financial responsibilities—details of sharing and building a life that we've eagerly embraced to attempt to secure a future for each other, to protect one another in as much as anyone can protect a loved one in this increasingly precarious world. Now my mother lives with us, and we try to find ways to extend that protection, that care, to her as well. We are a family, recognizably so, even if we are two men and an old woman who has come to accept her son's queerness, even if she doesn't understand it. She doesn't have to; we are family.

But David is different. He would seem from some perspectives an excess, because there is no accounting for his presence in our lives, in my life. And there's the rub. Even as I write about him, tell about this little bit of my life, I am still seeing through the eyes of others, hearing my story through the tropes and norms of a larger culture that sees relationality beyond the family as excess. I identify mother and Mack as family, while David is "different." But David is *not* excess to me, and he most definitely *is* family to me. Coming home recently from a trip with his parents to England, he texted me that he was on the plane, waiting to take off. All of the pictures he'd already sent, the postcards, the intimate threat of buying me a touristy t-shirt—of all the things he'd done to make me a part of his trip, this text said the most about how intertwined our lives are. He wanted me to know he was heading home.

Writing about him is simultaneously an attempt to honor and name what he is to me while also grappling with how my understanding of our relationship is always being written under the sign of pre-existing cultural norms. Amy Robillard writes eloquently in "Shame and the Personal Essay" that, even as teachers of writing, "we, too, at any stage of teaching, need to remind ourselves that our own perspectives are socially crafted and recrafted. And we need to share these reminders with students so that they can see that the perspectives of teachers—that group of people whose job it is to evaluate their abilities to see the perspectives of others—these too are crafted. And because they are crafted, they are subject to change" (715). Yes, indeed, I struggle to see and write my life through terms that make sense to me, even as I recognize that I can only ever use the terms given to me, however I might need to refit and remix them for my purposes and my needs. And in the process of such writing, I recognize how my views have changed—views on what makes a livable life, what I need to sustain myself, how I need to love others, how I need to let others love me. That learning to live is an ongoing scripting, a larger life-writing of which our textual narratives serve as powerful metonyms, offering opportunities for reflection...and then further crafting and recrafting.

So too with David, with our friendship, with a life we are writing in part together. I have chosen to integrate him into our family, and he has chosen to participate in that integration, and we invent, from A to Z, sometimes week to week, a relationship that is still formless, but whose form is palpable nonetheless. We can see the traces of it in our lives everywhere, much like John B. and Tyler left behind—

Traces of a Life

—in the spray-painting of their names together under a bridge in Woodstock, a scene that reads so much like two lovers carving their names in a tree. The marking of the bridge, the declaration of their intimacy rendered in the proximity of their names through graffiti—this is the scene that Tyler recalls with Reed as soon as he finds out that John B. has died. And Reed rightly returns to it late in the podcast, as though he acknowledges, finally in this small way, that the relationship was more important than not, perhaps more vital than generally recognized by the podcast.

And so too is the marking of the bridge, the specific *place* that John B. chose to stay in. One chrononormalizing narrative would have had John B. leave *S-Town*, take up life elsewhere, live more healthily somewhere else as a gay man. But John's commitment to his home is itself perhaps the reverse discourse we need to acknowledge, his insistence on living his life eccentrically in the place he was born. Reed reflects, finally, in the last episode, on how inviting and gracious John B. had been to him:

> John was depressed for sure, but still he didn't do what Cheryl's saying. He didn't hole up in a dark room with the blinds down. He may not have gone to the turnip green suppers, but he created his own place that was filled with sunshine. His 124 acres, which he designed to be incredible: bursting with beautiful flowers and an orchard, and an old preserved house, and a historic graveyard that he maintained, and a custom swing set. And, of course, a spectacular giant hedge maze, with 64 permutations of the solution, and one null set. And then John did share that with people. He didn't host big community events, but he made a point of inviting people over, giving them the tour he gave me, spending quality time with neighbors there.

However incomplete, John was building his future, in his own way, in his own time, in his own space.

Brian Reed ultimately asks if John lived a worthwhile life. In the final episode, he talks about the various clocks that John gifted folks, who are often extremely moved by them. One recalls John saying that "the measure of time had something to do with me." It's hard for Reed not to offer analysis and even judgment here:

> John was actually quite good at appreciating the time he had. That wasn't his problem. His problem was a proleptic one. He saw nothing but darkness in the future. Shit Town, for John, was not believing that anything good would last. That we would inevitably mess it up. Relationships that are meaningful, the earth as a place that can adequately support human life, even John's remarkable maze.

I'm not sure that someone who spent such time preserving clocks, building a maze, and cultivating his friendships "saw nothing but darkness in the future." He warned of catastrophe sure, but why rant and rave so eloquently if you don't think anyone is listening, if your rant won't ultimately make a difference? Reed rushes to judgment, and it's *his* version of this life I find myself rejecting; it's *his* version of the temporal arc of John's existence I find inadequate, not John B's. life. And who are we to judge, after all?

In many ways, this memoir-by-proxy measures a life, but its measurements are sometimes off, weighted too much in some direction, creating a portrait that doesn't quite seem balanced. To be sure, a life need not be "balanced," and perhaps the best ones aren't; their weightiness might not let them be, but they impress us nonetheless. We learn from them. In rendering them to others, in representing the complexity of a life, we should be wary of tipping the scales too far in one direction or another.

There's so much in this podcast I'm not addressing, and I'm so very cognizant of how much I've left unsaid, what surfaces I've barely scratched. I would consider my own rendering here unethical if I didn't leave it with an acknowledgement of how much hasn't been broached. Such an acknowledgement honors the density of a life and recognizes the necessary limits of representation. Ultimately, all I can do to try to honor John's life is to do what I've done—to tell a little of my own in relation to it, hoping to trouble the tropes that would otherwise turn his story into that of another homosexual case study, just the story of another dead gay man.

Note

1. Jonathan Alexander, Chancellor's Professor of English, University of California, Irvine. jfalexan@uci.edu

References

Bawarshi, Anis, and Mary Jo Reiff. *Genre: An Introduction to History, Theory, Research, and Pedagogy*. West Lafayette, IN: Parlor Press, 2010. Print.

Foucault, Michel. "Friendship as a Way of Life." *Ethics, Subjectivity and Truth: The Essential Works of Foucault, 1954–1984*, Vol. 1. Ed. Paul Rabinow. New York: The New York Press. 135–40. Print.

———. *The History of Sexuality Volume 1: An Introduction*. Trans. by Robert Hurley. New York: Vintage Books, 1990. Print.

Reed, Brian, narrator. *S-Town*, iTunes app, 28 Mar. 2017.

Roach, Tom. *Friendship as a Way of Life: Foucault, AIDS, and the Politics of Shared Estrangement*. Albany: State University of New York Press, 2012. Print.

Robillard, Amy E. "Shame and the Personal Essay." *JAC: Journal of Advanced Composition* 28.3–4 (2008): 713–26. Print.

Romano, Aja. "S-Town is a Stunning Podcast. It Probably Shouldn't have been Made." *Vox.com*. 1 Apr. 2017. Web. 29 May 2018. https://www.vox.com/culture/2017/3/30/15084224/s-town-review-controversial-podcast-privacy

"Wikipedia: S-Town." Wikipedia.com. Wikipedia. 27 May 2018. Web. 29 May 2018.

11. *Narrating Depression*

Amy E. Robillard[1]

A depression is literally a hole, an absence created by the pressure of another force pushing down, displacing what was once there, leaving in its place an emptiness.

Depression is also a force strong enough to accomplish this displacement.

It is a Monday and I am on campus only to meet with the two graduate students in the independent study I am directing on trauma theory. I am dressed down, not planning to see anybody else, deep in the throes of a depression that has been having its way with me for weeks now. Unbidden, images arrive in my head of me lying on the sidewalk and never getting up. Unbidden, images arrive in my head of me shooting myself. My husband tells me that he has not experienced such images arriving for him. "Do you ever just *see* images of yourself shooting yourself?" I had asked him. And then, when he said no, I wanted to take it back. Me neither, I wanted to say.

I hadn't planned to go anywhere on campus except my office, but then I needed something upstairs from the department office so, with ten minutes to spare before the graduate students arrived, I slowly walked upstairs and down the long hallway.

I am a good teacher. When I run into them, students are generally happy to see me. I am generally happy to see them. On this day, a day in the middle of the worst depression I had experienced since my early twenties, I ran into a former student on my way to the department office. The day I had planned on seeing nobody other than my two graduate students. "Hi, Dr. Robillard! How are you?" She was just so happy. And I had no filter. And I could feel my lack of filter even as the words came of my mouth.

"Ready to shoot myself in the head. And you?"

Depression is a force strong enough to displace whatever else was once in the spot it now needs itself to be. Depression empties out space for itself. It doesn't care what it has to displace in order to do so. It does not care that it displaces nearly twenty years of teaching and caring. The thing about depression is that it just does not care.

*

This was the semester of Hurricane Harvey, of Hurricane Maria, of the horrifying mass shooting that left 58 people dead in Las Vegas, of the church shooting in Texas that killed 26 people. It was the semester during which I was teaching three courses and an independent study and my antidepressants were about to bottom out. That's how my doctor put it when I finally saw him. They bottomed out. Apt.

The independent study was on life writing and trauma theory and our primary question was about how an understanding of trauma theory might inflect our understanding of what it means to write a life. If, as trauma theory tells us, trauma renders experience unspeakable and unnarratable yet we feel, at the same time, an *urge* to tell, to try to make sense, how might we begin to reconcile the urge to narrate the unnarratable?

We met every other Monday in my office. It's a large office, big enough to hold a large upholstered chair and a loveseat, so we had plenty of space to spread out and discuss the readings. We'd usually begin by discussing the cultural traumas happening around us and by applying the readings we were working through—Cathy Caruth, Shoshana Felman, Dorothy Allison, Bessel van der Kolk, Susan Brison—to them. But on this Monday I began by telling Gina and Teigha that I would have to cut our two-hour meeting short. I had to go to my doctor to see about my meds because if I didn't I was afraid of what might happen to me. "It's not pretty right now." And I left it at that.

I didn't tell them—or at least I don't think I told them—about how often I wondered about the point of anything, about why I continued to teach students about writing and language and rhetoric when any of them could be shot while going out for a cup of coffee with a friend or going to a movie or even while worshipping in church. I didn't tell them about how I wondered constantly about how they would cope when they got to this point in middle age when, that future they've been thinking about and preparing and talking all their lives about having finally arrived, they hit a wall, the wall of what-the-fuck-now. Is *this* how I'm spending my life? Where is the big payoff I was promised? Where is the peace?

The depression made itself known slowly, and one of the ways it did this was with its displacement of the silly little songs I would make up about our dogs, Wrigley and Essay. The depression forced these songs out and in their place left nothing. No longer was I walking around the house singing about how short little Essay was or about how much we loved our little girl named Wiggles. No longer was I making up stories about them that always began with "once upon a time." Nothing replaced them. In place of these songs and stories was nothing.

For more than 20 years, I think I had forgotten what it felt like to feel deeply, clinically depressed. The only way I could describe it to my doctor that day was to say that I felt unmedicated. I hadn't felt this bad since my early twenties. To want to hold a gun to my head, to wonder at the point of going on, to feel so heavy, to just want to lie down but also to want to eat eat eat because who cares if I gain weight because nobody looks at me anyway and isn't it just about time for me to die already? I wondered at the point of writing anything because how many people read it anyway? While walking the dogs, all I wanted to do was lie down on the sidewalk for a rest. And maybe not get up.

The difference between 22-year-old me and 45-year-old me was that I now knew for a fact that people cared about me. Though I may not have *felt* it, I *knew* it and I also knew that I couldn't very well shoot myself in the head and hurt the ones who loved me.

When you're in a deep depression, nothing happens. It is the opposite of narrative. Nothing leads you from moment to moment except the ceaseless-ness of time passing. Because nothing happens, there's nothing to *tell*, except maybe what no longer happens. But when you're in it, you're too low to see that there are things the depression has displaced. You're too low to see that perhaps those things are up there on the surface, just sitting there, waiting for you to climb up and reclaim them. The nothingness of depression threatens, instead, to suffocate you.

*

Rebecca Solnit writes, "An illness is many kinds of rupture from which you have to stitch back a storyline of where you're headed and what it means. Every illness is narrative" (138). I was still functioning, though not as myself. I was certainly ill. I would have to somehow stitch back a storyline from nothing.

*

For the four hours or so each Tuesday and Thursday that I was in the classroom, I still mostly managed to function as myself, inhabiting my teacher persona in ways that, I think, didn't let on the extent to which I was in the grips of a debilitating depression. I still taught lessons effectively, still connected with students in the ways I always had, still used persuasive rhetorical examples from current events, and still returned their written work quickly so they knew how they were doing in class. It was almost as though, for those few hours, I was okay. I could think about something other than nothing.

*

When I teach the undergraduate course on rhetoric, I introduce students to the concept of gaslighting on the day we discuss ethos for the first time. Having talked about how ethos is concerned with appeals to a rhetor's credibility, I save ten minutes at the end of class to talk with students about gaslighting as an abusive process in which one party seeks to destroy the credibility and standing of another, not just in the eyes of others, but in her very own eyes. In other words, gaslighting aims to persuade the target, or gaslightee, that she herself has no credibility, or standing to make claims. As Kate Abramson explains in her article, "Turning Up the Lights on Gaslighting,"

> The central desire or aim of the gaslighter, to put it sharply, is to destroy even the possibility of disagreement—to have his sense of the world not merely confirmed, but placed beyond dispute. And the only sure way to accomplish this is for there to be no source of possible disagreement—no independent, separate, deliberative perspective from which disagreement might arise. So he gaslights: he aims to destroy the possibility of disagreement by so radically undermining another person that she has nowhere left to stand from which to disagree, no standpoint from which her words might constitute genuine disagreement. (10)

I tell students that I want them to understand gaslighting as the erasure of reality, the destruction of a person's understanding of what is real, while rhetoric is a contest for what is real, and that contest has become particularly vicious in the era of Trump.

In Fall 2017, a couple weeks after I introduced the concept, an honors student named Stephanie Hedgespeth visited my office hours to talk with me about writing her honors project for the course on gaslighting. She was intrigued by the concept, she told me, because she believed that she was a victim of gaslighting herself. She told me a detailed story about her boyfriend cheating on her and then convincing her that she was wrong when she caught him lying about it, and in that moment all I wanted to do was scream. She was still with him. He was gaslighting her and she was still with him and she wanted my advice on how to write a paper about the rhetorical work of gaslighting and all I wanted to do was persuade her to dump the bastard. I took a deep breath while she asked me if she should write about her own experience as she analyzed the work of gaslighting or if she should just do a rhetorical analysis of the articles she'd brought with her (one of which was Abramson's). I sat back in my chair. I sat forward in my chair. I put my head in my hands. I took another deep breath.

"You're still with him?" I asked softly.

"Yeah. I know. It's not great."

"Okay. I'm not going to tell you whether to write about your own experience because you might begin to do that and find that it's too hard. I don't want you to feel like you have to, so I'm going to leave that up to you. Whichever way you decide to go with this project will be great. You'll learn a lot either way."

Stephanie is nodding. She's gathering up her articles and her notebook. She's telling me more about her boyfriend, about the ways he lied to her not very long ago, trying to persuade her that she was wrong about what she knew to be true and about how she sees it now. All I want to do is tell her to get rid of him. But I can't. That's not my job. My job is to help her with this honors project, so I reiterate what I've already said about it being her choice about whether to include her own experience in her paper.

I am familiar enough with the argument in composition studies against teaching personal writing that we shouldn't do so because we are not therapists. And I recognized, in that moment, that this is probably the kind of thing teachers who don't teach personal writing are wary of. But Stephanie hadn't written anything yet. And I wasn't playing therapist—though every fiber in my being wanted to tell her to break up with him in that moment, even if I had, anybody who has been to a good therapist knows that even that's not a therapist's job. No. What I was doing was listening to her story, considering what it meant for her project, and advising her on how to move ahead with that project.

Even as I was in the middle of the deepest depression I'd been in since my early twenties.

*

What was, perhaps, most terrifying about this depression was that I didn't want to write. What *could* I write? Nothing was happening to me. There was nothing to say. I was stuck in a hole, aspects of my life that I loved had been displaced, and I kept thinking about my dead mother. She had suffered so many all-consuming losses in her life, some of which I learned about only after she began her descent into dementia—another illness we understand conceptually as something into which we descend, the difference being that we do not have the language for climbing out of a dementia. It is only a continuous descent. I thought about my mother's depression, about the fact that she had never been to therapy or been medicated, about the fact that for more than twenty years I had lost touch with what it *felt like* to be deep in despair, to be uninterested in anything, to just not care. I had identified with depression because I'd been on antidepressants since I was 22, and I'd experienced mild depression from time to time, but if I was being honest with myself, I would have to say that I had forgotten what this felt like. I had forgotten what *nothing* felt like. And if my mother had felt this way for most of her life, well, I had not nearly given her the credit she deserved for sharing with me her louder-than-life laugh and her beautiful love for animals.

Because all I wanted was for it all to end. Everything. All of it. But there was another part of me, the part interested in self-preservation, that knew I couldn't let it. That part of me called my doctor's office and made the appointment for that Monday afternoon when he told me my meds had bottomed out. I told him I didn't have the words for how I felt except to say that I was angry all the time at the same time that I was about to fall to pieces at the same time that I didn't care about a goddamn thing. I couldn't think of a single thing that would make me happy. The image of the sidewalk kept coming back to me. "When I walk the dogs, I look down at the sidewalk and I just want to lie down and not get back up," I told him.

I did not tell him that I kept dreaming that I had to kill my dead mother.

"Your meds have bottomed out. They've stopped working. This happens," he assured me.

*

David Plunker's *New Yorker* cover, "One Day in a Nation of Guns," features 58 bullets against a red background, each bullet labeled with the name of a person who died at the hands of Stephen Paddock at an outdoor country music festival in Las Vegas on October 1, 2017. In my senior seminar I had interrupted the scheduled readings to set aside a week to talk about issues surrounding mass shootings, and I brought in this cover. When I asked students to interpret it, most saw it as a way of memorializing the victims of the shooting. Some said that it personalizes the issue, giving us a way to understand that these were real people who died, because most of us know people with the same names as those who died. Yes, I said. These are smart interpretations. But I want to push it further. "For me this cover suggests that there is a bullet out there with every one of our names on it."

The class was completely silent for a good two minutes.

Depression is a force with the power to displace pedagogical judgment with *nothing*.

*

I didn't tell my doctor that I kept dreaming about having to kill my dead mother. I told my students that I understood the *New Yorker* cover to be suggesting that there is a bullet out there with each of our names on it. I told a student in the hallway that I felt like shooting myself in the head. Depression muddles. It renders all situations arhetorical in ways that seem, at the time, inherently inconsequential. *Nothing* seems consequential, and rhetoric, by its very definition, is about consequence, about the effects of language in the world, but during this time I felt that nothing I said or did mattered and, therefore, audience, Kairos, the persuasive appeals—none of them lined up. Language did not travel in meaningful directions. I hurt people.

*

I do not remember how it felt to be 22 and deeply, clinically depressed, but I do remember the radical change that came over me when I first went on antidepressants. I was standing in line at the dry cleaners. The people in front of me were taking a very long time and I could *feel* the change in me as I realized that the old version of me would have been so very frustrated but all I felt was calm. I felt serene. I felt good with everything. When the man behind the counter apologized to me for the long wait, I told him it was no problem. I remember feeling like my body had been *infused with love*.

We *fall* into a depression slowly, but how do we climb out? Does it happen all at once? Or do we just notice it all at once?

Daphne Merkin writes in her memoir, *This Close to Happy*, that the subject of depression often brings out the partisan in people, "leading them to diehard positions, to swear for or against it as a real disease, for or against medication" (126). She writes that the stigma that surrounds depression persists in part because there is so much *nothing* there to point to. "If there is something intangible about mental illness generally, depression is all the harder to define because it tends to creep in rather than announce itself, manifesting itself as an absence—of appetite, energy, sociability—rather than as a presence. There is little you can point to: no obscene rantings, no sudden flips into unrecognizable, hyper-energized behavior, no magical belief systems involving lottery numbers or fortune cookies. It seems to me that we are suspicious of depression's claim to legitimacy because it doesn't *look* crazy" (16). If anything, what is noticeable in people who are depressed is the *difference* between the depressed versions of them and the newly medicated, suddenly energetic, infused-with-love versions of them. Depression displaces the valuable things in your life ever so slowly, so slowly that you sometimes don't even realize they're gone. The change registers only when the energy is suddenly *back*.

In the midst of my depression in the fall, as my doctor was tinkering with different medications, contacting my insurance company for me, writing to me through the practice's portal, and calling me directly once or twice, it occurred to me that there were minutes in his day during which he sat and thought carefully about what I needed. This realization made me weep. My doctor was trying to make me feel better and he had the tools he needed to do so. Though I was 45 years old and I knew, intellectually, that I was worthy of his care, I could not summon the confidence to feel that it was true. I did not feel worthy. His care made me weep because depression had displaced my ability to believe that my life was valuable.

Depression displaces, but it also steals. It doesn't just push things out of the way, up to the surface where we cannot see or grasp them. It hides them greedily in its pockets and walks away from us when we need those things most. We're left, at best, with their husks.

*

I hadn't felt so empty since I was 21 or 22, living in Alaska with my sister and her family, working at a law firm full-time, writing play reviews for an alternative weekly newspaper, and dating a man 13 years my senior. In the winter the days were short and terribly cold; the sun set near 3:00 and the cold air froze the snot in your nose the minute you walked outside. I sat in the car one evening while my sister ran in to the grocery store. As I watched the people go in to the store with their small children in tow wearing their bulky coats and their winter boots and as I watched the people walking out with their jugs of orange juice and milk and their plastic bags filled with loaves of bread and cartons of eggs, all I could wonder was how they managed to bother. How could they do this day in and day out? What was the point? I said as much to Sue when she got back to the car. She responded in a perfectly reasonable way, saying something about how this is what people did. "I think I'm really depressed," I responded.

*

The details of the different medications I tried until we found one that worked aren't interesting enough to relay here; suffice to say that Latuda was not the first medication I tried, and it wasn't my doctor's first choice for me, but after about three days on it, I felt that feeling again. I felt like I had been *infused with love.*

I loved everyone and every single thing about the life I lived. It was Christmas time and as I watched my husband roll oatmeal chocolate chip cookie dough into balls and place them on the cookie sheet, it was all I could do not to bust open with love for him. On the morning walk with the dogs, everybody had their garbage and recycling barrels out, and it occurred to me that, in all the years that I'd given goodies to the veterinarian and the mail carrier, I had never once prepared tins of treats for the people who collect the garbage and recycling. So I ran into the house, prepared gift bags of baked goods, wrote signs on bright green cardstock saying "Wait! Stop! Merry Christmas!" and set them atop the barrels for the city workers. I wanted everyone to feel as good as I did and I wondered about the *non*-transmissibility of affect. I wondered how I could get others to feel the way I felt in these moments.

I wonder, now, thinking back on my desire to share this feeling with others, if there isn't a way in which depression does such a hack job on us that, when it finally lifts—or when we finally climb out of that hole—we feel, on some level, that we need to show that we deserve to feel this good. I promise I'll be good!

I had no negative thoughts. It was as though somebody had taken an eraser to the part of my brain that harbored any thoughts of self-loathing, any thoughts that I wasn't good enough or smart enough or pretty enough or thin enough or *anything* enough and just wiped and wiped and wiped. They were all gone.

I had one fear, though, and that was that this feeling would somehow go away, that it would be taken from me.

And then, once my samples were nearly gone, my insurance company refused to pay for it.

My doctor told me, when he saw the medicated me, that he thought I was finally the person I was always meant to be. That we had finally found the exact combination of meds that worked to bring out the best in me.

And my insurance company refused to pay for this very expensive drug.

I joked with my therapist that I now understood why drug addicts went to the extremes they did to get the fix they so desperately needed. Except I'm not so sure it was a joke.

Depression doesn't just displace everything in one's life that once held meaning. Depression doesn't just steal those things from us when we need them most. Depression gaslights us, presenting us one reality only, a reality in which there is no narrative. Depression gaslights us into believing that this world of nothing—no feeling, no motivation, no meaning—is all there is and nothing will ever change that.

What is present now—*nothing*—is what the future holds. Nothing will follow from nothing. Your story will not progress, depression tells you.

Nobody will ever love you the way I do.

*

I hadn't heard much more from Stephanie as she worked on her honors project on gaslighting. I knew that she would come to me if she had questions, so I just assumed that she was doing fine.

In late November, she turned in her project at the end of class and I put it in my school bag without looking at it. Later, in my office over lunch, I took it out and as I read the first sentence, my heart soared. "On October

30th, 2017, I made one of the most difficult decisions of my life, ending my relationship of six years."

She had done it! She had gotten rid of the bastard! I probably let out a deep sigh of relief. I couldn't help but read her entire paper right then and there. Stephanie writes, "it is very difficult for a gaslightee to realize that they are being psychologically manipulated and abused. From my experience, I found it much more appealing to buy into the possibility of my own insanity than to consider the reality of my boyfriend's infidelity and dishonesty" (3). Stephanie also offers a terrific explanation of the psychology of gaslighting (citations are from Abramson):

> Because of this persistent desire to keep the relationship intact, many gaslighting victims begin to accept the idea that they may be as "crazy" as their partner insists. In situations where a person suspects that her husband or significant other is cheating on her, there is often no way to "prove" that an event occurred without outside corroboration (7). This inability to prove their own perspective to be true leaves the gaslightee feeling frustrated and hopeless, causing them to begin to doubt the reliability of their own perception. This confusion is heightened because "the only other person/s who could validate what they are hearing or seeing will not confirm their auditory/visual perceptions" (7). This is problematic because it does not allow for the gaslightee to begin grieving the inevitable loss of the relationship; rather the anxiety and denial causes the gaslightee to cling tighter to the relationship and to their unfaithful partner. Unfortunately, this instinct to salvage the relationship at all costs often comes at a high price: "gaslighted women have not only their wills, but their affective dispositions and even sometimes their character turned against them for their own destruction" (Abramson 16). Not only does the gaslighter "get away with" their infidelity, but they also steal their victim's sense of self, their entire ability to form a reasonable argument, and their independent perspective altogether. (4)

Gaslighting distorts reality, offering only the gaslighter's perspective, as the target's perspective is slowly destroyed.

Stephanie doesn't say how she found the strength to get out of the toxic relationship, only that she does. "Finally, I can say that I value my own sanity and my own worth more than the 'love' and affection of the person who caused me pain" (15). Perhaps it was studying gaslighting itself that helped her to realize that she was not alone, that her boyfriend's destruction of her reality was not normal, and that she could find a way out.

*

When you have felt as good as you have ever felt in your life, when you have felt so good that you want everyone you love to feel as good as you do, when you have felt so good that the grudges you once held simply fall away, it's easy to believe your doctor when he tells you that you're the person you were always meant to be. This is a reality worth believing in. Where before there was no narrative—there was just *nothing*—here, now, with this new medication, I not only had feeling back, but I had this new narrative of being the person I'd always been meant to be. I clung to it.

Even as trauma still rages around you, as mass shootings still take place regularly, as Trump gaslights the country daily, as natural disasters displace and kill people regularly, you still see the world differently. These are traumas that somehow don't manage to take you down with them.

I wrote earlier that depression gaslights, but I don't think that's quite true because to suggest that depression gaslights is to suggest that while you're in it, the perspective you're seeing from is distorted, less than real. But it is nothing *but* real. It's as real as it gets, and when you're seeing from it, it seems as though you will never see from a different perspective. Rather, depression is the feeling of everything being pointless, of it all being for nothing, of laboring and laboring—for even the smallest act takes an extreme expenditure of energy—for what in the end seems meaningless. Depression is a weight that pushes you down. It is the force that creates the literal hole from which it gets its name.

I wonder if, in comparing depression to gaslighting, I am doing work similar to what Stephanie did as she worked through her own experience of gaslighting with her boyfriend. She knew that something was wrong, and she recognized her experience in the concept of gaslighting. Though she does a thorough job articulating what gaslighting is and the ways in which she was gaslighted, she doesn't narrate how she managed to extricate herself from the relationship, only that she does. This isn't a criticism of her work; instead, it is a commentary on the ways we write on the edges of what we know. As I directed an independent study with two graduate students on the relationship between trauma and life writing while I was experiencing debilitating depression, I tried on a narrative of depression as gaslighting because I, too, was working at the edges of what I knew. This is what we do to try to climb out. This is what we do to try to name what is happening to us: we make approximate comparisons between what we do understand and what is blurry and unformed in our experience and we sometimes overreach.

We can know our experience only in retrospect. We can look back on what happened to us and say: this happened and then this happened and then this happened, and this is how I make sense of it. *When* it is happening to us, it is chaos. When we are in the pit of depression, there is nothing to lead us to believe that we will ever climb out. I wrote earlier that depression displaced the silly little songs I would sing to Wrigley and Essay. I didn't realize at the time that those songs had gone missing. I only realized after the fact, once the medication had kicked in and the songs came back, that they had been missing. Oh! But when you're in that pit, you don't know. It's only in looking back that you can see that they're gone. True, too, is that when the medication kicked in and I started to feel better, I got frustrated with some small household chore and I jokingly said to my husband, "Well, this makes me want to shoot myself," and I realized, only in that moment, that it had been weeks since I had said such a thing in earnest.

In her stunning essay, "Learning How to Tell," Lisa Schnell writes about the relationship between narrative and loss—"in fact, the plot of every novel…is in some significant way a story of loss" (277). Narrative, it seems, is a place "where things only ever go missing." Schnell continues: "Planting our narrative flags in its hospitable soil and claiming a piece of its ground as our own, though perhaps ultimately a futile gesture, is nonetheless what we must do to survive the pain of this life" (277). Narrating depression is nearly impossible while you're in it, as depression itself squashes our ability to tell. It squashes it, flattens it, even erases it, until we are left with nearly nothing. But it is still what we must do to survive the pain of this life. Even if it sometimes feels like we're telling a story of nothing, we need to tell. We need to learn how to tell. We need to resist the inner voices telling us that nobody is listening. We must do this work of narrating the loss that is depression; as Kathryn Schulz writes in her beautiful essay, "When Things Go Missing," "When we are experiencing it, loss often feels like an anomaly, a disruption in the usual order of things. In fact, though, it *is* the usual order of things."

The danger of such narration is this: Even what I've written in these pages strains toward a linear representation. I was ill and now I am better. But of course it is never that simple. I was ill and then I felt better and things I had lost came back to me and I lost other things and I will be ill again and I will struggle to narrate those experiences. "Entropy, mortality, extinction: the entire plan of the universe consists of losing, and life amounts to a reverse savings account in which we are eventually robbed of everything," Schulz writes.

There have been many times in my life when I believed that nobody else suffered the way I did, that nobody else felt so much nothing. I now know that this belief is defenseless, but I know this only because others shared their experiences in writing. Though that belief has gone missing, it returns every now and then, for what seems like no reason, alongside depression to persuade me that nothing I will ever do or say or think has any meaning at all. It pushes me down. It wants me to remain quiet. It wants nothing more than to silence me. If I lose my voice, I lose everything.

Note

1. Amy E. Robillard, Professor of Composition and Rhetoric, Illinois State University. aerobil@ilstu.edu

References

Abramson, Kate. "Turning Up the Lights on Gaslighting." *Philosophical Perspectives* 28.1 (2014): 1–30.

Hedgespeth, Stephanie. *Confessions and Revelations of a Gaslightee.* Normal: Illinois State University, 2017.

Merkin, Daphne. *This Close to Happy: A Reckoning with Depression.* New York: Farrar, Straus and Giroux, 2017.

Schnell, Lisa Jane. "Learning How to Tell." *Literature and Medicine* 23.2 (2004): 265–79.

Schulz, Kathryn. "When Things Go Missing." *The New Yorker.* 13 & 20 February 2017. https://www.newyorker.com/magazine/2017/02/13/when-things-go-missing

Solnit, Rebecca. *The Faraway Nearby.* New York: Viking, 2013.

12. Telling Other Stories: Some Musings on Rhetorics of Identity and Time in Memoir

LAURA GRAY-ROSENDALE[1]

We arrive at 6:15 a.m. in the ice cold, pitchy black, only a smattering of stars breaking through. We wait quietly in the dimly lit hallway, stripped of our boots, thick socks. As we enter the space, we are each handed a lit candle, our little bits of light in a new dark. Carefully we put away our coats, hats, and mittens. Silently we unfurl our mats, set the candles down in front of us, and collect our props. I sit on my mat, fold in on myself, forming a seed-like child's pose, then stretch my back and arms out long. I can feel my vertebrae unkinking from the night's sleep, my arm muscles growing taut, my bones straight and aligned above my head, my chest broad and expansive. I close my eyes. I breathe in through my nose, out through my nose. I feel the warmth of other bodies moving around me, settling in, and beginning to steady their breaths. We have all come here for one reason, the reason we wake up this early all year long, to take a big pause, to renew ourselves, to rededicate ourselves to a practice that gives to us, helps us to be our best selves, enables us to live lives in which we can be a little better at giving to others.

I open my eyes, sit up. Illuminated by our candles, our teacher moves to the front of the room, sits cross-legged, her back straight and long. In a soft voice, she reminds us. This is our Winter Solstice practice. It is the very longest darkness of the year. We need not fear this darkness. It is something to be grateful for, a moment to take stock, to recognize once again that out of darkness comes light. I come to a cross-legged position, sitting on a folded blanket. I breathe in. I breathe out. And in the dark, early morning silence, I settle into a place inside myself that is always there beneath the surface—a joyfulness, an unending. Right here.

Right now. There is only this immediate present. What has passed melts away. What awaits is but glimmery hope.[2]

*

A few years ago, I published a memoir about a stranger sexual assault that happened to me while I attended university titled *College Girl*. Right after it came out, sexual assault became a very visible issue in the national conversation and on university campuses. I found myself traveling around the country giving talks about it, offering readings from my book. It described a set of experiences that had been formative in my identity, had radically changed how I looked at the power of rhetoric and its relationship to the world. The story was, of course, true. It also had a natural plot trajectory, a structure that made sense, real characters who were vibrant. I wrote it in large part because many of our students who have experienced sexual assault don't have a lot of professors who publically identify themselves as survivors and who are now on the other side of those experiences. It was very important to me that I do so. I wanted them to understand that they are not alone, that they could find a way through. As a person and as a writer, I also needed to tell that story at that time in my life and in those specific ways.

I have always known that I would write that book. Though at many moments I was not sure *how* I would write it as trauma itself often resists our abilities to represent it in narrative, I have always known exactly *why* and *for whom* I would write that book.

But when I began writing pieces of that book many years ago—sketchy drafts of pieces were composed as early as in my late twenties—I never expected that several other crucial, difficult events would occur in my life. I have scribbled words about these events in journals. I have typed language about them in documents no one else has ever seen. And sometimes these events have suggested themselves as subjects I should write about for some audience other than myself. However, I have never been quite sure how or even why to write about them for a larger audience. And, until now, until well after the publication of my memoir *College Girl*, I have never chosen to do so.

This essay tells pieces of these unpublished stories. Interspersed are other very recent moments captured, snapshots of movement, bliss, and joy, also part of the life I am living. They are meant to both speak with and across those other pieces. Along the way, I also theorize about the complex nature of the memoir genre, about identity itself, about why we necessarily need to share certain identities at certain moments, in certain ways, and in certain contexts, and other identities at other moments, in other ways, and in other contexts—and the potential effects of doing so. What is the nature of writing about traumatic experiences? As Leigh Gilmore argues so eloquently in *The*

Limits of Autobiography: Trauma and Testimony, "language is asserted as that which can realize trauma even as it is theorized as that which fails in the face of trauma," or writing about trauma raises the "impossible injunction to tell what cannot ... be spoken" (7). How does one write about that which defies being put into language somehow, that which resists being written? And, is it different when we are dealing with a physical and psychological trauma like sexual violence that—in my case—may be well in the past, time- and space-bounded, rather than those events that are closer in time or still ongoing within the present? When do we reveal various parts of ourselves to various audiences and with what potential costs and benefits? I also write about how these experiences continue to shape me as a person. And, finally, I describe how they impact the ways in which I teach the rhetoric of memoir.

*

It's been the mildest of winters in Flagstaff. It's a morning in early January and we just got our first snow. I get up at 4:30 a.m. like an itchy-excited child on Christmas morning. I pull on my snow boots, my thick furry hat, my big black gloves, and sky blue down jacket. In the deep black, flashlight in hand, I hit the trail. I cannot see very far in front of me, just enough to make out one other set of track marks in the snow, a rabbit's. The trees are caked with a thick powder, branches weighed down spring up, give way, send a shooting cold down on my head, the back of my neck. I giggle. The sky begins to light up as I climb higher on the trail, the dense, dark blue giving way to a peep of yellow, then drifts of pink and orange. But it is still dark amongst the trees where I walk. I top out on the Pipeline Trail. I can just make out movement to the left of the trail in the trees. A herd of over twenty female elk and their babies stand in amongst the trunks. They watch me. I watch them. They watch me watching them watching me. No one moves for what feels like a long, long time. I hear my voice speak. "Good morning to you all!" My face is hurting from smiling so hard. By the time I say goodbye to them, the sun is coming up in earnest. I round the bend, pass by houses, greet the barking dogs in the long back yard, make my way home.

*

Something strikes me as I begin to tell this story. Part of me is afraid to write it down, as if writing about it could somehow make the past present again. I was 34 years old, right before my 35th birthday. My husband (also an English Professor) and I were just about ready to head out on our first sabbatical—to take a camping trip to Alaska, read and write along the way. The kid question was still out there for us at that point. Would we or wouldn't we?

I was in the shower. And then I felt it. It was a tiny little pebble underneath my right breast. I asked myself. Was I feeling what I thought I was feeling? I came out of the shower and showed my husband. He felt it. It was probably nothing, we both agreed. But I should get it checked out just to be sure. I went to a surgeon. It was determined that they had to go in and see what this thing was, take a sample. I can remember that snowy world, coming out of anesthesia. "It doesn't look like anything," the kind, white-haired surgeon leaned over and said to me. "But we will run pathology just to be sure."

I was at work. It was June. My breast hurt a bit from the surgery. As usual, I was running the STAR (Successful Transition and Academic Readiness) Writing Program. As usual, I had taken the one car we owned to work that day. As usual, I was grading in my office. There was a knock on my door. I opened it. There stood my husband, his face looking strangely ashen and something else. Tear-streaked. "What are you doing here? How did you get here?" He had taken a bus, he said. He had needed to get here right away, he said. "Sit," he said. "Sit." "Why? What?" I said. He didn't know how to tell me what he had to tell me. How does anyone know how to say such a thing to another person? "The surgeon's office called. You have it," he said through sobs. "It's cancer."

"No," I said. "No, damn it." My wail shot through to my core. Cancer meant death to me. How long would I have? And, then, just like that I knew what I had to do. I had to get out of there. Right then. I had to move. He could read my mind. Somehow he's always been able to do this. "Do you want to go up to the mountains?" he asked. "Yes," I said. "The mountains." And he drove us down the highway and up the steep Snowbowl Road to the Kachina Trail. I don't know what we said to each other on that drive. It's a haze. But when we got there it was all high ferns, silvery aspen trunks. The heels of my shoes kept poking into the earth as we walked, my legs wobbling so badly that at moments I could barely stand. Slowly he unpacked it for me. I had breast cancer. It was an aggressive kind. I would have to have surgery to check whether it had spread to my lymph nodes. I would have to have chemotherapy to kill those rapidly dividing cells.

We put our sabbatical on hold. For a while the news was bad and just kept getting worse. It was not only aggressive. It had some characteristics associated with a far poorer prognosis. The researcher that he is, my husband read and read and read. He condensed and deciphered medical articles for me, constantly sharing what he had learned. I had choices to make in consultation with my very smart, tremendously supportive oncologist. While it had not yet spread to my lymph nodes, they had found evidence of it in my lymphatic vessels. Would I have a lumpectomy? Would I have a mastectomy? Would I have a double mastectomy? If I got a mastectomy, did I want reconstruction? I had real trouble imagining myself without breasts for a while. But having a double mastectomy would make the chances of my cancer coming back far, far less than any other choice I could make. I had to look into it.

I can recall going to the plastic surgeon's office. He pulled out a big book of boob pictures. This was his work, he said. These were examples of what he could do with reconstruction. Some of the pictures of the breasts with place-holding expanders in them were strange, clownlike. But the finished products with implants were not that bad, I began to think. I would have scars forever. But he could make me look sort of like myself again. I made a decision that much of my family did not understand, many of my friends did not understand. I chose the most drastic option in order to save my life. My husband and oncologist stood by my decision. What I wanted to do should be done.

I woke up in a hospital room filled with flowers. My chest was wrapped up in thick bandages. I had trouble comprehending what might be underneath there, though on some level even in the twilight caused by morphine, I knew. My breasts were gone. There were drains implanted to take the blood and other fluids away. Expanders had been put in under the skin in their place. The expanders would be filled a little bit every few weeks to get my body ready for the implants. The surgeon had also put a port into my chest so that they could administer the chemotherapy drugs more easily.

I had had long hair for many years. I knew it was all going to fall out. So, I went to a hairdresser and asked for a short cut. What she gave me was long in the front, short in the back. I didn't look like myself to myself. But I knew that it was a step along the way, a step I had to take. In time, after all of the vomiting from the first chemo and the first clumps of hair came out in the shower, we would shave it off, my brother the pathologist and my husband the professor, both teary, taking turns until all that was left was tiny stubble. I looked ridiculous to myself. My face was tan from the summer sun. My scalp was bright white.

I was stripped of my hair, my breasts. I was filled with expanders and ports. I would throw up almost anything I ate in the days following chemo. My weight hovered around 88 pounds. In many ways, I felt like a skinny, spewing monster. But every morning I would go upstairs to my office and look at the wall where I had placed the cards everyone had sent me, where I put inspiring quotes meant to see me through. I would tell myself that I could do this thing. I would tell myself to just put one foot in front of the other. And that I did. During my chemotherapy, we hiked and camped as much as we could with our dog, Max. Even when my feet were covered with thick blisters and bleeding from the chemo, I had to walk. Movement gave me solace. Movement told me that I was still alive.

I would continue my course of chemotherapy, driving each time down through the red rock beauty of Sedona with my husband. By the end I had no eyelashes. By the end I had no eyebrows. I looked stranger still to myself then. It was winter and I wore lots of hats. They could cover my bald head. But nothing could disguise these changes to my face that made me look truly sick, alien. Time passed. My last chemotherapy came and went. I had the surgery to put in the implants. And slowly the hair began to grow back—curlier and darker than before. I can recall hiking in Buffalo Park with one of my girlfriends. "Love your hair," a woman said as she passed us. "I wish I had your guts." I smiled and laughed. My guts, I thought. Chemo chic, I thought.

The next year would be spent on sabbatical, driving up to Alaska and then back down to the desert in Arizona, living in our new camper that we splurged on just for this occasion. How long of a life would we have together anyway? Why not spend the money? And the hair continued to grow back. It was a funny, brushy mess. But still. It was hair.

I would get genetic testing and learn that I had an abnormal BRCA gene, but that its abnormality was not deemed to be "significant." I would talk with other oncologists. I would learn that getting a hysterectomy would shut down the estrogen that could feed my breast cancer. The kid question would be answered for us. In the next few years a drug would come on the market for people whose tumors had markers like mine, Herceptin. I would be able to go to my oncologist to get infusions. And these infusions would make my prognosis even better. Over time, my visits to my oncologist became fewer and fewer. Three months changed into six months. More time passed. Before I knew it, I was five years out. Then ten. Now fifteen. I am a breast cancer survivor who has lived years beyond her cancer.

My hope, of course, is that it is long gone, that I will never have to face breast cancer again. But I don't know the future. It could come back. If it does, it will likely have spread to other organs, found other places to live. In short, the story of breast cancer, another story of psychological and physical traumas, may not be over for me. This is part of why I have found it hard to publish anything about this until now and why I have yet to write any memoir about these experiences. I find it hard to gather the words to tell the story. I find it hard to locate the language. And, part of me wonders this, too. If I share these identities with you now—the cancer ones—will I bring them back with me into the here and now? Will I ever rid myself of them, really?

When I think about writing the story of my breast cancer for a larger audience, many things occur to me. I feel the pull of all of those other narratives about breast cancer that are out there—especially the breast cancer memoir narratives with the sickly-sweet happy endings, the ones with the terribly tragic endings too. I feel the pull of the massive cultural narratives around raising awareness, all of the pink ribbons, the pink Kitchenaid mixers, the pink everything else.

And I also wonder about other things as well. Can I write a story of my life—this breast cancer story—without knowing or, more important yet, trusting its tentative conclusion? It is also a kind of trauma that is closer to me in time than my sexual assault. That closeness in time can sometimes make it feel fresher, like a wound that has had less of a chance to begin scabbing over. It's harder somehow to write about these things. With sexual violence, experiences may come back to me as aftereffects in terms of my psyche such as with triggered PTSD symptoms. Experiences may come back to me in terms of my body as remembered sensations. Sexual violence exerts its power over its survivors for many years, certainly, and its effects are far-reaching and never ending. But, for me at this point, the events of sexual violence themselves are not ongoing and they are not recurring. In contrast, cancer is that monster that can lurk with its few cells left behind, beginning to divide again and again until it is once more ever present. The difference is that cancer may be undoing my body even as I write this. Unlike with sexual violence where I have a better sense of the events and their parameters, cancer recurrence is something about which I might have little knowledge and might be able to exert very minimal control.

What do I stand to lose in writing about this to an audience now? I fear that I might not get it as right as I want to, that language may fail me or that I may fail language. I fear that the identities I construct for you here—my selves—while seemingly in the past, could be returned to at any time. I fear that as much as I like to think that I have left cancer world, I have not really left it after all.

*

We are camping at McDowell Mountain Regional Park. We are avoiding the winter mud of Flagstaff, the cold temperatures. It's early morning, my favorite time of day. The desert is bone dry. The saguaro cacti look terribly thin. The jojoba plants are shriveled. I see one lone yellow brittle bush flower. The hedgehog and prickly pear cacti won't bloom until March, April. There has been so little rain this year. There have been sweeping fires in California. I give thanks that Arizona has not had those kind of fires, at least not yet. A howling starts up. I can hear the coyotes talking to each other across the desert, the pups yipping away, the adults all soulful sound. Noise reverberates through the canyons. Then the sounds die down. I walk on the Granite Trail, watching the clean gravel path beneath my feet, devoid of all mud, all snow. I make my way to the Wagner Trail, pass buckhorn cacti and lots of cholla cacti, throwing off little spiky baby plants. And

I wend my way back through the campground, back to our camper, back to the hot cup of coffee.

*

"How are you feeling?" she asked. "Fantastic," I said. "Any pains or aches?" "Not a one." "Do you have good energy?" "Yes. I exercise every day. I run. I lift weights. I do yoga. I hike." "You look really fit. That's great." She paused. "Hmm ... that's strange." "What?" "Well, you have a high platelet count," she told me. She glanced back through my records, flipping to some twelve years back. "It looks like you have always had a high platelet count." She stared at me with wide blue eyes. "I want to look into why that might be." I said that sounded good to me. She'd need to take a sample from my spine. "It might hurt for a while," she said. "That's totally fine," I said.

Several weeks later one of my girlfriends drove me down to my oncologist's office in Sedona. We talked the whole way down the switchbacks about the silliest things. I wasn't thinking about what was coming. When we got to my oncologist's office she had me lie down on my stomach. My friend sat in the room while my oncologist took that sample. My back throbbed. Then we drove back, talked the whole way up. Days passed. Things got busy. I forgot about the sample. I was in the middle of a university-level meeting. My phone buzzed. I saw that it was the oncologist's office. I said nothing, just quietly left the room. As I answered the phone, I plopped onto a couch in the main part of the student union. It seemed like she was talking really fast. I know that wasn't really how it was. The world just sped up for a moment.

"It's smoldering right now. It might not fully manifest itself for five years, if we are lucky. Maybe ten," she said. "Multiple what?" I said. "Myeloma. It's a cancer of the bones." She mentioned something about me having bad light chain ratios. I pictured chains of light pouring through my bones, sneaking out through the joints, seeping out of my skin. She said that she was so sorry. I told her it was okay. I wasn't sure why I said this thing. It was not okay. I was not okay. I got off the phone. I sat there for ten minutes, just sinking into that couch, as if it might swallow me whole. What on earth was happening? Could this really be true? Could I really have cancer again—this time a different cancer, a cancer I knew virtually nothing about? I called my husband and I told him. "My God," he said. "Come home," he said. I made my way to the car and I did just that. I drove home.

In the weeks to come my husband read everything he could find about multiple myeloma. He deciphered things for me. He shared what he'd learned. We discovered that it's usually diagnosed in people in their seventies. It is a cancer that lives in the bone marrow. We learned that, over time, it can cause severe bone pain, bone fractures, deterioration of the bones entirely.

And then something made sense. I had once heard a woman at the oncology center say, talking about her parents' multiple myeloma, "In the end, they were just bean bags. I had to carry them around with me everywhere." My future—a human bean bag. My future—high dose chemotherapy and stem cell transplants. There was a specialist in multiple myeloma at the Mayo Clinic in Scottsdale, my oncologist told us. He worked with patients who were younger, like myself. We should go to see him.

I remember thinking about the money quite a bit. This wasn't covered under my medical insurance. I knew we'd have to pay a lot to see this man. Still, we knew we had to do it. He had a good energy about him—very positive, optimistic. He ran through much of what we knew already about the disease, cementing in our minds what could happen in the future, pointing out that as long as I was "smoldering," there would be no need for treatment. Just eat well. Rest. Exercise. "Go out and live your life!" he announced, smiling. "Can I still run?" "Yes." "Can I still lift weights?" "You should." He sent us on our way, noting that my oncologist in Sedona could be my primary oncologist unless my blood levels changed.

So now, every three months I get my blood tested. They take five vials. Their main objective is to check to see whether my light chains—these are in fact proteins made by plasma cells—have changed in terms of their ratios. It's been over two years. So far, the changes have been within normal parameters. If that shifts, however, I'll enter back into cancer world again. So, I do everything I love while I can—the running, the hiking, the weight lifting, the yoga. I may have years stretching ahead of me before my life changes drastically again. I may have months.

This more recent cancer is even harder to write about, I find. Writing a full memoir about it would be strange, feel like little parts strung together. There would likely be holes, a series of incomplete images. It's not in the recent past, in danger of returning. It's my here and now—my every day. It's my present condition. This cancer is like a wound whose dimensions I cannot even see fully yet, do not yet understand. In many ways, it's a story of psychological and physical traumas yet to come. So, I cannot know what all of the aspects of the story are. I don't see a plot trajectory or even a full list of characters in my mind. Most times I don't want to imagine a conclusion to this story since its end will likely occur with my own. In this case, unlike with breast cancer, I don't fear a return to earlier identities. I don't have that luxury. These identities, these selves, are with me right here, right now. I am a person living with cancer. I am not someone who survived it, who has moved on with her life. Instead, I am living in it and living with it. And not only do I feel like it's hard to locate the language to do the telling. I feel like the truth and the situation are changing, too, flipping and slipping in the midst of my very writing. What is true right now may not be true in quite the same ways just a short time from now.

*

The mud is gone. The forest floor is baking pine needles and packed earth. I'm wearing a T-shirt, a skort that has a special pocket for my phone. I put in my head phones. I set up the GPS on my phone to clock my mileage, my pace, my route. I turn on my electronica playlist. I walk a mile to warm up. It's straight uphill, so I don't mind the walking. When I reach the top of the hill, I suck some air deep into my lungs. I breathe out. And I begin. My gait is slow at first. There are many more hills to climb and these ones are for running. I wend my way through the scrub oaks, through the pines. I pick up my feet over rocks, over fallen branches. And I reach a crest. I stop. I turn around, look back at the winding trail, at all of the treetops moving softly in the breeze. And hot damn. I love where I've come from. I love where I am going.

*

I think about how my own experiences with writing memoir impact the ways in which I teach courses in the rhetoric of memoir at the undergraduate and graduate levels. I often begin with something like this premise from Mary Karr's *The Art of Memoir*, the notion that "memoir wrenches at your insides precisely because it makes you battle with your very self—your neat analyses and tidy excuses" (xxi).

I don't tell my students not to write about things that have recently happened to them or are happening to them so as to avoid this messiness. Instead, I prepare all of my students by encouraging them to find support along their journeys—from me, from family, from friends, from classmates, from counselors. They will need this help no matter when the events occurred. I tell them that those identities that they are trying to convey through language in their texts are necessarily also in-process and changing. For those of us who attempt memoir, we cannot fully represent our lives or ourselves as in any way a done thing. We may also not be able to fully take up residence yet within the selves that we create through our writing. When what's being depicted is in the present, we may also not yet feel like fully trustworthy narrators of our own experiences. Or, we may not yet be completely under the right conditions to do a more finalized telling. As I noted, from this close distance, it can be hard to make out the pieces, the right approaches to take.

This doesn't mean that we shouldn't try, however. If we want to, we absolutely should. But, as we do so, we need to come back to those questions I mentioned at the beginning of my essay about whether to write memoir as well as *how, why,* and *for whom*. In the case of my sexual violence narrative in

College Girl, for example, I asserted that while I did not know *how* to write the narrative, I did know *why* and *for whom.* Though it took some time for me to discover *how* to do it, since the other parts were in place, once I began to understand this, already knowing the other parts made it possible for me to begin to craft the narrative in a fuller form. However, in the case of my illness narratives, the *how* and the *why* still remain questions for me. As the *for whom* comes into greater focus, writing a memoir about those experiences for a larger audience may make more sense to me and the other pieces may also begin to fall into place. If I can wrap my mind around survivors of cancer and the general public as my audience for my story as well as my real reasons for wanting to reach them, the *how* to reach them question will likely become much, much clearer.

Only through beginning to write and think about such things even when we do not have all of the pieces figured out will we begin to sketch out the parameters of narrative and start to get a sense of the implications of such experiences on our lives. Only through doing this will we begin to see characters emerging. This is what Vivian Gornick in *The Situation and the Story: The Art of Personal Narrative* describes as "a mind puzzling its way out of its own shadows—moving from unearned certainty to thoughtful consideration to clarified self-knowledge" (36). This is writing to learn or discover at its very finest, I think. We need to test, to draft, to erase, to draft again. And, as I tell my students, whatever we produce as a final product is really just another rough draft. It's not the end all and be all. Instead, hopefully it's something we'll write now, set aside, and return to later.

Sven Birkerts' little book *The Art of Time in Memoir: Then, Again* always sticks with me when I think about elements of time and writing memoir. He notes that "the memoirist writes, above all else, to redeem experience, to reawaken the past, and to find its pattern; better yet, he writes to discover behind bygone events an explanatory narrative" (25). When the past is close by or the past is in fact quite present, it can be hard to see those patterns. It can be hard to make out the explanatory narratives. But it is often through writing that we can better come to understand what we are experiencing, its import, and our place within that story taking shape. And it is through looking at our pasts—even if they are extremely recent—that we can begin to imagine our possible futures.

It seems strange to write what I am about to write. After all, I've spent a lot of time in this essay describing my own experiences and writing about the genre of memoir itself. But, I don't know whether I'll ever publish a complete memoir about the pieces I've covered here. In these pages, I have begun to do some of the telling, begun to draft bits of my selves, begun to sketch out some characters, begun to lay down some plot points, begun to reflect a bit on what's occurred. Doing so has brought up various memories, rekindled various identities. It's certainly given me some perspective on the events as they have unfolded or are as yet unfolding.

For now, though, I have the complete work out there that I want to be out there, the one memoir I have always known that I had to write, *College Girl*. I may never need to write another. Or, perhaps in time, I may sense that these other stories call out to me, that those questions about *how, why,* and *for whom* to write it make more sense to me. The stories may have an urgency that I can no longer ignore, emerge clearly with their characters and their plots, demanding to be heard more fully. I may have a better sense of the shape such a memoir might take, how I might do a fuller telling. If that happens, I will go there again—I will write my life in a more complete way for others. In all likelihood, if I do so, these stories will look different from their shortened depictions here and more different still from that first memoir I wrote. After all, I wrote it for specific reasons, in a particular time and place. I had certain goals and needs as a writer. I held certain identities then and even now that will likely not be the case in the near future.

So, I don't yet know, cannot yet know. I suppose only time will tell me. But, as I have learned from my yoga, my hiking, and my running, through my movement in this world, even in the face of difficulties, there is great joy. And just writing about these things—even if I never do anything more with such writing—has tremendous value in and of itself. I am writing my way toward a better understanding. And, along that road, I am also writing my way toward more compassion for myself. I am writing my way toward greater compassion for others. I am writing my way into where I have been, where I am now, and where I am going.

I breathe in. I breathe out. I settle into a place inside myself that is always there beneath the surface—a joyfulness, an unending. Right here. Right now. There is only this immediate present. What has passed melts away. What awaits is but glimmery hope.

Notes

1. Laura Gray-Rosendale, Professor of Rhetoric, Writing, and Digital Media Studies and President's Distinguished Teaching Fellow, Northern Arizona University. Laura.Gray-Rosendale@nau.edu
2. I would like to thank Ari Burford and Joni Haug for their thoughts on earlier versions of this text.

References

Birkerts, Sven. *The Art of Time in Memoir: Then. Again.* Minneapolis: Graywolf Press, 2008.

Gilmore, Leigh. *The Limits of Autobiography: Trauma and Testimony.* Ithaca: Cornell University Press, 2001.

Gornick, Vivian. *The Situation and the Story: The Art of Personal Narrative.* New York: Farrar, Straus and Giroux, 2002.

Gray-Rosendale, Laura. *College Girl: A Memoir.* New York: Excelsior/SUNY Press, 2013.

Karr, Mary. *The Art of Memoir.* New York: HarperCollins, 2015.

Contributors

Jonathan Alexander is Chancellor's Professor of English at the University of California, Irvine, where he is also the Founding Director of the Center for Excellence in Writing and Communication. The author, co-author, or editor of fifteen books, Jonathan is currently focusing scholarly attention on the rhetorics of life writing in particular and the notion of the "popular" more broadly.

Elizabeth Boquet is a Louisiana writer living in Connecticut, where she is Professor of English at Fairfield University in Fairfield, CT. She is the author of *Nowhere Near the Line* (Utah State University Press, 2016), and her creative nonfiction has appeared in *The Bitter Southerner, Full Grown People, Dead Housekeeping,* and *Louisiana in Words.*

D. Shane Combs is Assistant Professor of English Composition and Professional Writing at Central Methodist University. His work blends his three favorite academic endeavors: life writing, pedagogy, and mentoring. His writing has appeared in *Composition Forum, Writing on the Edge, and Assay: A Journal of Nonfiction Studies,* among others. He is currently working to develop an affective-relational pedagogy and to eventually find his way back to a mountainous area, at least for vacation.

Laura Gray-Rosendale is a professor in Rhetoric, Writing, and Digital Media Studies, and she is a President's Distinguished Teaching Fellow at Northern Arizona University. Her research and teaching interests focus on memoir and theories of autobiography, history of rhetoric and composition, literacy studies, and popular culture studies. She directs the S.T.A.R. (Successful Transition and Academic Readiness) English Program, a curriculum that addresses the needs of students who are first-generation and/or in economic need. Along with various articles and book chapters, she has published the following books: *Rethinking Basic Writing*, *Alternative Rhetorics* (with Sibylle Gruber), *Fractured Feminisms* (with Gil Harootunian), *Radical Relevance* (with Steven Rosendale), *Pop Perspectives*, *College Girl* (winner of the Gold Medal Independent Book Publisher's Award in Memoir), and *Getting Personal: Teaching Personal Writing in the Digital Age*. Currently she is the guest editor on two special volumes (on graduate education and basic writing) for the *Journal of Basic Writing*. She has begun work on a new book tentatively titled *Living in Motion: Writers' Stories of Triumph, Joy, and Healing*.

Bump Halbritter is Associate Professor of Rhetoric and Writing and Director of the First-Year Writing Program at Michigan State University. His research and teaching involve the integration of video-based, audio-visual writing into scenes of college writing and scholarly research. Bump's 2013 article, "Time, Lives, and Videotape: Operationalizing Discovery in Scenes of Literacy Sponsorship," co-authored with Julie Lindquist, received The Richard Ohmann Award for Outstanding Article in *College English*. Bump's book, *Mics, Cameras, Symbolic Action: Audio-Visual Rhetoric for Writing Teachers* received the *Computers and Composition* Distinguished Book Award for 2013.

Brooke Hessler has been a high school dropout and a tenured professor, a corporate ghostwriter and a short-order poet. She specializes in helping educators connect the dots between digital storytelling, critical reflection, and Universal Design for Learning. An award-winning teacher of community-engaged writing, Brooke has mentored hundreds of students in the U.S. and Singapore as story-workers and oral history activists. After serving 14 years as Carrithers Chair of Writing at Oklahoma City University, Brooke followed her bliss to the San Francisco Bay Area, where she is Director of Learning Resources at California College of the Arts and teaches writing, digital storytelling, and yoga for mindful learning to studio artists and designers.

Rona Kaufman is an associate professor of English at Pacific Lutheran University, where she teaches writing, memoir, and the English language and directs the First-Year Experience Program. Her work has appeared in *ISLE*, *JAC*, and other publications. She is the co-editor of *Placing the Academy: Essays on Landscape, Work, and Academic Identity*.

Julie Lindquist is Professor of Rhetoric and Writing at MSU, where she teaches courses in writing, rhetoric, literacy and composition studies, and research methodologies. She is the author of *A Place to Stand: Politics and Persuasion in a Working Class Bar* (2002) and, with David Seitz, *Elements of Literacy* (2008). Her writings on rhetoric, class, literacy, and writing pedagogy have appeared in *College Composition and Communication*, *College English*, *JAC*, and *Pedagogy*, as well as in several edited collections. Her article "Time, Lives, and Videotape: Operationalizing Discovery in Scenes of

Literacy Sponsorship," co-authored with Bump Halbritter, was awarded The Richard Ohmann Award for Outstanding Article in *College English* in 2013.

Sam Meekings is Assistant Professor of Writing at Northwestern University in Qatar. He is the author of *Under Fishbone Clouds* (called "a poetic evocation of the country and its people" by the *New York Times*) and *The Book of Crows.* He has a PhD from Lancaster University, and has taught writing at NYU (Global Campus) and the University of Chichester in the UK. His website is www.sammeekings.com.

Richard E. Miller has delivered over one hundred invited talks across the country and abroad on a range of topics related to literacy, technology, and higher education. His new book, *On the End of Privacy: Dissolving Boundaries in a Screen-Centric World* (UPitt 2019), explores how education is being changed by the proliferation of hand-held devices that enable instant publication and global distribution of anything that can be seen or heard. Richard recently spent three years on the faculty of the Doctoral Program in Social Work, where he designed and then helped to implement a three-year curriculum in multimedia composing.

Karen-Elizabeth Moroski is an Assistant Teaching Professor of English and Co-Curricular Programs Coordinator for Writing and Languages at Penn State University, University Park. Her research centers on writing studies, writing centers, queer theory, trauma and affect: she wants to better understand how we tell our stories and why, and what happens to us through that "telling." She serves on the executive board of the Mid-Atlantic Writing Center Association, leads the Digital Content Team for the International Writing Center Association, and is an Associate Editor for WAC Clearinghouse. Karen lives in Pine Grove Mills, Pennsylvania, with her wife Chelsea and their two terribly behaved cats.

Amy E. Robillard is Professor of English at Illinois State University, where she teaches graduate and undergraduate courses in rhetoric, composition, and life writing. She is the author of *We Find Ourselves in Other People's Stories,* and the editor, with Ron Fortune, of *Authorship Contested: Cultural Challenges to the Authentic, Autonomous Author,* and, with Rebecca Moore Howard, of *Pluralizing Plagiarism: Identities, Contexts, Pedagogies.* Her personal essays have been published on *The Rumpus* and on *Full Grown People.*

Lisya Seloni is Associate Professor of TESOL and Applied Linguistics in the Department of English at Illinois State University, where she teaches courses on second language writing, TESOL methods, and materials and cross-cultural issues in teaching English as an international language Her research explores ethnographic approaches to second language writing, academic socialization, and issues related to sociopolitical context of English language teaching and linguistic landscape in the city. She is specifically interested in the ways translingual writers construct knowledge and text in various writing environments across the disciplines. She is the co-author of *Ethnolinguistic Diversity and Literacy Education*. Her most recent publications have appeared in *Journal of Second Language Writing*, *English for Specific Purposes*, *Language Policy*, and *Journal of Language and Politics*.

Jessica L. Weber created and currently directs a workplace writing center for the Federal Reserve Bank of Philadelphia. Her efforts have been featured by *Harvard Business Review*, *The Write Life*, and *Ragan*. She is currently enrolled in Texas Tech University's PhD program for Technical Communication and Rhetoric. Though her professional focus has been on teaching and tutoring writing to adults in workplace settings, she is a personal essayist at heart. She lives in South Philadelphia with her rescued blue pit, Juniper.

Index